SPEECH COMMUNICATION
A Contemporary Introduction

SECOND EDITION

SPEECH COMMUNICATION
A Contemporary Introduction

SECOND EDITION

Gordon I. Zimmerman
James L. Owen
David R. Seibert
University of Nevada, Reno

WEST PUBLISHING COMPANY
St. Paul New York
San Francisco Los Angeles

50 West Kellogg Boulevard
P.O. Box 3526
St. Paul, Minnesota 55165

Printed in the United States of America

Library of Congress Cataloging in Publication Data

Zimmerman, Gordon I
Speech communication.

Bibliography: p.
Includes index.
1. Oral communication. I. Owen, James L., joint author. II. Seibert, David R., joint author.
III. Title.
PN4121.z49 1980 808.5 79-24516
ISBN 0-8299-0326-7

CREDITS

4 Arthur Grace, Stock, Boston; **16** © Ken Graves/Jeroboam, Inc.; **33** Elizabeth Hamlin, Stock, Boston; **41** Richard Kalvar, Magnum; **46** © Hank Lebó/Jeroboam, Inc.; **54** Susan Miller; **58** Gregg Mancuso; **62** Peter Menzel, Stock, Boston; **68** Susan Miller; **58** Ellis Herwig, Stock, Boston; **84, 91** Susan Miller; **100** Frank Siteman, Stock, Boston; **111** Owen Franken, Stock, Boston; **122** © IPA/Jeroboam, Inc.; **129** Richard Kalvar, Magnum; **136** Robert Eckert, Ekm-Nepenthe; **142** Mark Chester; **155** Owen Franken, Stock, Boston; **163** Peter Southwick, Stock, Boston; **178** Donald Patterson, Stock, Boston; **184** Robert Eckert, Ekm-Nepenthe; **214, 218** Ellis Herwig, Stock, Boston; **228** © Hap Stewart/Jeroboam,, Inc.; **236** Mark Chester; **244** Frank Siteman, Stock, Boston; **250** © Ilka Hartmann/Jeroboam, Inc.; **263** Elizabeth Hamlin, Stock, Boston; **268** Mark Chester; **277** Gregg Mancuso; **283** Mark Chester; **296** Patricia Hollander Gross, Stock, Boston; **300** Channel Five Group W Stations; **310** Jerry Berndt, Stock, Boston; **313** The Milk Advisory Board; **326** Gilbert S. Nearman; **331** Michael E. Bry, Icon; **343** Mark Chester; **349** Anestis Diakopoulous, Stock, Boston.

Pages 7, 52, 118 Cartoons by Don Dougherty. Reprinted by permission of the artist.
Pages 20, 198, 220, 322 Cartoons by Clem Scalzitti. Reprinted by permission of the artist.

Page 34 From "Mental Maps," *Newsweek*, March 15, 1976, p. 71. Copyright 1976 by Newsweek, Inc. All rights reserved. Reprinted by permission.
Pages 36-37 From Williams, F. and R. C. Naremore. "On the Functional Analysis of Social Class Differences in Modes of Speech," *Speech Monographs*, 36 (1969) pp. 77-102. Reprinted by permission.
Page 87 From Sieburg, Evelyn, "Confirming and Disconforming Communication in an Organizational Context," *The Personnel Woman*, 18, February, 1974, pp. 4-11.
Page 89 From Dance, Frank E. X., and Carl Larson, *The Functions of Human Communication*. New York: Holt, Rinehart and Winston, 1976. Reprinted by permission.
Page 166 From Phillips, Gerald, *Communication and the Small Group*, Indianapolis: Bobbs-Merill, 1966, pp. 7-8. Reprinted by permission.

TO OUR PARENTS

CONTENTS

PART TWO PUBLIC COMMUNICATION 177

Chapter Seven Speech Development 179

Chapter Eight Delivery Strategies and Problems 215

PREFACE

The purpose of this textbook is to improve understanding and skills of speech communication. The focus is clearly on the student's communication needs. We have no interest in attempting a definitive statement on speech communication theory and research, nor do we want to encumber a speech fundamentals course with a bulky, all-encompassing overview of the field. We want to help students improve communication.

To accomplish this purpose, we employed the joint input of three authors with extensive backgrounds in speech fundamentals instruction. This consensus strategy permitted varied information and frequent feedback on the best approaches for each chapter.

We developed chapter topic areas on the basis of a nationwide survey of instructors in speech communication. We patterned the book after the collective approach of speech instructors generally, according to the ways in which they actually teach the basic course. We omitted topics that sometimes appear in basic texts but probably do not help the beginning student achieve the objective of speech improvement.

The book has two main parts. Part One is a contemporary analysis of concepts often covered in courses on communication theory and interpersonal communication. We discuss the verbal, nonverbal, and intrapersonal dimensions of comcommunication at the dyadic and small group levels. Our concern is not merely with *initiating communication* but also with *listening and responding* to the messages of others.

Part Two addresses more traditional themes of public communication, with materials appropriate for courses on speech fundamentals or public speaking. We examine very practical problems of speech preparation, delivery, informative and persuasive strategies, and selected problems of public presentations. The most important feature of this section is its close integration with concepts in Part One. We view public communication as different perhaps in form but not in substance from other communication events and tasks. Our discussion of theory and practice of speech communication is conceptually consistent throughout the book, making it especially appropriate for the growing number of speech communication courses that combine skills training in both interpersonal communication and public speaking.

Each chapter includes study questions and suggested readings. An accompanying *Instructor's Guide* provides teaching strategies and suggested projects and exercises. It also includes sample test questions.

Once more we acknowledge the many speech communication faculty from both two- and four-year colleges who provided incisive prepublication reviews for the first edition. Major reviewers were: William E. Arnold, Arizona State University; Clarence H. Baxter, Jr., Sinclair Community College (Ohio); Gary D'Angelo, University of Washington; H. W. Farwell, University of Southern Colorado; Lucia S. Hawthorne, Morgan State University (Maryland); James A. McCubbin, Bloomsburg State College (Pennsylvania); Donald B. Morlan, Eastern Illinois University; Thomas J. Murray, Eastern Michigan University; James W. Pence, Jr., University of North Carolina; Jim Towns, Stephen F. Austin State University (Texas); and Loretta A. Walker, Utah Technical College.

We are especially grateful for the guidance we received from three communication scholars whose experience with the first edition influenced the revisions in this edition: Don B. Center of the University of Texas at San Antonio; Harry Hazel, Jr. of Gonzaga University at Spokane, Washington; and Bill Henderson at the University of Northern Iowa at Cedar Falls. Each supplied us with incisive but supportive criticism that we believe has substantially improved the "teachability" of the present volume.

Our gratitude extends to our students and teaching fellows at the University of Nevada, Reno, whose study of the first edition resulted in many helpful suggestions for revisions that have been incorporated in this volume.

Finally we wish once more to thank Mrs. Betty Ghiglieri for her valuable assistance in preparing the manuscript for the first edition and to Mrs. Merle Owen for her equally valuable assistance in preparing the manuscript for the second.

GORDON I. ZIMMERMAN
JAMES L. OWEN
DAVID R. SEIBERT

SPEECH COMMUNICATION
A Contemporary Introduction

SECOND EDITION

The speech communication faculty of a large university in the Midwest met to consider possible changes in their curriculum. The chairperson asked, "Does anyone have a suggestion for new courses?" A young instructor replied, "Yes. I'd like to suggest a course called 'Interpersonal Communication.' " A skeptical and somewhat impatient senior professor replied, "*Interpersonal*? What other kind of communication is there?"

Indeed, the professor had a good question. The term *interpersonal* implies "between people," and when we think of communication we think of people sending and receiving messages. What other kind of communication is there? Realistically, when two people talk with each other, or when several people discuss a topic in a small group, or when one person talks to a large audience, all are engaging in interpersonal communication.

In Part One, we are concerned primarily with a more specialized definition of interpersonal communication, one that perhaps the young instructor had in mind: "the face-to-face interaction between people who are consistently aware of each other. Each person assumes the roles of both sender and receiver of messages, involving constant adaptation and spontaneous adjustment to the other person" (Giffin and Patton, 1976, p. 11). The key terms are *face-to-face*, *aware of each other*, *sender and receiver*, *adaptation* and *spontaneous adjustment*. Even this definition is quite broad, however, because most of our interaction with others fulfills the criteria of the definition. This broad perspective does suggest an important fact. A large amount of our *behavior* is interpersonal communication.

Communication may appear to be a simple process, something we do every day and usually fairly well. Typically, we give it little conscious thought and only rarely admit, "What we have here is a failure to communicate." Actually, the communication process is complex, and truly effective and rewarding communicative transactions are rare. We should give regular and serious attention to our communication with others, for good interpersonal communication, when it does occur, is highly rewarding.

In this text, we focus on the communicator as (1) a unique individual, (2) a partner in a one-to-one transaction, (3) a participant in a small group, and (4) a speaker or listener in a public address setting. There is a great deal of overlap in these areas of study. For example, *intrapersonal* communication is defined as the communication that takes place primarily within an individual, yet our understanding of a person's intrapersonal communication requires that we look at the experiences he or she has gained through interaction in dyads, small groups, and speaker-audience situations. In turn, our understanding of the interaction of people in various communication settings requires that we understand something of the unique ways that individuals are organized at the intrapersonal level.

Each communication setting presents unique considerations. At the intrapersonal level, we focus on important dynamics of the individual communicator; at the dyad level, we focus on the issues that surface when two communicators confront and interact; and at the small group level, we look at the different types of small groups and the various roles that evolve when individuals interact in a group setting. At the public address level, the subject of Part Two, we focus on the different purposes and settings for public presentations and the more formalized roles of speaker and audience.

THE INTERPERSONAL COMMUNICATION PROCESS

Part One explores in depth the interpersonal communication process. In Chapter One, we identify key terms and offer a simple model of communication. In Chapter Two, we examine communication that occurs *intra*personally (within the person) and affects the ways in which the individual deals with information and with other people. Our comprehension and use of verbal language are central elements in intrapersonal communication. Chapter Three explores *nonverbal* communication —ways in which we communicate by means other than spoken words. Chapter Four looks at the process nature of communication through an explicit examination of the speaker and listener roles and their dynamic interaction. In Chapter Five, we apply the concepts discussed in the first four chapters to the *dyad*, the one-to-one communication setting. Chapter Six expands the analysis further to interpersonal communication in small groups.

As you read Part One, you will undoubtedly find many applications to your own life. The examples in the text should help you become more aware of, and skillful in, this difficult process we call interpersonal communication. One textbook and one speech communication course cannot possibly cover the topic completely. Communication study should be a lifelong effort. We hope, however, that Part One will be an important first step.

1 INTRODUCTION TO SPEECH COMMUNICATION

PREVIEW

Most of us spend a major portion of every day communicating with other human beings, initiating messages for the consumption of others, and interpreting messages sent by others. Communication is an activity so commonplace that we tend to take it for granted. Yet it is probably the most demanding and complex behavior that we exhibit. We have the capacity to continually improve our communication skills throughout our lives. It is a difficult undertaking, but if we persevere it can be immensely satisfying. Indeed, the study of communication can be an adventurous exploration into a fascinating frontier—the untapped potential of the human mind.

We begin our study of communication with a discussion of some basic concepts useful in communicating about communication. Chapter One introduces some of these key concepts, which form the basis for further inquiry into the problem of improving communication skills.

OBJECTIVES

To equip you with basic terms for thinking and talking about human communication

To encourage you to improve on your own communicative competence

To identify some basic principles of human communication

To indicate some frequent problems in communication

ONE Dusk settles around a mountain cabin in which a young man and woman are reading light fiction. The young woman shivers slightly in the draft of cool evening air coming through the open window. Her husband notices her shivering and quietly slips to the window to close it.

A student pilot taxis carefully toward the end of the runway for his first solo flight, acutely aware of the different quality of engine noise in the cockpit now that the instructor is no longer in the right seat. The tower operator's voice, calm and businesslike as always, crackles over the radio: "Cessna Two Three Golf, what are your instructor's directions?" The student replies, "Tahoe Tower, Two Three Golf, I'm supposed to make three takeoffs and landings, two touch-and-goes, and a full stop." The tower operator responds, "Roger, Two Three Golf, report downwind when you're abeam the tower, and good luck."

With slightly sweaty palms and queasy stomach, a college student takes her place behind the lectern, looks around at her classmates, and begins to deliver her speech. After a minute or so her nervousness subsides as she recognizes signs of attention and interest in her audience.

A DEFINITION OF COMMUNICATION

What do these three incidents have in common? They are all instances of human communication. Moreover, each one exemplifies effective communication – communication that is both productive and satisfying for the individuals involved. The communication is *productive* in that it helps someone accomplish a task, achieve an objective. It is *satisfying* because these tasks, when accomplished, help fulfill one or more of the participant's needs.

Communication obviously occurred in two of the three incidents, but you may be wondering about the one in the cabin in which no *spoken* messages were exchanged. Even this incident demonstrates communication within the broad definition serving our present purposes: *Communication is the process in which persons assign meanings to events and especially to the behavior of other persons.*

PURPOSES OF COMMUNICATION: CONTENT AND RELATIONSHIP

Presumably you are reading this book because you desire to improve your communication skills. If that is your goal, we suggest that you begin by thinking about the functions and purposes that are served by communication.

As a practical matter, over half the employed citizens of the United States produce nothing but symbolic products—words, numbers, images, and so on for the utilization of others, and for the management

"Earl, I'm very fond of you, but I simply cannot continue this relationship until I know where your head is at!"

of others' work. Chances are, you will make your living with your communicative skills. This is obviously the case for journalists, teachers, entertainers, and ministers, but it also holds for managers and supervisors — anyone who must exercise influence over others through the preparation of reports and directives, oral or written.

Your own communicative skills and those of others around you will exert an enormous influence on the way you earn your livelihood — even if you're among the few who have something to show at the end of a day's work, something you made with your hands.

As social creatures, human beings also depend on one another to fulfill their needs. This interdependence requires that we cooperate with each other, and cooperation depends on the quality of relationships we establish through communication.

An exhaustive list of communication purposes can be divided into two broad categories corresponding to our practical and social needs: *content* and *relationship*. First, we communicate to accomplish tasks that are essential to fulfill our needs — to feed and clothe ourselves, to satisfy our curiosity about the environment, and to enjoy being alive. Second, we communicate to establish and maintain relationships with others. Thus, communication has both a *content* function, which involves the exchange of information necessary to accomplish tasks, and a *relationship* function, which involves the exchange of information about where we stand with others. Of course, communication does not serve either purpose independently of the other: it serves both simultaneously (Watzlawick et al., 1967).

Examine your own communicative behavior in terms of these two broad categories, asking yourself: "How does my behavior help me and others to get the job done?" and "How does my behavior affect the quality of my relationships with other people?" If you earnestly pursue these two questions, you'll be well on the way toward discovering what you must do to improve your communicative performance.

IMPORTANCE OF COMMUNICATION

If you had not already achieved a considerable degree of competence in communication, you wouldn't be able to read this book. You can read and write and speak well enough to be admitted to college. In fact, you may be thinking that you already know *how* to communicate and that what you need now is more knowledge to communicate *about*. If you think harder, though, you'll realize that the acquisition and sharing of knowledge is so intimately bound up with communication that it's impossible to separate the two. The brilliant nuclear physicist Niels Bohr (1961) saw the relationship between knowing and communicating when he said:

> . . . as the goal of science is to augment and order our experience, every analysis of the conditions of human knowledge must rest on considerations of the character and scope of our means of communication.

The practical value of developing and improving our communicative skills and techniques is obvious. Each of us, no matter what our individual goals, must achieve minimal levels of competence in communication just to survive as a free and independent person. Beyond these minimal levels of competence, however, our worth to ourselves, to one another, and to all human civilization is directly linked to our communicative abilities. Do you aspire to a difficult profession? To realize your goal, you must not only master the knowledge needed, but be able to communicate that you have done so. Do you aspire to become an effective advocate of social change? A good parent? A responsible member of society? These goals are absolutely unattainable without a high level of communicative competence.

None of our technological advances would have occurred without the means to store and exchange information efficiently and rapidly and to cooperate with one another for mutual benefit. No matter which human achievements you deem valuable — NASA's exploration of space, modern medicine, progress toward equal opportunity, or whatever — all have occurred as a direct consequence of exceptionally skillful communication.

Similarly, although not every major problem confronting humans is caused exclusively by a "breakdown in communication" as is often naively assumed, inadequate communication is frequently a contributing factor to personal and social failures. This becomes apparent from any careful interpretation of historical events such as the Viet Nam War, the Watergate scandal, the Bay of Pigs fiasco, the U-2 incident, Japan's attack on Pearl Harbor, or the mass extermination of European Jews under the Third Reich.

The discovery and implementation of solutions to our problems — indeed, the very recognition of our problems — are based on our willingness and skill in communicating with one another symbolically. Clearly, it is imperative that we acquire a better understanding of how communication works and of what we can do to make it work better.

ELEMENTS OF THE COMMUNICATION PROCESS

There are six major elements in the process of communication. Each is defined below as an aid to understanding the material covered in later chapters. Figure 1-1 is a simple model of communication in which these six elements are identified.

SENDER, SOURCE, OR SPEAKER

The terms *sender*, *source*, and *speaker* are used interchangeably. They refer to an *individual whose behavior communicates*. It is important that you recognize that the spoken message is only a part of the total message sent when persons interact with one another. Thus, it is the sender's *behavior* that communicates.

RECEIVER, LISTENER, AUDITOR, OR INTERPRETER

The terms *receiver*, *listener*, *auditor*, and *interpreter* are also used interchangeably. They refer to an *individual who assigns meaning to the behavior of a sender*.

MESSAGE

The message is *that portion of the sender's behavior to which a receiver assigns meaning*. You're accustomed to thinking about a message as something written or spoken. However, messages may take forms other

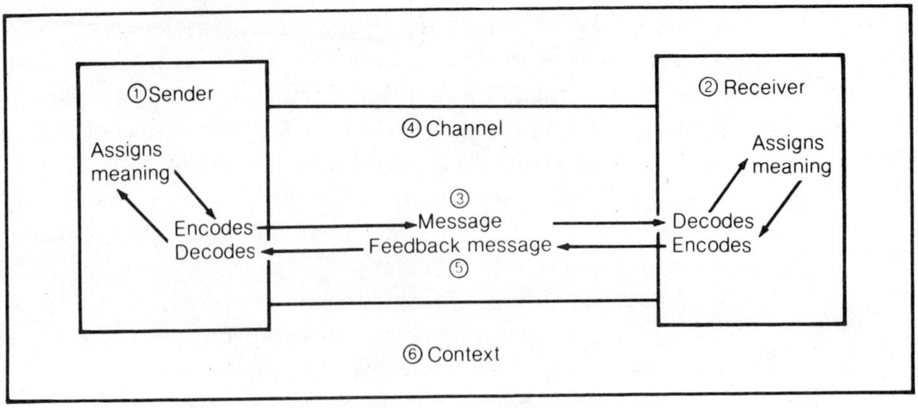

FIGURE 1-1

than the shared code of language and speech, and such *nonverbal* messages contribute much to the meanings assigned by interpreters. Chapter Three introduces the study of nonverbal messages and the kinds of meaning they can stimulate.

CHANNEL

The term *channel* refers to the *medium through which messages are conveyed from senders to receivers.* The primary channels of interest are the senses of vision and hearing. Most of the messages we receive are conveyed through patterns of light and sound, received through the eyes and ears. As we shall see, however, touch and smell may also be channels in human communication.

Frequently, messages between individuals are mediated by several additional channels, such as electronic media, paint on canvas, or print on a page. Such additional channels permit message transmission between communicators separated in space and time. Regardless of the number and nature of media and channels involved, the important thing to remember is that the message received is a product of the behavior of the sender.

FEEDBACK

Feedback refers to a *message initiated by a receiver in response to a message received, which influences the subsequent behavior of the original sender.* Not all responses are feedback. A message is feedback only (1) if it is actually a response to a sender's message which would not have occurred in the absence of the original message, and (2) if it actually influences the original sender's subsequent behavior. Furthermore, feedback may or may not be intentional. For example, if you are giving a speech and someone in the back row is lulled to sleep by your talk, you may or may not notice. If you notice and adjust by raising your voice to awaken the sleeper, you are responding to feedback. If you fail to notice, there has been no feedback.

CONTEXT

The term *context* refers to the *situation in which a message is conveyed from sender to receiver.* Context includes a number of elements, such as the setting in which the communication occurs, the means of message transmission available, and the various expectations of the senders and receivers. More specifically, a communication context includes such factors as the physical environment, the time of day, the number of people present, their dress, formal and informal rules of conduct for the situation, and even the labels used to describe the situation.

We are all required to communicate in a variety of contexts each day. Each context calls for a different repertory of communication behaviors and requires sensitivity to the unique demands of the situation. For example, consider the influence of context on the participants' communication behavior in the following situations:

1. a party held outdoors in a public park for twenty-five members of a women's softball team, dressed informally
2. a library tour for a first-year communication class
3. a formal state dinner in Washington, D.C., for the staff of a foreign embassy
4. a small group of students meeting in the student union coffee shop to prepare for a class presentation
5. that same group's presentation before the class

The context of a message is crucial to the kind of meaning that will be assigned to it. To illustrate, suppose you encounter two men, one of whom fires a small pistol in the air while the second, who is wearing a black and white striped shirt, stops running at the sound of the gunshot. In the context of a football game, these behaviors communicate nothing frightening. In a farmer's field near the state prison, they will produce totally different meanings.

A DEFINITION OF MEANING

We said that there are six basic elements in the communication process. To define them, however, we need a seventh term: *meaning*. When we refer to the meaning of a message, we are referring to some interpreter's *response* to that message. The distinction between the *content* and *meaning* of a message is an essential one. They are *not* the same thing. When we select words to encode messages, we attempt to select words that will cause our listeners to assign meanings consistent with our intended purposes. Frequently, a message fails to produce the appropriate response. When this happens, the content of the message has failed to produce the intended meaning.

In general, messages can produce three kinds of meanings (responses) in their interpreters: *thinking*, *feeling*, and *acting*. Morris (1946) has identified three kinds of messages according to the type of meaning responses they produce: *designative*, *appraisive*, and *prescriptive*. *Designative* messages produce thinking responses, which include perceiving, observing, or experiencing objects and events. "This book is printed in black ink" is a designative message because it causes an interpreter to respond on the level of observation — to look at the book and think about whether the message is accurate.

Appraisive messages cause the listener to respond on a feeling level — to evaluate or judge something. "This book is printed with attractive type" is an appraisive message. This message speaks to more than just the observable characteristics of the book: It speaks to someone's feelings about what is attractive and what is not.

Prescriptive messages cause the listener to respond by acting — not just to observe, think, or judge, but to *act*. "Read this book" is an example of a prescriptive message.

Awareness of these three response categories is useful in helping us prepare messages consistent with our communicative purposes. We send messages designed to stimulate various responses. However, messages do not have automatic effects on their interpreters, partly because interpreters have the capacity to choose how they will respond to a given message. A designative message may stimulate feelings and judgments and even incite a receiver to action, while a prescriptive message may fail to do so. Suppose someone told you, "Your car headlights are on in the parking lot." This is a purely designative message, but one that might cause you to respond with "Oops, that's no good!" (a feeling response) and send you scurrying out to turn off the lights (an acting response).

Small children tend to respond only to the literal, explicit content of messages. For example, a father may enter his child's room and announce, "There are clothes and toys scattered all over this room" (designative message), or "This room is a mess!" (appraisive message). If the father's intent is to get the child to pick up, he will frequently have to prescribe, for the child will typically interpret the designative or appraisive message at face value and fail to recognize and respond to the prescriptive implication in it. In general, the more mature the interpreter, the more likely his or her response to a given message will go beyond the *explicit* content of the message and reflect what the message *implies*.

To a large extent, communicative competence involves knowing the receiver's needs with respect to the three kinds of meaning responses — that is, knowing whether, within a given context, the receiver needs a message stimulating him or her to think, feel, act, or do a combination of these things. For example, when the immediate context of communication calls for rational analysis, as in explaining a mathematical concept, there is a need to stimulate thought. When the context is emotional, as in expressing one's condolences to someone who is grieving, there is a need to stimulate feelings. In a time of grief, it is inappropriate to send messages about the clinical details of death, but highly appropriate to empathize. Finally, when the context requires that the receiver act, there is a demand for prescription. The receiver needs guidance on what to do. When someone is learning to drive a car, fly an airplane, or write a term paper, a lengthy treatise on the theory of internal combustion engines or linguistic theory will not meet the learner's needs unless it helps him or her perform the acts required to get the job done.

Often a receiver needs a combination of messages — designative, appraisive, and prescriptive. For example, when you go to a physician with a complaint, you are ultimately seeking a prescriptive message: "Do these things and you'll get better." You may also look for messages that describe what is wrong with you: "You've got a common, rarely dangerous, viral infection." You may also want some indication that the doctor empathizes with your discomfort: "It's a miserable bug, but nothing we can't clear up with proper rest and medication." Many communication problems can be avoided if senders are sensitive to the needs and expectations of receivers with respect to designation, appraisal, and prescription.

Much of the material in this book is prescriptive. It is intended to tell you what to do to improve your communication skills and to stimulate you to act on the advice. Much of it is also designative, calling on you to observe and think about communication events to understand how they work.

We believe that most people want to know at least some of the theoretical (designative) support for the advice they receive. We, the authors, share some beliefs about human communication — crucial beliefs that have shaped our thinking about communication in important ways. These provide the basis for much of the advice given here. It is appropriate that we share those beliefs with you, so you'll know where we're "coming from."

COMMUNICATION THEORY: SOME BASIC PRINCIPLES

ALL BEHAVIOR COMMUNICATES

In its broadest sense, the study of communication is the study of what happens when people behave in each other's presence or leave evidence of their behavior where others can find it. If we think of communication as limited to what individuals *intend* to communicate, we overlook some extremely important aspects of the process. For example, the man who lights up a fat cigar in a restaurant may not intend to communicate anything to someone seated at the next table, but nonetheless a message is conveyed and a meaning may be assigned. Irrespective of our intentions, our behavior is subject to interpretation by others.

The speaker addressing an audience may spend a great deal of time and effort polishing his speech, but he may fail to influence his listeners because he is careless about some of the other messages sent inadvertently during his delivery. If he fidgets and shuffles his feet to the point of distraction, if his dress and grooming are inappropriate for the occasion, or if his style of speaking detracts from his credibility, then the meanings assigned to the *verbal* portion of his behavior may be adversely affected. Remember that a listener has the right and the responsibility to assign meanings to the total behavior of the communicator. You cannot reasonably expect people to "just listen to my words and ignore the rest of what I'm doing." Listeners, not speakers, decide what is relevant to the assignment of meanings.

This is not to say that all behavior automatically communicates. The point is that any and all behavior *may* communicate. Behavior that goes unnoticed will not stimulate meaning; behavior that draws attention to itself certainly will.

WE CANNOT NOT COMMUNICATE

It is a mistake to believe that by sitting still and keeping silent, we can avoid communicating. When we withdraw from active interaction with others, we are actually communicating a great deal. Passive, silent behavior may stimulate a variety of meanings. At best, it may lead others to conclude that we are shy or reticent. At worst, it may signify that we are lazy, stupid, incompetent, or indifferent to others.

There is even a principle of law that assigns a shared meaning to silence under some circumstances. Silence implies consent. Our silence

may be interpreted as indicating our approval of a situation in which we're involved. You may have seen the play or movie *A Man for All Seasons*. This is a story about Sir Thomas More, Archbishop of Canterbury during the reign of Henry the Eighth. Henry sought More's approval of his divorce from the queen in order to marry Anne Boleyn, his mistress. More did not approve of the divorce, but chose to remain silent, believing that his silence would give implicit consent and spare him from Henry's wrath, which usually involved the headsman. Henry finally solved the problem by having Sir Thomas beheaded. Your silence may not cost you your head, but you should recognize that it conveys a message and may not produce the meaning you intend.

MESSAGES DO NOT HAVE MEANINGS

Meanings are assigned by interpreters as responses to messages. It is commonly understood that words have meanings and that the proper meanings of words can be found in the dictionary. This is a serious misconception. Words do not "have" meanings any more than sharp knives "have" cut fingers. Rather, words stimulate receivers to assign meanings. Messages do not convey ideas from one mind to another; they elicit ideas in their interpreters. In short, messages *cause* meanings, but do not carry them.

When someone says that words have meanings, he means only that their interpreters are highly likely to assign certain commonly shared meanings to those words. Words communicate accurately only if they elicit the same meanings in both sender and receiver.

A college professor once spent many months drafting a manuscript for a new textbook. He gave the manuscript to his secretary with the instruction "Burn this for me, will you?" He intended for the secretary to photocopy the manuscript, and he was using the office jargon "burn." You guessed it. Months of hard work went up in smoke in the incinerator.

Another unsatisfactory communication occurred in Japan some years ago. A Navy aircraft squadron contracted with a Japanese machine shop to build a nosewheel strut for one of its airplanes. The original strut had developed a tiny, perfectly straight hairline crack at one end. The Americans stressed the importance of replacing the strut with a perfect copy — precisely machined to the dimensions and specifications of the original. When the Americans returned to pick up the new strut, they got exactly what they had demanded — a perfect copy of the original strut, *including the crack*. The Japanese machinists were justifiably proud of their work and announced that the crack had been most difficult to duplicate.

These communication failures were caused by ambiguous or incomplete messages that failed to produce appropriate interpretations in their receivers. They may seem to be extreme examples, but they illustrate common occurrences. You can probably recall incidents from your own experience in which misunderstandings have resulted from the assumption that messages are conveyor belts on which meanings travel intact from mind to mind.

COMMUNICATION IS A PARTICIPATIVE PROCESS

The key words here are *process* and *participate*. Let's begin with the notion of process. A process is not a tangible thing, but a pattern of dynamic relationships among things, a patterned sequence of events. Even the simplest communication between two persons, "Pass the salt," involves a complex chain of events if the receiver complies with the request. Furthermore, it is difficult to determine precisely where and when a given communication event begins and ends. For some purposes, we can say that the above event began when person A asked for the salt and ended when person B surrendered the saltshaker. But we cannot account for the event entirely in terms of what happened between the asking and the passing. Both person A and person B drew on past experience to encode and decode the message and respond appropriately. As another example, consider a speaker giving a speech. When does the communication between speaker and audience begin? When the speaker takes his position behind the lectern? When he enters the room? When his services as a speaker were initially engaged? And when does the communication end? Unless the speaker's message is forgotten the instant he stops speaking, audience members may continue to assign meanings to his message months and even years later. Can we really say that the communication process ended at the conclusion of the speech?

How we punctuate or identify critical points in the communication process (such as beginnings and endings) is crucial to our understanding of the process. A small boy once demonstrated a precocious wisdom about process as follows:

MOTHER: *(Noticing the black eye and bruised knuckles of her son after he has been playing with a neighbor's child)* Did you and Eric get into a fight?

BOY: Yeah.

MOTHER: Who started it?

BOY: Well, I guess I started with the hitting part, but *he* started with the talking part.

Another aspect of the communication process is that the various components are constantly undergoing change. This is especially true of the most important parts of the process, the communicators themselves. For example, when someone sends a message that is especially important for some receiver, the receiver's orientation toward the sender changes dramatically and vice versa. The sender and receiver experience change as a consequence of the communication between them. Extremely important communication events illustrate this principle: proposals of marriage, disclosures of love and affection, messages that truly inform, persuade, or inspire. Listed below are some common and simple messages that produce life-changing consequences for senders and receivers:

"I love you."
"We find the defendant *not guilty*, your honor."
"Congratulations . . ."
"We deeply regret to inform you that . . ."
"It is our pleasure to inform you that your application has been approved."

When we say that communication is a process in which senders and receivers *participate*, we mean that *both* sender and receiver must participate actively for effective communication to occur. This may seem obvious, but we believe that many individuals tend to view communication as a lopsided process in which senders do most of the work and receivers sit back and soak up the message. It doesn't work that way, or at least when it works that way it doesn't work very well.

Listening and responding appropriately to the messages of others is demanding work, especially where there is an opportunity for constructive feedback. An actively participating listener assigns meanings to a sender's message on the basis of his or her own previous experiences, both with language and with nonlinguistic perceptual stimuli. Senders rarely express their own meanings as perfect messages—

perfect in the sense that they produce the intended meanings for the listeners. Productive and satisfying communication does not occur unless listeners work diligently in assigning meanings. It is misleading to think of communication as something done *by* speakers *to* listeners, because there is so much room for variation in assigning meanings to a given message, and so many different ways for senders to encode messages reflecting their own meanings. Barnlund (1968) defines communication in two deceptively simple phrases as (1) the process of creating a meaning, and (2) an effort after meaning. Combining the two, we see that communication is a *creative effort* for both senders and receivers.

It is easy for us to lose sight of this important principle and relax when we think it's someone else's turn to be "on stage." When it's our turn to be "on" — to deliver a speech, participate in a discussion, or chair a meeting — we usually feel some tension and excitement as the adrenaline begins to flow. When we're not "on," we tend to relax, and if we relax too much, we don't fulfill our obligations in the effort after meaning. Think of it this way: When you're engaged in the process of communication, trying to understand the messages of another human being, you're *always "on."*

COMMUNICATION BARRIERS

We've said that human communication involves a complex chain of events. There are many points in the chain where things can go wrong. The following areas require careful attention from anyone wishing to participate effectively in the process of human communication.

ENCODING

Encoding and decoding both involve several steps, although they occur in senders and receivers so rapidly that they are not experienced separately. When we try to put an idea into words, we are trying to capture a meaning in language that will elicit a similar meaning in someone else. We frequently grope for words that will do the job. There are many different ways to encode the same idea, but the words we select contribute to subtle nuances of meaning for the listener. For example, when General Douglas MacArthur retreated from Corregidor near the

SR 5·13·78

beginning of World War II, his parting words were "I shall return." This potent phrase is well remembered. His words would probably now be long forgotten had he said "I'll be back."

In some communication situations, we have time to select carefully the words we use to capture our meanings; in others, we must encode our messages as we think, rapidly and spontaneously. When you have the time to be selective, *take* the time to be selective. A skilled carpenter would not think of driving a nail with a screwdriver, and a skilled speaker should not misappropriate linguistic tools. You'll find that the time spent in carefully preparing messages for formal occasions will enhance your encoding abilities in spontaneous communication.

TRANSMISSION

When we speak and write, we are creating signals for transmission to others. The audible signals of human speech make up an incredibly complex pattern of sounds, capable of creating many subtle nuances of meaning. There is much more information in the spoken message than that attributable to the words themselves. Creating intelligible sounds — sounds recognizable as words — is only the beginning in the task of speech communication. Remember that listeners assign meanings to a number of variables accompanying the sounds of speech: pitch, rate, inflection, volume, pauses, and a variety of gestural and postural behaviors.

CHANNELS

Frequently, our communication signals must compete with other signals, often called *noise*, in the channels through which we interact with others. By noise, we mean something more than the simple distraction of a passing jet or a jackhammer competing with a spoken message. Noise takes many forms in the process of communication. For example, a daydreaming listener creates noise in his own head, noise that competes with incoming speech sounds from others. Similarly, if a speaker becomes self-conscious and begins to worry excessively about how others evaluate her, her worries may constitute internal noise that disrupts her speaking at both the encoding and transmitting levels.

A certain amount of noise is inevitable in every communication channel. Some sources of noise can be controlled, while others may be difficult or impossible to control or even detect. For example, we can move to a quieter room to deliver a speech, but we can't always control the daydreaming of a listener or calm our own anxiety. If senders and receivers are to *participate* in the process of communication, *both* must deal with the problem of noise.

DECODING

The decoding process may not be completed if the receiver is able to recall the exact words of a message but unable to assign a meaning to those words. Consider, for example, the statement, "Brothers and sisters have I none, but *this man's* father is my father's son." Who is "this man"? Decoding may not even get as far as message recall, especially if the message is in technical language. Read the following sentence just once, and see if you can repeat it and assign a meaning to it. It is the definition of a statistical concept: The sum of scores in a distribution divided by the total number of scores. Did you have trouble getting the message and its meaning in just one reading? The concept defined is one with which you're probably familiar—the arithmetic mean, or simple average of a set of numbers.

If you had trouble with either or both of the previous examples, you can always go back and read the message again on the printed page. Spoken messages do not afford the same opportunity, and this is why speakers should compose messages that are more *redundant* than is necessary in writing. *Redundancy* is the repetition of information. Redundancy can be increased by repeating the same message or by restating the same idea several different ways. Human languages are approximately 50 percent redundant as they appear in normal speech and writing; that is, about half of the cues convey all the essential information. To illustrate:

The English language is about 50 percent redundant.	=	English is half redundant.

Or even

E gli h is h lf r d nd t.

We can decode and assign appropriate meanings to nonredundant messages, but it is difficult to do so, and many subtle meanings are lost when redundancy is decreased. The skillful communicator uses redundancy to help the interpreter decode and assign appropriate meaning to the message.

Similarly, the actively participating listener uses redundancy to help in the decoding process. Since half of the incoming message carries no additional information, the receiver has time to mentally repeat and perhaps paraphrase the incoming message, leaving out nonessential details. We really don't understand something unless we can at least recommunicate it to ourselves, and if we can do that, we can communicate it to someone else. There is wisdom in the old adage that we don't know what we know until we try to explain it to someone else.

APPROPRIATE FEEDBACK

When a receiver has decoded a sender's message and assigned a meaning to it, he may respond with a message of his own. We have already said that feedback, by definition, influences the subsequent behavior of the original sender. Thus, feedback serves basically to inform the sender of the consequences of his communication and to give him guidance as to how to proceed. No simple rules govern the communication of effective feedback, but there are three basic kinds of feedback messages that can be adapted to a wide variety of circumstances and purposes.

Imagine that you, as a receiver, have only three possible feedback messages that you can give. Instead of a voice, your transmitter is a traffic signal with red, yellow, and green lights.

Red means: Stop! I am unable to assign an appropriate meaning to your last message.

Yellow means: Proceed with caution! I think I have assigned an appropriate meaning to your last message, but I won't be certain until I hear more.

Green means: Go ahead! I'm certain I have assigned an appropriate meaning to your last message, and I'm ready for you to move on to your next idea.

Being limited to just these three feedback messages would severely limit the kinds of things a receiver could communicate to a sender, but these three simple messages are precisely what a sender needs for effective communication. They are crucial to mutual understanding. They do not indicate whether the receiver likes or dislikes or agrees or disagrees with the sender or his ideas, but they do give the sender an indication of whether his message is producing the intended meaning in the listener.

Feedback messages take a variety of forms, both verbal and nonverbal. Furthermore, the amount and quality of feedback we receive profoundly affect the growth and development of our communication skills. In other words, our skills in communication do not develop without high-quality feedback from other persons in our environment. In our role as listeners, we have an essential responsibility for nurturing the communicative behavior of others.

Learning to give and receive feedback intelligently is one of the most difficult communication skills to master. In two-way communication, every message should serve as feedback after the dialogue has begun. Every message should (1) be an appropriate response to the other person's message, and (2) give the other some indication of how to proceed. Remember that feedback, in one form or another, is the *only* indication of whether or not a communication has been effective. Remember the burned manuscript and the cracked nosewheel strut. Appropriate feedback would have given these incidents happier endings.

SUMMARY

This chapter has advanced some elementary concepts and principles about human communication. These concepts and principles are extended and elaborated many different ways in the chapters ahead. As you continue reading, it may help if you refer to these ideas from time to time to help you organize your thinking about the communication process.

We've introduced a simple model of communication and defined its elements: sender, receiver, message, channel, feedback, context, and meaning. We've said that all behavior communicates and that we cannot *not* communicate. We've said that messages do not have meanings, but rather that meanings are the responses of interpreters to messages. We have characterized communication as a participative process and shown how each element of that process is associated with specific barriers to effective communication.

We've found the ideas discussed here extremely useful in thinking about human communication and in discovering ways to improve our own communication skills and those of our students. We're still working hard to improve, and we hope you will, too.

QUESTIONS

1. Try to recall some incidents from your own experience in which communication failed. Can you find an incident to illustrate each of the communication barriers discussed in this chapter?
2. Why do our attempts to avoid communicating frequently communicate things we do not intend? Offer some examples from your own experience or observations. What were the consequences for the persons involved? How could such problems be avoided?
3. What are your greatest strengths and weaknesses as a communicator? What kinds of feedback have led you to these conclusions?
4. What are some of the communication skills demanded of you in connection with your current activities? What kinds of demands do you anticipate ten years from now? Twenty years from now?
5. Suppose you are asked by your instructor: "Would you rather be graded in this class on the basis of what you *really know* about the subject, or on what you are able to communicate about what you know?" Consider this question in light of what you know about communication, and offer a reply to the instructor's question.

SUGGESTED READINGS

Barnlund, Dean C. Toward a meaning-centered philosophy of communication. *Journal of Communication* 12(1962): 197–211.

Gerbner, George. Communication and the social environment. *Scientific American* 227(1972):152–160.

Goldmark, Peter C. Communication and the community. *Scientific American* 227(1972):143–150.

Miller, George. *The psychology of communication*. Baltimore: Penguin, 1969.

Miller, Gerald R. *An introduction to speech communication*, 2nd ed. Indianapolis: Bobbs-Merrill, 1972.

2

INTRAPERSONAL COMMUNICATION

PREVIEW

When an individual responds communicatively, he or she does so as an entire being. He or she responds with thoughts, with feelings, and on occasion with overt communication acts. The uniqueness of a person's thoughts, feelings, and behavioral acts is influenced by past communication encounters; in turn, the way that an individual is organized intrapersonally is an important basis for his or her performance in future communication settings.

In this chapter we will focus on the individual. We will consider some of the ways in which an individual's intrapersonal behaviors are influenced by his or her social community. We will also consider the nature of private intrapersonal behaviors as a basis for communicating with others.

OBJECTIVES

To discuss the *process* nature of human communication

To describe the role of the language community in shaping the individual's communication behavior

To describe the organization of an individual's intrapersonal behaviors and their role in communicating with others

TWO Human communication is a process. By process we simply mean that the individual and the community interact; they act upon and respond to each other. And it is through this interaction that things really happen; both the individual and the community are changed; they co-determine each other's behavior.

Since the focus of this chapter is on *intrapersonal* communication, our current goal is to direct attention to the effects of the *communication process* upon the *individual*. Specifically, our goal is to examine the ways in which the individual is changed through interaction with his or her language community and how those changes can influence the general well-being of a person as well as his or her effectiveness as a communicator.

Through communication an individual can be changed in the ways in which he *feels*, the ways he *thinks*, and the ways in which he might *act*. Communication exchanges can result in the learning of new attitudes about the communication process as well as new strategies, styles, and skills that can increase the individual's overall satisfaction and effectiveness in future social encounters.

In studying intrapersonal communication we can employ a *developmental* approach and focus on an individual's *history* of communication with others and the ways in which the individual is changed by that history. Also, we can adopt a *structural* approach and study the *current organization* of an individual's communication behaviors and the ways in which an individual is likely to respond because of that organization. In this chapter we will look at intrapersonal communication from both the developmental and the structural points of view.

INTRAPERSONAL DEVELOPMENT

From the *developmental* point of view we can define intrapersonal communication as a study of the ways in which we *develop* repertories of *thoughts*, *feelings*, and *behavioral acts* due to our unique history of interaction within a social community.

Communication behavior is essentially social behavior. Although our basic *capacity* for communication can be attributed to our unique genetic history, the particular *form* and *scope* of a person's communication can be attributed to historical influences on his or her language communities. It is no accident that people who grow up in an English-speaking community speak English while individuals who are raised in an

Hispanic community speak Spanish. The effects of the language community upon the individual go far beyond vocabulary and grammar. The language community helps determine what we see, how we feel about what we see, and how we are likely to respond to the world around us.

A speaker's language behavior evolves from a considerable amount of *social interaction* and *instruction*. Children imitate the language of their parents and others in their immediate environment. The child is encouraged to use language, is provided with models, is corrected when mistakes are made, and is rewarded when he or she gets it right. After the community is successful at getting the child to generate a lot of talk, the next problem is to get the child to modify his or her talk and to keep quiet! The child must learn to distinguish between those occasions where certain forms of talk are encouraged and those where talk is discouraged.

COMMUNICATION AND CONSEQUENCES

A language community is influential in shaping the communication behavior of an individual because it provides the individual with *consequences*. When the community ignores or punishes a particular behavior, it tends to reduce the recurrence of that behavior. When the community rewards a particular behavior, that behavior is strengthened and its recurrence is more likely.

Over a period of time, a child learns certain communication behaviors and the consequences of those behaviors. For example, a child may learn that the word "drink" when spoken in the presence of the mother will lead to a glass of water, whereas the word "apple" will lead to a round, red object. Eventually a child learns to put words into sentences much like those used in his language community. When he deviates from accepted language structures he is usually corrected. Through this social process of *acting* and *receiving feedback* an individual develops communication behaviors, both verbal and nonverbal, which are similar to the communication behaviors of others in his language community.

INTERPERSONAL VS. INTRAPERSONAL COMMUNICATION

The child's first communication behaviors are essentially interpersonal. That is, the child interacts with the community as an active participant and responds as a listener or a speaker. Eventually, however, the individual is able to assume the roles of both speaker and listener without the presence of another person. When a child is alone, he may ask a question "out loud" and then answer his own question. Or, as the child matures he may simply "think" in the sense of carrying on a "private" conversation with himself.

Interpersonal communication is unique in that it leads directly to *consequences* provided by the social community; in contrast, if a person maintains the privacy of his intrapersonal communication he is relatively free from social consequences. For example, a person can think unpopular or unacceptable thoughts and not get punished. Hostile or overly aggressive feelings can also be disguised.

It is doubtful, however, that even our so-called "private" intrapersonal behaviors are totally free from social consequences. To disguise our true thoughts and feelings in the presence of a discriminating observer is often difficult. Additionally, in intrapersonal communication we function as both speaker and listener and many of our private listening behaviors have been learned from our social community. As a private listener we provide consequences for some of our own thoughts in much the same way as a listener in our community provides consequences for those thoughts. We probably do something like this when we "feel guilty" for certain private behaviors, even though no one else in the community is aware of them

Our private conversations also provide the basis for much of our public conversations which clearly do result in consequences. There is a direct tie between the quality of our intrapersonal communication and the quality of our public communication.

THE DEVELOPMENT OF "SELF"

From a communication point of view we can define a person's "self" as the individual's repertory of intrapersonal behaviors. A person's self is in process, but at a given moment can be described in terms of how the individual thinks, feels, and is capable of behaving with a variety of overt acts.

Through social interaction and instruction an individual can develop an expanded and more discriminating repertory of communication behaviors. Through specialized instruction an individual can learn to develop more "fine-grained" descriptions of events, and can learn *rules* about the relationships among those events.

The material in this book, as well as the discussions and activities in the course in which it is used, can offer new and more discriminating ways of looking at human communication, can facilitate constructive

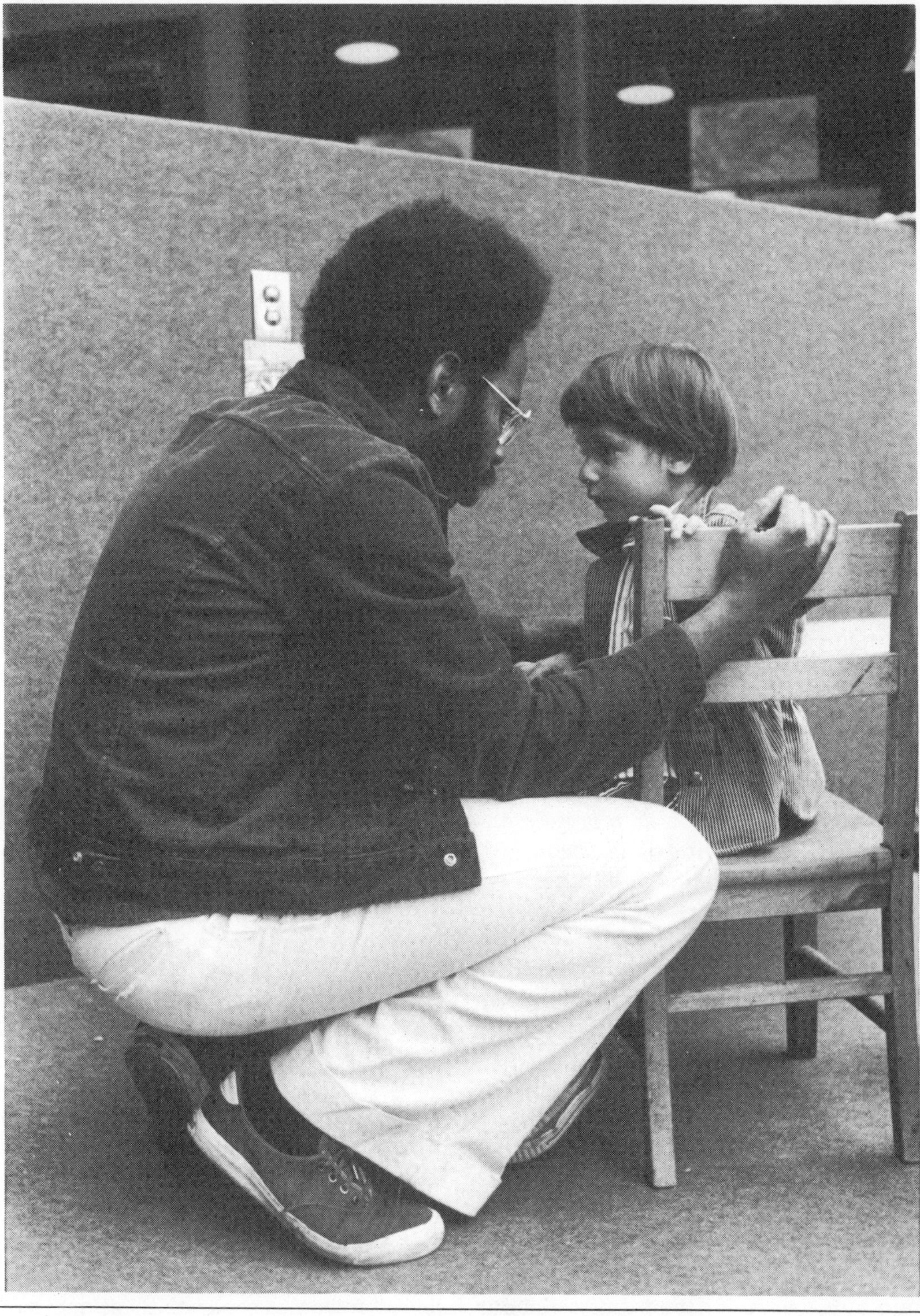

attitudes about one's own communication abilities and potential, and can assist in the development of new and useful communication skills.

As this learning process continues, the individual becomes more autonomous and *self-sufficient*; he can solve more of his own problems, and is capable of more appropriate and more rewarding actions.

Evidence of this increasingly autonomous behavior is clearly demonstrated when an individual is able to think through and solve a problem. In mathematics, for example, an individual might engage in verbal behavior (thinking) that results in the generation of *new* verbal behavior (the correct answer). But a person might also think about his or her physical poise behind a speaker's stand and conclude that certain distracting mannerisms should be modified. In this case, thinking would result in nonverbal outcomes, that is, a more poised and less distracting presence behind the speaker's stand.

An individual learns communication behaviors through social interaction as a "public" speaker and a "public" listener and then learns to employ these behaviors at the private or intrapersonal level. In turn, the quality of a person's "private" intrapersonal communication becomes an important factor in the quality of one's public communication.

It is difficult, if not impossible, to separate the individual from the community. Clearly, people do "think through" and solve problems. They also write and edit "original" speeches. But even here the behavior of the individual is highly influenced by concepts, rules, and skills learned from the community. It is in this sense that we describe communication as a *process* in which people *act upon* and *respond* to each other. And it is through this basic communication process that we *co-determine* each other's behavior.

THE STRUCTURE OF INTRAPERSONAL COMMUNICATION

From the structural point of view, we can define intrapersonal communication as a study of the ways that a person is prepared to respond due to the unique organization of that individual's personal repertory of *thoughts*, *feelings*, and *behavioral acts*. When an individual responds communicatively, he responds as an entire being: he has *thoughts* about the topic at hand, he has *feelings* about that topic, and he *responds* according to his own unique patterns of communication acts. Although people respond simultaneously with thought, feeling, and behavioral acts, for the purposes of our discussion we can separate these subjects and treat them individually. Accordingly, the nature of each of these responses is explored below.

THOUGHT (COGNITION)

Thinking may be described in terms of the ways in which we *conceptualize* events and their relationships and in terms of the *language* we use to describe those events and relationships.

Intrapersonal Concepts A recent study by the Los Angeles City Planning Commission aptly illustrates the differences in our individual perceptions. Members of the Commission asked people from various ethnic and economic groups to draw a map of the city. Each individual was asked to include as much detail as possible. Study findings showed the following (*Newsweek*, March 15, 1976, 71):

> . . . upper-class residents from Westwood had an extensive knowledge of the city, including the location of such features as beaches, airports, universities and museums. But, Black residents of Avalon (near Watts) perceived L.A. as consisting only of the inner city with a few main streets. Maps made by Hispanic residents of Boyle Heights contained, in addition to their own neighborhood, only City Hall, Union Station and the bus terminal. Both poor Blacks and Hispanic citizens were aware that the city is, in fact, larger than their own neighborhoods, but depicted the other areas only with empty circles.

Each individual develops not only a concept or "mental map" of the city in which he lives but an entire cultural perspective made up of concepts that pertain to a multitude of other events. Concepts pertain to what we *see* and how we draw boundaries around what we see. Our mental maps vary in *completeness* and *incompleteness*, in *accuracy* and *distortion*, and in the extent to which they are *shared* or *not shared* by others in our environment. Just as our mental maps of a city largely determine the ways in which we will use a city, our mental maps of self, of others, and of the world around us provide the basis for the ways we communicate with ourselves and others and how the world communicates with us.

The ways our unique concepts directly influence communication are illustrated by the experiences of an American social worker assigned to a Peruvian village. Studies had shown that contaminated drinking water was the source of many of the villagers' diseases, and the social worker was training the Peruvian women to boil water as one means of

reducing illness in the village. As a part of her program of change, the social worker explained the nature of the harmful bacteria and how the women could eliminate the bacteria by boiling water used for drinking. An extensive effort to communicate this "simple" information, however, persuaded only a handful of women to boil water! Why the failure of communication? Attempts to answer this question led to several discoveries. First, the Peruvian women had no concept for "bacteria," nor could they imagine how something invisible to the eye could be harmful. Furthermore, the villagers believed that "warm" was for the sick and "cold" was for the healthy. Accordingly, their customs dictated that they serve cold water to the healthy and warm to the ill. To boil water for a healthy person was to contradict basic concepts that were well established in village traditions (Rogers and Shoemaker, 1971). Thus, the breakdown in communication was traced to the differences in the concepts or mental maps held by the social worker and the villagers: The villagers had no concept for "bacteria," and the social worker did not share their concept that "warm" was only for the sick.

The study of intercultural communication reveals a multitude of differences in the concepts we hold. For example, our concept that a cow is something to eat is abhorrent in India where cows are sacred. While these great differences in concepts are clearly apparent across cultures, they are sometimes less perceptible within a single culture, perhaps partly because we frequently stress our similarities while avoiding our great individual differences. They exist nevertheless and contribute to many of our communication breakdowns.

We can explore a person's intrapersonal thinking in terms of the concepts he builds and uses. Those concepts differ in their scope, form, and universality:

1. For a given person, a concept can be *existent* or *nonexistent*. In the case of the Peruvian villagers, for example, the concept of "bacteria" was nonexistent.
2. Concepts vary on a continuum from *simple* to *elaborate*. For example, the concepts of male and female are relatively simple. More complex concepts are involved, however, in descriptions of the interaction patterns of men and women.
3. Concepts vary in terms of their *universality*. For example, "bacteria" is a widely shared concept in our society. The concept of "cognitive dissonance" exists in our society also, but it is a less conventional term — that is, it is shared and understood by only a relatively small number of people.

If we recognize that communication occurs between two or more people when they are able to *share meaning*, it is clear that communication depends strongly on the conceptual habits of the participants. When we talk to another person or to a group, we are talking not to a standardized thinking machine but to a unique individual or a collection of individuals, each of whom has evolved his or her own ways of seeing and responding to the world.

Intrapersonal Language Language events include words as well as the grammatical or syntactical rules that govern their usage. Additional formal language systems include logic and mathematics. Informal language systems — those not governed by prescriptive sets of rules — include numerous forms of nonverbal communication.

Since much of the business of intrapersonal communication is conducted with the use of language, *language facility* may be a basic determinant of an individual's ability to manage intrapersonal communication. As we increase our repertory of language symbols, we can "label" a wider range of informational events. Similarly, as we increase our store of language structures such as grammar, logic, and mathematics, we expand our ability to analyze and synthesize a wider range of relationships among language symbols.

In effect, then, we can describe the nature of a person's intrapersonal communication in terms of the complexity of his language code. Some individuals may be capable of *restricted* coding; others may be capable of both *restricted* and *elaborated* coding. A restricted code includes relatively simple syntactical patterns, whereas the elaborated code involves more complex ones. The individual with a restricted code will employ similar language patterns on a frequent basis, and the person who possesses the more elaborate code will evidence a much greater variety of speech patterns (Bernstein, 1971, 125–128).

Williams and Naremore (1969, 98) have developed a fairly detailed classification of restricted-elaborated codes. Examples of their five classes of codes are given here:

Impulsive "ouch," "wow," "oh," "ah," screaming, laughter, crying, swearing, etc.

Contactive "hello," "hey," "John?" "waiter!" "How do you do?" "you know," "do you hear me?"

Conversive cocktail party chatter, language exchanged between persons just introduced, elaborated greetings and farewells, simple yes-no answers, names, etc.

Descriptive/directive Recounting some event which has been experienced; delineating in verbal terms a "picture" of something; telling a person how to play a game, step-by-step; giving instructions to a traveler; commanding some action

Elaborative Interpretation, or explaining one's understanding of the meaning of some event which has been experienced, or of some concept or idea (e.g., what "freedom" means). Narration, or developing a topic in story form (e.g., retelling the story of a movie or TV show). Persuasion, or inducing direction in thinking or behavior by overt verbal appeal (e.g., a mother reasoning with her child)

Williams and Naremore suggest that nonverbal codes may be as expressive as verbal codes for the fundamental task of *impulsive* communication. Some of the *contactive* or "linkage" functions of human communication can be performed as well by both verbal or nonverbal codes. For the *conversive*, *descriptive*, and *directive* functions of communication, nonverbal codes can complement verbal codes. For the *elaborative* tasks of reasoning, argument, and complex explanations, however, nonverbal codes have minimum relevance. Complex thinking tasks require clarification and rational analysis of information and arguments, and the more elaborate verbal codes are necessary to accomplish these tasks.

FEELING (AFFECT)

Most of our feeling responses can be described in terms of two basic dimensions: their "strength" (from weak to strong) and their content (from negative to positive). Accordingly, we can have weak to strong feelings about a person or an event, and we can feel positive to negative about that person or event.

Human feelings are a vital part of each person's intrapersonal life. It may well be that our *feelings* about ourselves, others, and the world around us provide a basic index of the meaningfulness of our lives and the extent of our personal and social adjustment. A number of scholars in psychology and speech communication have argued that the well-adjusted communicator is one who has developed positive feelings about himself and others.

While some of our feelings, like those experienced while walking barefooted on hot pavement, are natural consequences of our physiology and the environment, many are learned through communication with other people. Through new communication experiences, such feelings can be relearned or altered, or new ones can be acquired. One mechanism by which feelings are generated is *feedback* from others in communication settings. Further, different kinds of feedback can generate different feelings. If we receive considerable positive feedback, we are likely to feel better about things; if we receive considerable negative feedback, we are more likely to feel badly about things.

The nature of feedback depends both on the person we receive it from and on our own perspective and behavior. If most of our contact is with highly critical people, for example, we are more likely to receive a greater amount of negative feedback. At the same time, if we continually approach others with antagonistic or unattractive behaviors, our own behaviors can be the source of the negative feedback. Thus, each individual has a degree of control over the feedback he receives and over some of his own feelings as well. He can be selective in his encounters with people and in the ways he approaches them. We can increase the odds of receiving useful feedback by emphasizing exchanges with responsible persons who are likely to provide a realistic and constructive balance of positive and negative feedback. We also can reduce the odds of generating negative feedback by recognizing and modifying some of our behaviors that interfere with effective interpersonal contacts.

Feelings can be viewed as (1) a source of information and (2) a basis for action. For example, if one backs into a hot stove, one's feelings would provide information about that stove — hot as hell — and generate an action — like getting away fast. In such a case, feelings can be a reliable and useful source of information. They can also be unreliable and misleading, however. For example, an individual may possess considerable skill in communication, as well as potential skills and abilities not yet discovered or developed. He nevertheless may develop very negative feelings about his ability to communicate.

Reliance on our feelings is a fairly effortless means of responding to the world. It may be tempting to let feelings become the primary basis for many of our decisions about each other and about the world. Feelings are a vitally human part of our existence; however, they cannot provide the amount and quality of information that is available through our thinking processes. In fact, they may provide a limited and distorted basis for many of our evaluations. Further, they do not provide an adequate basis for complex analysis and problem solving, which require the more advanced thinking processes.

Juries are frequently admonished to determine the guilt or innocence of accused persons on the *objective facts* of the case as opposed to their feelings about the accused. The jurors are so instructed because of the inherent unreliability of feelings as a basis for determining a person's guilt or innocence. If we have negative feelings about a person, it may be difficult to separate them from our consideration of pertinent facts about that person. Nevertheless, an awareness that feelings provide limited and sometimes unreliable or irrelevant information should motivate us to go beyond our "feeling barometer" and seek relevant objective facts as a central basis for the important conclusions we draw about each other.

In general, how one's set of feeling responses compares with those of others is likely to depend on the extent of shared experiences among the persons involved. For example, members of a particular minority group are likely to share certain experiences that are common to that group and may result in similar feelings. At the same time, people who live under very different circumstances may find it difficult to understand each other's feelings. The most earnest attempt to put oneself in another's situation may provide only a limited understanding of the other's experiences and the feelings generated by those experiences.

BEHAVIOR (ACTION)

At the intrapersonal level, individuals are not only predisposed to think and feel in certain ways, they are also prepared to behave or act in certain ways. One's repertory of potential acts constitutes the third area of a person's organization at the intrapersonal level. Behavior is the area of communication that is directly observable by others. It is through communication acts that we have an effect on others and others have an effect on us.

Overt communication responses are numerous. They include our use of all forms of verbal and nonverbal messages: words and syntactical structures, posture and gestures, voice and style of speaking, interpersonal and organizational roles, communication strategies, and the ideas and values that make up the content of our messages.

A person's communication acts are typically evaluated in terms of two basic criteria: *intelligibility* and *appropriateness*. Intelligibility is a measure of understanding. Appropriateness pertains to a communicator's ability to meet social standards of acceptability. In general, a person can satisfy standards of intelligibility and acceptability if he can read the spectrum of individual and social expectancies and can draw from an appropriate set of potential communication acts.

At any given time, an individual is capable of responding communicatively in certain ways. But through the continued development of communication knowledge and skills one can develop a wider range of adaptive communication responses that provide opportunities for more effective participation in a variety of communication settings. Most individuals are quick to learn intelligible and appropriate responses within their immediate home and community environments. For example, a child soon learns that she or he is expected to raise a hand before speaking in a classroom. The child also learns to employ messages that make basic desires and needs intelligible to others.

As an individual enters new and more complex environments, effective communication requires the ability to read the grid of more varied and subtle expectancies and to draw on an expanded repertory of communication acts. For example, a person in a midmanagement position will need to understand and respond to subordinates, peers, and superordinates. He will also need communication skills that are appropriate for different types of dyads, small groups, and public speeches. Virtually all management tasks are communication tasks, and the more complex problems of management require an expanded repertory of intelligible and appropriate communication behaviors.

Some of our current response tendencies may make a positive contribution toward effective communication while others may not. A person who cannot read the grid or who has a limited or rigid set of communication responses will tend to respond in the same basic ways in spite of the differences among people and settings. Accordingly, his responses are less likely to satisfy normative standards of intelligibility and acceptability. A reasonable goal is to retain and enhance those communication behaviors that make positive contributions to individual and social needs and to minimize or eliminate behaviors that do not.

A PROGRAM FOR SELF-IMPROVEMENT

A person's intrapersonal behaviors include thoughts, feelings, and a repertory of potential communication acts. The form and scope of these behaviors develop as a natural consequence of interaction within one's general language community and influential subdivisions of that community.

Some of our learned behavior may lead to shared meaning and effective action while others may lead to misunderstanding and unnecessary conflict. In developing a program for self-development a first step should be to examine one's current communication behaviors and their usual consequences. A second step should be the development of a specific plan for self-improvement. Progress toward both goals might be accelerated through a consideration of the following questions:

1. What are some of the important social factors that influence my current thoughts, feelings, and communication acts?
2. What are some of the important consequences of my current style of communication?
3. Which of my current behaviors seem to lead to misunderstanding or unnecessary conflict?
4. Which of my current behaviors leads to more effective and constructive interaction with others?
5. Whom should I turn to for the most useful feedback and advice?
6. What is a reasonable plan for additional instruction in spoken and written forms of human communication?
7. How can increased communication effectiveness contribute to my personal satisfaction and well-being?
8. How can increased communication effectiveness contribute to my professional goals?

SUMMARY

In this chapter we have described human communication as a *process*. By process we simply mean that people are continually acting upon and responding to each other. The communication process is *dynamic* in the sense that it provides consequences. Through communication people are changed; they are changed in the ways they feel, think, and act.

The study of intrapersonal communication is concerned with the effects of communication upon the individual. When approached developmentally, the focus is on the individual's history of communication with others and the effects of that history on the individual's current repertory of thoughts, feelings, and potential acts. When approached from the structural point of view, the focus is on the current organization of an individual's repertory of thoughts, feelings, and potential acts and the effects of that organization on the individual's likely responses to current and future communication settings.

In this chapter intrapersonal communication was described as a relatively private process, but one that is based on what we have learned from public communication processes. It was concluded that one's history of social interaction provides the basis for much of our intrapersonal behavior, and in turn that the structure of our intrapersonal behavior provides a basis for a person's performance in current and future communication encounters.

Intrapersonal thinking was described in terms of an individual's conceptual orientation and language facility. Feelings were described as a source of information and a basis for action. One's repertory of communication acts was described in terms of their potential intelligibility and appropriateness.

Finally, it was noted that an individual's current communication behaviors are in large part a product of learning. And, through additional experience and instruction an individual can modify existing behaviors and learn new ones. When this process is successful the individual can enjoy a marked improvement in communication satisfaction and effectiveness.

QUESTIONS

1. How does a person's organization at the intrapersonal level affect his participation in dyads, small groups, and public address settings?
2. How can an individual's participation in dyads, small groups, and public address settings affect the nature of his intrapersonal communication?
3. What are the natural limits of our ability to communicate with the world in which we live?
4. How might an extended visit to a different culture affect our communication behaviors?
5. Why is the social community effective at shaping many of our intrapersonal communication behaviors?

SUGGESTED READINGS

Catania, A. Charles. *Learning*. Englewood Cliffs, New Jersey: Prentice-Hall, Inc., 1979.

Cronkhite, Gary. *Communication and awareness*. Menlo Park, Calif.: Cummings, 1976.

Dance, Frank E. X., and Carl Larson. *The functions of human communication*. New York: Holt, 1976.

Faules, Don F. The impact of values on organizational communication. In J. Owen, P. Page, G. Zimmerman (eds.), *Communication in organizations*. St. Paul, Minn.: West, 1976.

Giffin, Kim. Social alienation by communication denial. *Quarterly Journal of Speech* 56 (1970):347–357.

Wilmot, William W., and John R. Wenburg. *Communication involvement: personal perspectives*. New York: Wiley, 1974.

BREAKING WINDOWS
YOU MAY SAY WAS AN
ACT OF POLITICAL
FRUSTRATION, BUT,
STEALING THE MERCHANDISE
FROM THE WINDOW DISPLAYS
WAS NOT. PEOPLE WHO STOLE
MY MERCHANDISE CAN BRING
THEM BACK WITHOUT FEAR OF
BEING CHARGED.
Braun

3

NONVERBAL COMMUNICATION

PREVIEW

When most people think about communication, they think of speaking with *words*; when they think about a speech class, they envision students trying to improve their *verbal* abilities. But while the verbal message continues to be the focus of courses in speech communication, we must recognize that we are continually sending and receiving many messages that are not expressed in words. These messages are nonverbal. They prompt us to develop significant meanings and responses for our perception of the behavior and the environment around us.

Words interact with nonverbal messages so intricately that we really cannot understand the communication process without also knowing one of the crucial components of that process—the message that is truly "beyond words." Students are better off if they develop a good awareness of the nonverbal dimension of communication before practicing the kinds of verbal skills discussed in later chapters.

OBJECTIVES

To identify many different kinds of nonverbal factors that affect the communication process

To enhance the development of skills in perceiving and interpreting nonverbal cues in our environment

To increase awareness of our personal nonverbal messages

THREE A candidate for U.S. senator had to make a decision. His campaign was well financed and had a good staff, but he had no experience in public affairs and was not well known. Though he was an attractive man, he was a marginal public speaker and had little grasp of the intricacies of public issues. What should be his campaign strategy? The candidate and his staff decided on a media campaign. There would be no mass rallies, no public speeches at high schools or service clubs, no difficult question-and-answer sessions. Instead, most voters would learn of the candidate through television, radio, and newspapers. They would see him in thirty-second or one-minute television spots, in full-page newspaper ads, or on large posters or billboards with color photographs of his handsome face. They would see him shaking hands with senior citizens, schoolchildren, factory workers, leaders of minority groups, and famous politicians. They would watch the family man as he romped with his happy children and chatted with his pretty wife at their tasteful suburban home. They would read a personality profile in a news magazine and see old photos of the candidate in his military uniform and as a janitor working his way through law school. The evening news would report on his appearance at a local shopping center, public barbecue, or sports event. Makeup experts, fashion coordinators, photographers, and other consultants would ensure that the candidate's hair was always neatly trimmed, his clothes carefully tailored, his face well-tanned. The candidate would appear smooth, confident, relaxed, congenial, trustworthy, and competent. And he would be elected.

A young executive replaced the retiring branch manager of a large insurance company. On arriving at her new assignment, she saw a discouraging situation. Productivity in this branch had consistently been the lowest in the company. Absenteeism and employee turnover were high. Most employees sat at gray desks arranged in rows and facing the same direction with the supervisor watching from behind. A time clock welcomed the workers to the drab, barren offices. Talking was permitted only in relation to specific job duties. The noise of typewriters and photocopy machines was monotonous. The floor, walls, and windows were dirty. In general, the office complex was a depressing place to be. The new executive began to make changes. Employee committees were asked to suggest changes in the working environment. Partitions were installed and desks rearranged to provide semiprivacy for smaller work teams. Plants, curtains, carpeting, and attractive furniture were purchased. Quiet recorded music was piped to all offices, and the lighting was improved. Rooms were repainted. An extra janitor was hired. In sectors where employees met the public, a dress code was established. Coffee corners were set up for casual employee conversation. The time clocks were removed, and area supervisors were asked to keep informal records of employee attendance. A permanent employee committee was established to develop ideas for continually improving the work operations and environment. The branch office became a pleasant place to be. Absenteeism declined, and morale improved. Within a year, office productivity had increased to offset the cost of the changes.

Professor Bland is a brilliant mathematician. Several books and scholarly papers have made him a nationally respected scholar. With his students and colleagues, however, his reputation is quite different. He speaks in a rapid, high-pitched, often stammering whine, and his gestures are nervous and repetitious. As he lectures, he rarely looks at the students; as people talk to him, he looks to either side and never establishes direct eye contact. He paces back and forth. Professor Bland sighs and frowns whenever a student seeks clarification of lecture material. When people talk to him in his office, he often glances at his watch as they are explaining their problems. He interrupts others in midsentence and often impatiently and abruptly changes the subject. He bathes infrequently, his hair is disheveled, and his clothing mismatched, wrinkled, and usually dirty. When greeting colleagues, his handshake is limp and brief. He has much to contribute to his field. His words are carefully chosen and sometimes beautifully arranged; his ideas are profound. Yet nobody can stand to be around him. People avoid Professor Bland like the plague.

What is happening here? What do these three examples have in common? Obviously, they all involve human communication, but we believe that their most significant messages are conveyed by *nonverbal* communication—by means other than words. In the first case, the candidate depended not on verbal messages on the issues, but on public impressions of his "image" as revealed through visual appeals. In the second, the executive did not verbally command or even request improved employee performance; rather, she changed the nonverbal environment so that it began to say something different: "This is a good, comfortable place to work, and we are glad you are here." In the third example, a man with enormous intellectual and verbal competence failed to recognize his nonverbal behaviors and characteristics, negating the potential productivity of his interpersonal encounters.

Nonverbal is a term that describes "all communication events which transcend spoken or written words" (Knapp, 1972, 20). In Chapter One we drew an important distinction between behavior that we perceive and behavior that goes unnoticed. In this chapter, we emphasize that nonverbal communication includes only the events, behaviors, and characteristics *that we perceive and give meaning to.* It is difficult to know precisely when a communication event begins and ends, particularly when the event consists of nonverbal behavior. When does a gesture or facial expression begin? When do we first notice the nonverbal environment — the room, furniture, space, background noise? When do we stop noticing a person's clothing, grooming, or posture? In practice, we can define and understand nonverbal communication only in general terms, because it is virtually impossible to know precisely the specific boundaries of behavior we perceive.

TYPES OF NONVERBAL COMMUNICATION

What are the behaviors and features — the messages — of nonverbal communication? Several different nonverbal events usually interact to form the perceived message. Thus, while we may suggest several categories of nonverbal communication, discussed below, each category inevitably overlaps one or more of the others.

PHYSICAL FEATURES OF THE HUMAN BODY

A perhaps regrettable trait of human beings is that we develop important meanings from a person's physical features. A tall man with slender waist, muscled torso, and square shoulders may appear confident, strong, and attractive. If he is too big and too muscular, however, we may think him muscle-bound and simpleminded. A short, thin man with stooped shoulders may suggest a timid, unassertive person, though we might also guess him to be intelligent. A woman with the so-called hourglass figure may be viewed as sexier and less intelligent than one with straighter lines. Facial features of both men and women — eyes, nose, mouth, and shape — prompt immediate judgments of pretty, ugly, plain, handsome, funny, or sexy. Thinness and fatness are characteristics that we almost always notice in others and use as an index of attractiveness. Hair style (or baldness) is also important. If you ever look at a personal photograph taken several years ago, your hair style may be the first thing you notice.

The tendency to take nonverbal meanings from physical features can be insidious, cruel, and dangerous. Brown- and black-skinned people have suffered for hundreds of years because of the unfavorable meanings given their racial characteristics. Yet, ironically, among Caucasians a deep tan may seem more attractive than a pale skin that may suggest weakness and anemia. The absence of typical bodily features also creates meaning, often with unfortunate overtones. Missing or shrunken limbs from amputation or birth defects, blindness, and paralysis may prompt a variety of responses from the receiver, most of them emotional reactions to characteristics that should not affect communicative transactions but often do.

There is evidence (Knapp, 1972, 63–79) that the meanings we associate with physical features significantly influence our judgments of credibility, intelligence, attitudes, dating and marriage decisions, personality, and ability. Sadly enough, many of these same features are elements over which a person has very little control. Still, we diet, exercise, lift weights, use cosmetics, groom, and even undergo plastic surgery in attempts to change our physical features and encourage positive responses from others to the nonverbal messages conveyed by our appearance.

BODILY MOVEMENT AND POSTURE

Closely related to our physical features are bodily movement and posture. We use the term *kinesics* to denote the broad category of observable physical motion that communicates — that is, to which people give meaning. The three types of observable physical motion discussed here are facial, gestural, and postural. Note, however, that although we can categorize types of bodily movement, *they are all closely linked. It is usually difficult to determine which discrete portion of the total movement or position is essential to our interpreting a particular meaning. Furthermore, physical movement and features interact in conveying a total bodily message.*

Facial Expression In general, the face provides crucial nonverbal cues in communication. In phone conversations, for example, the absence of facial expression significantly decreases the number of cues that the listener can receive and interpret. Facial expression may also be the most precise indicator of a person's inner feelings. For example, we can usually interpret another's happiness, anger, fear, sadness, surprise, pain, or affection simply by observing his or her facial movement. Facial expression can also be quite ambiguous, however, giving a variety of possible interpretations. For example, judges try to appear totally passive as they listen to courtroom testimony, even though they

undoubtedly feel surprise, disagreement, happiness, boredom, anger, concern, or enthusiasm. (Of course, the jury members *take meaning* from this passive expression; they do interpret the judge's mood, though probably less accurately than with more active facial movement.) An example of a misleading expression might be that of the celebrity who smiles whenever in the public eye. This so-called painted-on smile may deceive the observer, though some of us claim to be experts at detecting phoniness.

Notice how closely facial *movement* interacts with facial *features.* A smile or frown (movement) on a round, chubby face (features) may suggest a different meaning than a similar smile or frown on a narrow, gaunt face. Obviously, both movement and features interact as we receive and interpret these nonverbal messages.

The focal point of facial communication is the eyes, usually the most expressive part of the face. Eye contact is obviously a key signal in our communication with one another. *Length of gaze*, the duration of uninterrupted eye contact, can suggest a number of messages. For example, if your eyes and a stranger's meet for only a second or two, you both may receive the message, "I see you, you are unfamiliar, and I do not wish to interact with you." If the gaze lasts considerably longer, the message may be, "I've seen you somewhere before" or "You look interesting and I'd like to meet you." Courting behavior, flirting, and other romantic interaction depend on the skillful use of eye contact. The avoidance of eye contact can be equally communicative: "I don't like you so I'll pretend not to notice you," or "I want this conversation to end so I'll look away," or "I am shy and self-conscious," or "I'm thinking about something else." Of course, eye contact *alone* cannot give the receiver a reliable indication of another person's thoughts, feelings, or truthfulness. But these nonverbal cues are crucial to the understanding of the total facial message.

Gestures In speech communication, we most often think of gestures as arm and hand movements. However, gestures also include a wide range of behaviors such as shrugging the shoulders, cocking the head to one side, kicking a leg, swishing the hips, or tapping the toes.

Gestures may simply add emphasis to audible messages, as when a speaker uses a chopping motion with his hand every time he stresses a word with his voice, or they may convey more elaborate meanings to different observers, depending on the context of the message. The following nonverbal gestures, for example, are open to a variety of interpretations:

a step backward
a step forward
arms outstretched, palms up as if pushing
arms partially forward, palms down
one arm partially extended, hand and index finger shaking
arms folded, one foot tapping
fists clenched, arms down
fists clenched, arms partially forward
one arm outstretched, sweeping from one side to the other
swinging one leg, as if kicking at the dirt
arms close to body, hands folded

None of these gestures has inherent meaning. Message content depends largely on context—a gesture is perceived and interpreted by *unique human beings* in *unique situations.*

Posture Posture is defined roughly as body position and stance. We can describe different postures as formal, relaxed, rigid, defensive, aggressive, suggestive, sexy, slouched, awkward, and the like. Not only is a specific posture important nonverbally, but postural shifts can

also be revealing. Notice what happens, for example, when a military officer approaches a group of recruits in casual conversation or when a person whom we consider an enemy moves too close. Like many other species, human beings do a great deal of deliberate posturing that conveys to others our attitudes, intentions, and roles.

A special type of physical communication is *sign language*, the specific and identifiable movements of fingers, hands, and arms to denote letters, words, or phrases. Used for communication by and with the deaf and mute, this form of message is not nonverbal at all, since the sign gestures are as uniform and unambiguous as actual written verbal messages. Sign language can instead be thought of as a different form of verbal communication.

VOCAL INFLECTION

The human voice is an instrument for uttering language symbols, or words, in the primary form of verbal communication—speech. The voice is also part of the nonverbal arena, however. We use it to give special forms and patterns of inflection to verbal sounds. Communication scholars often use the term *paralanguage* to describe the vocal (audible) cues that accompany spoken language. *Paralanguage* does not refer to words themselves, but rather to everything that we can hear about the *way* in which words are spoken. Paralanguage or vocal inflection becomes nonverbal *communication* when we perceive the sound and assign meaning to it.

Emphasis, loudness, and force are all terms that refer to an important element of vocal inflection—increased volume. A change in volume usually signals a change of meaning. Consider, for example, the sentence, *I want you to go*. If the *I* is emphasized, the meaning might be, "I don't care if *John* wants you to stay; *I* want you to go." If *want* is accented, the sentence may mean, "I'm not *ordering* you to go, but I *want* you to go." If *you* gets the stress, it may mean, "I know *John* offered to run the errand, but I want *you* to go." Using force on all the words with special emphasis on *go* may indicate anger: *"I want you to GO!"* Variables other than volume that may affect the meaning of the verbal message are *pitch* (highs and lows of the voice or tones), *rate* of speech (fast, moderate, slow), and voice *quality* (raspy, nasal, hoarse, gravelly, breathy).

Some vocalizations do not modify verbal symbols but are rather discrete sound units. Laughing, crying, burping, hiccupping, grunting, sighing, audible yawning, swallowing, coughing, moaning, loud inhaling or exhaling, and throat-clearing all may suggest significant meanings. We may clear our throat to get someone's attention, grunt to imply agreement, or breathe deeply to show impatience or exhaustion. Some utterances like *oh-oh*, *um*, *ah-HA*, *er*, *a-a-a-ah*, *o-o-o-oh*, *oo-oo-ooh*, or *uh-huh* are often used in lieu of actual words or even whole sentences. For example, on the proverbial "morning after," a slow, pained groan may be the only vocal cue necessary to describe one's condition.

The *pause* is usually classed as an element of vocal inflection. Whether silent or audible (*er*, *uh*, *um*), the pause may connote indecision, reluctance, confusion, or a variety of potential meanings. Pauses may also simply be habitual and mean nothing at all to most listeners. For an example of a meaningful pause, suppose you ask a friend for a loan of ten dollars. A quick "Well, sure!" may imply that he has no reluctance to grant you the loan. But a hesitant "Well, uh . . . sure" may suggest quite another meaning.

As with bodily movement, all specific characteristics of a particular inflection pattern will interact to modify the spoken language. We do not usually take meaning solely from, say, the speed of delivery; instead, we take it from a combination of speed, loudness, pauses, and changing pitch levels. Interacting vocal cues are among the most subtle and complex elements of speech. In fact, paralinguistic meanings are often the last and most difficult phase of learning a second language. Notice, for example, how many jokes in English depend to some extent on vocal inflection. People for whom English is a second language may laugh politely, but chances are that they do not completely appreciate the humor. And even for native speakers, we sometimes say, "You just don't know how to tell a joke," meaning that the speaker has not mastered the intricate vocal shadings that are the source of the humor.

TOUCH AND SMELL

Human beings assign meanings to touching behavior (*tactile* communication) and to odors (*olfactory* communication). Both are primitive forms of messages that each of us experiences from birth. Most of us receive significantly less information through touching and smelling than through seeing and hearing, but some tactile and olfactory messages can still be crucially important.

Among Americans, touching is generally less acceptable than in other cultures around the world. Touching is usually confined to close interpersonal relationships as between family members, lovers, or close friends. Formal or impersonal touching includes handshakes, pats on the back, or kisses on the cheek. Touching that goes beyond these societal conventions carries significant communicative implications. For example, men touching men, other than in a simple handshake, is taboo to some people, a suggestion of homosexuality. A nudge or shove may indicate hostility and prompt a fight. A kiss or a hug that lasts longer than usual may stir romantic interests or rumors (in observers).

We know that the meaning interpreted from tactile messages depends partly on the amount of physical contact — how long, how much pressure, how frequent — and partly on the regions of the body that are touched. Touch can be a fairly accurate indicator of emotional messages such as anger, love, affection, sympathy, and happiness. It is perhaps regrettable that in our culture we rarely get close enough to people to permit the richness of tactile communication to develop.

Olfactory messages, or communication through smell, may also be much less common in America than elsewhere. Body odor is given a negative connotation, so we bathe every day and cover our bodies with perfumes and deodorants, brush our teeth and use mouthwashes, buy breath-freshening candies, use scented hair sprays, and wear clothing that has been deodorized. But the perfumed smells that replace natural body scent nevertheless may be given meanings, such as sexy, pretty, nauseating, offensive, or pleasant.

Artificial scents in our environment also tend to reduce our sensitivity to olfactory communication. We try to eliminate natural household odors with perfumed sprays and exhaust fans. We clean our rugs and furniture. We substitute fresh foods with processed, canned, and frozen products almost devoid of natural odor. We even try to deodorize our pets. Some smells in our environment are clearly offensive, but the increasing standardization of smells through commercial products may be depriving us of meaningful nonverbal information.

We receive many messages through our senses of touch and smell — messages subject to different interpretation by different people. What nonverbal messages might be suggested by the situations below?

While talking to another person, you notice an offensive odor.

Just before you are introduced to give a speech, the person sitting next to you reaches over and squeezes your arm.

A new business acquaintance shakes your hand with a strong and almost painful grip.

You observe two women walking arm in arm along the sidewalk.

Your partner on a first date kisses you lightly on your ear.

Waiting for dinner at a friend's home, you smell something burning.

OBJECT LANGUAGE

The nonverbal cues discussed above are associated with a communicator's bodily characteristics and personal behavior. *Object language*, on the other hand, involves the physical things in our environment — things we see and use — that become nonverbal cues.

Perhaps the most relevant communicative objects are *artifacts,* the clothing, jewelry, and other accessories that we use to present and describe ourselves to others. Artifacts help define who we are and who we want to associate with. The owner of a sporty, colorful, stylish, flowing wardrobe might have little in common with the wearer of tight, straight, formal, plain clothing. The man who wears traditional jewelry — wedding ring, wristwatch, key chain, cufflinks, and tie clasp — might feel uncomfortable around a man with one earring, several rings, necklace, beaded belt, and sequined shirt.

Artifacts have another important function, however. They also suggest our moods and our behaviors. The following situations, for example, call for different types of clothing consistent with the participants' emotions and activities:

business conference
tennis match
funeral
family picnic
cocktail party
rock concert
Army Reserve meeting
intramural softball game

That we would dress according to what we expect to be doing seems obvious. Less obvious but intriguing is the proposition that our clothing might actually influence how we behave and how we feel. Do artifacts ever *cause* us to do certain things? It seems that they do. For example, people who have been in law enforcement, the military, or on athletic teams have noted that they interact differently with others when they put on their uniforms. Certainly, others who take meanings from those artifacts behave differently, too.

Other objects like cars, houses, furniture, art, food, and sundry consumer goods may convey meaning. *Status symbols* are nothing more than objects to which we expect the perceiver to assign favorable meanings. We like to surround ourselves with objects that not only make us comfortable but also communicate nonverbally. The leather-jacketed motorcyclist, the blue-jeaned and sandaled owner of a Volkswagen van, and the business-suited Cadillac owner are all sending messages through object language.

Some argue that we should not evaluate or relate to each other on the basis of physical features or objects, that we should always try to perceive and understand the "real person" underneath. Such an argument is well meaning but, we believe, unrealistic. People inevitably take meaning from objects in their environment. More important, however, is the question, "What is the 'real' person?" Isn't it in part the one who *selects* the artifacts, who *buys* products, who lives in the environment that he has helped create? From this perspective, object language is not a facade that hides a person, but instead a fairly consistent indication of the way that person wants to be perceived.

SPACE

The distances between ourselves and others, as well as the space around us, frequently become important nonverbal messages. The term *proxemics* (think of *proximity*) is used to describe our perception and use of personal and social space for communication. One key dimension is the *distance between people.* We all have a kind of personal territory, and like other animals, we can sense invasions of that personal space and seek to defend it.

A noted researcher in nonverbal communication, Edward Hall (1959), categorizes and defines four spatial relationships between communicators. He also discusses *close* and *far* phases in each category, suggesting that such variations depend on the relative intimacy between communicators. *Intimate distance* occurs from actual touching to about eighteen inches apart; sensory awareness of the other person is very high. *Personal distance*, about eighteen inches to four feet, is the typical space for conversation between people who are personally acquainted. *Social distance* (four to twelve feet) suggests a more impersonal relationship as in everyday work activities. Business offices are typically set up to conform to social distance. *Public distance* (twelve feet to the limits of hearing or seeing) gives participants the option of attending to or ignoring the messages of others, and sensory input is minimal. No close interpersonal contact or recognition is expected. Public speeches are examples of the use of public distance. A crowded environment, like a packed elevator or bus, can also modify the boundaries of each distance category.

Size of space also communicates. A large office, an expansive backyard, a roomy car, or a massive lecture hall will prompt different meanings than their opposites. Both in our homes and in most organizations, we can accurately assess the rank or status of people simply by the amount of space they control and how private that controlled space is.

In addition to distance and size, the *flexibility* of environmental space may be important. Hall identifies and defines three types of space according to their relative flexibility and the messages they may impart. *Fixed-feature space* has permanent features that tend to dictate how much of the space should be used. For example, we do not take a bath in the kitchen or prepare meals in the bathroom. We do not conduct a public meeting in a small office or hold an interview in an auditorium. The inflexible features of particular settings usually prompt us to create meanings and decide appropriate behavior for each setting. In *semifixed-feature space*, objects such as furniture may occasionally be moved to alter the nonverbal environment. Anyone who has ever rearranged a living room or office knows how that exercise may change not only our moods but also the typical ways in which we behave and interact with others in the altered space. The third category is *informal space*, which deals *not* with physical objects but with the way we *use* the space around us while interacting. The messages suggested by the distance between communicators, discussed above, are examples of how we communicate by means of informal space.

Whether our environment is fixed or flexible, it will frequently affect our communication behavior. Sommer (1969) explores in depth the impact of spatial factors on communication, noting that these factors tend to promote or discourage close communicative interaction, depending on the communicators and the setting—for example, small groups and informal encounters in the classroom, in offices, and even in the home. As with other forms of nonverbal communication, spatial messages are interpreted by the perceiver who answers the question, "How am I expected to behave in this environment?"

TIME

The dimension of time has at least two nonverbal connotations in communication. First, time as *a specific point on the clock* carries significant

meaning. For example, we may notice when someone is late for an appointment and begin thinking of possible reasons: "It's 1:30 and Jane isn't here yet; I hope nothing's wrong." We may notice that it is noon and suddenly become hungry. We may be pleased to get a friendly phone call in the early evening but irate if it comes at 2:00 A.M. We may begin to equate a person's punctuality with dependability, tardiness with irresponsibility. Americans tend to be preoccupied with clock time; our personal and institutional lives depend on timepieces to "tell" us when to begin and end most of our everyday activities.

A second way of thinking about time is *duration*, or time span. Closely related to clock time, and often measured by it, time span may suggest potent messages. "You haven't written in three weeks; that means you don't love me anymore!" "You've been swimming for over an hour; you must be getting cold." "How long has she been lecturing? Seems like forever!" "He grabbed my hand and held it for the longest time. I wonder what he was trying to tell me?" "There hasn't been a major earthquake in this area for over thirty years." A situation or a behavior is not only communicative in itself, but also significant in terms of the length of time involved.

SILENCE

As if nonverbal communication were not complex enough, merely the *absence* of audible messages also may carry meaning. Silence may also be called *tacit* communication. When a person who could communicate orally chooses to remain silent, either briefly or at some length, that choice has message content we may interpret.

Jensen (1973) suggests five communicative functions of silence. First, it may serve as a *linkage* between people. Moments of silence shared between two people may suggest an invisible bond of trust and compatibility. Silence may also suggest the *absence* of a linkage, however, as when one fails to respond to a spoken message from another.

Second, silence serves an *affective* function in that it has impact on our emotional interaction. For example, "holding our tongues" during a violent argument may prevent even greater anger, while giving someone the "silent treatment" may cause increased hostility.

Third is the *revelational* function, which can either reveal or keep something hidden. If we remain silent in response to questions, we hide explicit information. For instance, if we ask "How was your day?" and get no response, we do not receive explicit information. On the other hand, we may then think, "I'll bet she's upset from a rough day; I won't bother her." Not revealing some information was the basis for developing another message. Silence may also reveal personal traits, such as moodiness, shyness, thoughtfulness, hostility, arrogance, or any number of other characteristics.

A fourth function is *judgmental.* We use silence to suggest good or bad, agreement or dissent. For example, some argue that not speaking out against social evils is implied agreement with those conditions. We use the "silence implies consent" premise in our daily lives, as when we say, "If no one objects, I'll go ahead and do it." Silence may also show a negative judgment, as when a teacher or parent glares silently at an unruly child.

Finally, silence serves an *activating* function. It can move us to do or think certain things that might not occur while talking. The familiar phrase "Let's stop talking and start working" implies that silence may better activate physical effort than continued oral communication. The person who says "Let's take a breather" and is met by silence from the others may be prompted to continue working!

GENERAL CHARACTERISTICS OF NONVERBAL COMMUNICATION

We have seen that nonverbal aspects of communication take many forms having tremendous complexity, variety, and communicative significance. Nonverbal communication also has a number of general characteristics that apply to the variety of individual elements discussed above.

Nonverbal communication is usually interdependent with verbal interaction. As we speak and listen, we observe cues in other people and in the environment. For example, the comment "I'm really tired today!" may be accompanied by sagging shoulders, sad facial expression, and a slow, quiet vocal inflection that reinforce and amplify the verbal message. Similarly, the comment "I like you; you're fun to be with" can best be interpreted in the context of a face-to-face awareness of the other person's behavior. Hence, when we study nonverbal communication—how specific personal and environmental cues affect meaning—we must remember that such a process can be truly understood only when we appreciate interrelationships among all messages, verbal and nonverbal.

Nonverbal messages are frequently more significant than verbal messages. That is, we may give considerably more attention to nonverbal cues.

Mehrabian (1968) suggests that from his experimental studies the "total impact" of a message is derived from 7 percent verbal cues, 38 percent vocal cues, and 55 percent facial cues. Percentages vary, of course, and, with the close interrelationship between verbal and nonverbal cues, we can probably never know precisely how much of the meaning we create in a given situation is based on nonverbal factors. In any case, one should never underestimate the relevance of nonverbal messages, even though the initiator of a message may place the greatest emphasis on the spoken or written words.

We cannot avoid nonverbal communication. In Chapter One we noted that we cannot *not* communicate. If we are being heard, seen, smelled, or touched, or if our absence or silence is noticed by others, meanings will be created. Communication occurs whether we like it or not. For example, suppose Jane decides, "Every time I meet with the group I always say the wrong thing, start arguments, or put my foot in my mouth. So today I'll just keep silent and try to listen pleasantly to the others." In other words, Jane tries not to communicate. For an hour she makes no verbal input. After the meeting, some group members chat. "What was bothering Jane today?" "She was really in a foul mood, wasn't she?" "If she isn't willing to participate, I wish she wouldn't come." "She's so arrogant, so aloof; does she think she's better than the rest of us?" "I think her feelings were hurt. I argued against her last time, and now she's pouting." Obviously, group members were receiving and interpreting many messages from Jane. And if she decided not to attend the next meeting, even more "messages" would be created.

Nonverbal communication is especially potent and accurate at the subjective or emotional level. When we want to communicate logical, factual information, we usually rely on verbal or mathematical symbols. "Population increased 21 percent over the past ten years with the largest growth in metropolitan areas." But the expression of emotional information is frequently nonverbal — through behaviors that suggest happiness, sadness, anger, moodiness, fear, confusion, love, melancholy, contentment, enthusiasm, boredom, disgust, frustrations, and so on across the spectrum of human emotions. Davitz (1964, 178) reports studies showing that emotional meanings could be communicated accurately with several different types of nonverbal behaviors or media. Our accuracy in interpreting the emotional condition of another person probably improves if the nonverbal behavior is *involuntary* — if the person "sending" the cues is unaware of his behavior and has no conscious strategy for projecting a particular look or image. Because we emit some involuntary cues no matter how hard we try to control them, it is difficult to deceive others about our true feelings.

Nonverbal factors define relationships between people. Our clothing, offices, homes, physical traits, animation, and vocal patterns tell others who we are. Others interpret our cues and use them to determine how they should interact with us. How does one know to begin a conversation with a stranger? To avoid antagonizing someone who appears upset? To treat certain people with formality and respect? To terminate a conversation? To touch another person? Chances are that the elaborate meanings involved in most interpersonal relationships evolve primarily from nonverbal cues. Without those cues we would drift more uncertainly in a trial-and-error process of determining how we should behave.

NONVERBAL CUES AND COMMUNICATION PROBLEMS

If we can observe, categorize, and explain nonverbal behavior, why do we still have problems interpreting the messages of others? Why is it still so difficult to establish shared meanings between people if nonverbal factors are such a rich source of information? The answers to these questions lie in the nature of nonverbal cues themselves, particularly their susceptibility to widely varying interpretations and their potency at the emotional level. These characteristics and their implications are explored below.

LOW RELIABILITY OF MEANINGS

One key problem with nonverbal messages is *the low reliability of their meanings*. Similar nonverbal behaviors or characteristics, when perceived at different times and by different people, frequently result in widely varied meanings. We selectively perceive some portions of the nonverbal environment and behaviors and filter out other parts. Also, we attribute great significance to some cues and very little to others. Only rarely will a nonverbal message elicit identical responses from different observers. True, certain kinds of messages have high reliability. Facial and vocal cues usually prompt accurate assessments of a person's emotional condition. A room with desk, filing cabinets, calculator, conference table and chairs, typewriter, and clerical supplies obviously suggests "business office" to most people. Nodding the head means *yes* and gesturing toward a door means *you go first*. But despite the clarity of these simple messages, unreliability is a frequent problem.

INTERDEPENDENCE OF DIVERSE CUES

Perhaps the greatest source of poor reliability of some messages is the interdependence of many diverse cues. In an earlier section, we tried to identify specific cues, but we also cautioned that such cues are rarely perceived in isolation. For example, we don't just see a head nod but also a facial expression, body posture, and clothing that may intervene to present a total message that we interpret. How, then, can we say we "know what it means" when a person smiles? What if he is also extending his hand? Backing away from us? If the situation involves a formal reception, and the smiling face greets one person after another, what does the smile mean then?

The fact is that while we try to codify nonverbal cues and even catalog pictures of typical nonverbal behaviors, we shall never have a nonverbal dictionary like we use for verbal symbols. A dictionary might suggest two meanings for the word *orange*: a color and a type of citrus fruit. Every time we see or hear *orange* we ascribe one of those two meanings. But what meaning do we ascribe to the property of orangeness, like a room with orange walls and furniture or orange clothing? And what do we think of when we see oranges on a tree? What is the inherent nonverbal meaning of orange? How do we *respond* to it? We cannot write down in a dictionary, "Whenever you see an orange-colored room, you will think warm and pleasant thoughts." The intricate complexity of cues, the unique situation, and the unique person account for the unreliability and inconsistency of interpretations.

UNNOTICED NONVERBAL CUES

Communication problems also may result from a *failure to notice nonverbal cues*. We might call this tendency *out-of-awareness* — events occur, situations exist that we do not perceive. One person might say, "Did you see how nervous John got when he saw Margaret?" Another responds, "No, he seemed relaxed to me." In truth, some people are naturally more skillful than others at picking up subtle cues and processing them meaningfully. And even those who notice cues in others may be blind to their own nonverbal messages. In verbal communication, we know what we write and speak, and we are generally confident

that we know what we mean by a particular set of words. But nonverbal behavior is so subtle and unconscious that we may not stop to think about the messages we might be sending. If communication problems occur when people interpret the *same* set of *verbal* symbols, think of the potential for error when, due to missed cues, we interpret *different* sets of *nonverbal* events.

NONVERBAL-VERBAL CONTRADICTIONS

Nonverbal messages may contradict verbal messages. One person at a formal party, for example, may greet another with "It's good to see you," while facial expression, formal distance, and vocal inflection seem to say, "For the sake of decorum I'll be cordial with you, but I really don't like you very much." Another example is the teacher who announces: "I hope we can develop rapport with each other. Let's avoid the formalities and be on a first-name basis. Come talk to me about any problems you may have and think of me as a friend." For the students, however, there are continual reminders of the teacher's rank and status: the grading system, giving assignments and setting deadlines, a formal classroom arrangement, the teacher's formal clothing, a difference in age, formal language and precise inflections, and the teacher's traditional office arrangement. The verbal communication says, "I want to be your friend." The nonverbal message is, "I am much different from you."

Which message — verbal or nonverbal — do we judge more credible? No definitive answer is possible. We suspect, however, that in most situations the quantity and clarity of nonverbal cues, combined with past experiences in which people have used verbal messages to manipulate or mislead, may tip the balance in favor of the nonverbal. Of course, nonverbal cues can mislead as well — witness people who use cosmetic techniques to hide their true age or who show off fancy cars to give the appearance of wealth. Too, in many situations, verbal messages may carry the intended meaning. The communication breakdown occurs when the receiver of contradictory messages selects the wrong cues as being the most accurate.

INDIVIDUAL DIFFERENCES

Accurate interpretation of a given individual's nonverbal behavior depends upon the extent to which one is familiar with the individual.

The better you know someone, the more likely it is that you accurately interpret that person's nonverbal cues. Be skeptical about the widely held belief that some nonverbal behaviors exhibited nondeliberately have inherent or intrinsic meanings; they don't. Simplistic notions about specific facial, gestural, or postural cues can lead to trouble. Don't assume, for example, that just because a member of the opposite sex has his or her legs crossed towards you, you are sexually attractive to that person. Look for the totality of cues being exhibited—in context—and bear in mind that individuals vary considerably in their nonverbal behavior just as they do in their verbal behavior. In assigning meaning to nonverbal cues treat each individual as the unique person he or she is.

One thing that can improve your accuracy in interpreting nonverbal cues is to look for *changes* in a person's nonverbal behavior. Changes in routine patterns of behavior are reliable signals that something is going on. For example, a person's pattern of gazing (eye contact) might change during testimony in court. Ironically, and contrary to popular notions about the meaning of eye contact, a sudden shift *toward* steady eye contact *might* provide a clue to that fact that the witness has just begun to conceal the truth.

INTERCULTURAL VARIATIONS

The generally accepted meanings of many nonverbal cues are determined by a *culture*—a group of people who share common geographical, racial, religious, or social heritage. An *intercultural event* is an interpersonal transaction between two or more people of different cultural backgrounds. *Differences between cultures* can cause communication problems.

The most obvious problem in intercultural events is language. When we are unaware of the other person's verbal symbol system, we may rely on rough gestures or sign language, an imperfect system that limits our communication potential. Even if a person of one culture has learned the language of the other, his speech may suffer from a heavy accent and limited vocabulary.

Most intercultural events in this country involve a shared language—English. Yet we still encounter problems because the subculture of an individual teaches specific "meanings" of various nonverbal events. White middle-class Americans, for example, take positive meaning from direct eye contact. A black child, on the other hand, may have been taught that to look an adult in the eye shows disrespect. Suppose that boy is scolded by a white teacher and looks at the floor. The teacher demands, "Look at me, Tommy, when I'm talking to you! Show me respect!" Tommy continues to look down, not daring to violate the norms his parents taught him. The teacher becomes even angrier at Tommy's impudence. Each is acting "out-of-awareness" of the nonverbal meanings of the other.

Within a culture, like "general American," there are many subcultures, special variations caused by an assertion of ethnic heritage or religious background or even special lifestyle. Thus, in North America we encounter such ethnic subcultures as Afro-American (black), American Indian (native American), Mexican American (Chicano), or Asian American (Chinese, Japanese, Vietnamese, Korean, and other groups once termed *oriental).* Pockets of European cultural identity in this country include the Jewish community, Italian Americans, Polish Americans, Irish Americans, and French Canadians. Even religious, social, and political groupings can take on subcultural characteristics — for example, the environmentalists, the feminist movement, the drug culture, the counterculture, the "anti-Nuke" groups, the New Left and other antiwar groups of the 1960s, and the "establishment" organized around business and government.

While this continent is blessed with rich cultural diversity, the implications for nonverbal communication are significant. Review again the many categories of nonverbal factors. In each may be several potential communication problems due to special cultural interpretations. Depending on one's cultural background, what might be the "meaning" of the following events?

A young black male walks with a rhythmic strut past a white policeman; the young man wears sunglasses, high-heeled shoes, and a brightly colored hat.

A Mexican American with heavily accented English speech and a college degree walks into the office of a Midwestern executive to apply for a job as computer analyst.

A student of Navajo descent wears a tribal headband and beads to his graduation exercises at a suburban high school.

A woman wearing jeans, T-shirt, sandals, sunglasses, and no makeup walks into the Sunday services of a suburban Protestant church.

A black man and white woman stroll across campus holding hands.

Two young men stroll across campus holding hands.

A Chinese American woman with a slight accent is promoted to vice-president in a large stock brokerage company.

A middle-aged couple, walking into their son's college apartment for the first time, smell burning incense, hear rock music, see multi-colored lights and psychedelic posters, and notice a woman's nylons hanging over the shower rod.

These and other communication events with nonverbal cues are troublesome because our personal reality, imposed on us by our subculture, determines the meanings we assign to what we perceive. This problem, combined with other barriers — low reliability, failure to notice cues, and verbal-nonverbal inconsistency — are obstacles to developing shared meanings.

IMPROVED NONVERBAL COMMUNICATION

Nonverbal information can both clarify and confuse; it can be a blessing or a curse. What can be done to improve nonverbal communication events? The complexity and spontaneity of such events suggest that we shall never be totally accurate in sending, receiving, and interpreting cues. As outlined below, however, there are several ways in which we can improve our handling of nonverbal cues.

1. Look for cues. Seek them out. We miss some messages simply because we are not observant enough. A theater professor once had his students spend several hours in a bus station watching people so that their stage interpretations could be more varied and fluent. The students watched for body posture, mannerisms, conversational styles, facial expressions, and clothing. On a more informal basis, individuals can train themselves to really *see* the people and the environment for the first time.
2. Tell others about your reception of nonverbal cues and the meanings you are forming. "I noticed that you seemed uncomfortable when I mentioned the new proposal. You shifted nervously and you were frowning." For many people, it may be the first time they realize that others notice their nonverbal behavior.
3. Seek verbal feedback, especially when you think your nonverbal cues may be ambiguous or contradictory. Feedback that we receive naturally may be incomplete, haphazard, and confusing. We should seek it more actively. "Did you think I appeared angry with the

group?" "Do you think my office encourages free and open communication?" Some feedback, of course, is not too reliable. Others don't always level with us; they tell us what they think we want to hear. So feedback from several sources may be necessary to clarify nonverbal messages.

4. Even without feedback, try to increase awareness of personal nonverbal cues. We are not suggesting that you stand in front of a mirror practicing a winning smile. Rather, we believe that before, during, and following a communicative transaction, you should become consciously involved in interpreting your personal messages. What information do you hope to initiate with your appearance and behavior? How are you behaving at the moment? How did others respond to your nonverbal cues? What might you change in future encounters?
5. Do some personal analysis of how you typically interpret nonverbal messages. We really cannot be confident about understanding others until we first understand ourselves and the way we interpret information. How do you tend to stereotype particular types of clothing? Bodily features? Certain cultural groups? Do you react positively or negatively to certain kinds of behavior? In what ways do movies and television dramas condition you to read cues? In what ways has your background determined how you will respond to silent messages?

In conclusion, return again to the three examples that introduced this chapter. The political candidate, the executive, and the professor were all intimately involved with nonverbal messages. If you can now analyze those events in depth, then you will have taken an important step toward improving your communication skills.

SUMMARY

We have explored the varied communication events that transcend the spoken or written word. Nonverbal messages may originate from several sources: bodily features, including shape and skin color; bodily movement and posture (kinesics), especially facial expression and eye contact; vocal inflection or paralanguage; communication by touch (tactile) and smell (olfactory); object language like clothing and other consumer goods; spatial communication through interpersonal distances and room characteristics; time; and silence.

Despite the variety of nonverbal cues, together they have some common features. Nonverbal communication is interdependent with verbal messages but occurs more frequently. It cannot be avoided: we cannot *not* communicate. Nonverbal communication is especially accurate at the subjective or emotional level. Most importantly, it is instrumental in defining our relationships with other people.

Important problems exist in our ability to perceive and interpret nonverbal messages. Either we do not notice important cues or those cues are unreliable and contradictory. Since we all ascribe meaning according to our cultural backgrounds, intercultural nonverbal transactions can be especially difficult. The best solutions to nonverbal communication breakdowns are to increase awareness of nonverbal cues, both in ourselves and others, and to use verbal interaction more actively to check and supplement nonverbal messages.

QUESTIONS

1. What do the following terms have to do with nonverbal communication: *kinesics*, *proxemics*, *paralanguage*, *tactile*, and *olfactory*?
2. Why is the statement "Meanings are in people, not in messages" especially appropriate in reference to nonverbal communication?
3. What is meant by the *interdependence* of verbal and nonverbal stimuli? Why must we use caution when we study specific verbal or nonverbal messages?
4. What are some of the barriers to shared meaning in the area of nonverbal communication?
5. How can we improve nonverbal communication, both as initiators and perceivers of cues?

SUGGESTED READINGS

Ardrey, Robert. *The territorial imperative*. New York: Atheneum, 1966.

Birdwhistell, R. L. *Kinesics and context*. Philadelphia: University of Pennsylvania Press, 1970.

Hall, Edward T. *The silent language*, Garden City, N.Y.: Doubleday, 1959.

———. *The hidden dimension*, Garden City, N.Y.: Doubleday, 1969.

Harrison, Randall P. *Beyond words: an introduction to nonverbal communication*. Englewood Cliffs, N.J.: Prentice-Hall, 1974.

Knapp, Mark L. *Nonverbal communication in human interaction*. New York: Holt, 1972.

Mehrabian, Albert. *Silent messages*. Belmont, Calif.: Wadsworth, 1971.

Sommer, Robert. *Personal space*. Englewood Cliffs, N.J.: Prentice-Hall, 1969.

4

LISTING AND RESPONDING

PREVIEW

Many individuals think of a listener as a relatively "passive" communicator who is on the receiving end of speaker messages. Accordingly, they view the listener's primary tasks as "attending to" and "trying to remember" speaker messages. In this chapter, the listener is viewed as an active communicator who not only *attends to* and *retains* speaker messages but also *mediates* and *responds to* them.

A speaker is an *initiator* who produces a topic, directs attention to certain items of information, engages in various persuasive tactics, and expresses judgments. A speaker exercises a measure of control over a listener in the sense that the messages have their effects upon the listener. But listeners are not passive victims. Through the use of various verbal and nonverbal strategies a listener can function as an effective respondent who exercises considerable countercontrol over the nature and quality of the speaker-listener interaction. Accordingly, this chapter focuses on the communicator in the role of *listener respondent* and considers the various respondent strategies and skills that determine the effectiveness of that role.

OBJECTIVES

To provide a model of listening and responding

To review listener strategies for attending and responding

To consider the listener's role in people- and task-oriented settings

FOUR During a social get-together of undergraduate and graduate speech majors, an undergraduate approached one of our graduate students with the comment, "You know, you graduate students act as though you are something special; you must think that you are superior or something."

The undergraduate served as an initiator and set the stage for a variety of possible responses. The graduate could have responded by trying to "deck" the undergraduate; he could have responded with an equally demeaning evaluation of undergraduates, or he could have simply turned and walked away. But the graduate student did none of these things; he simply smiled and said, "Tell me more." That response seemed to catch the undergraduate off-guard and he felt compelled to "say more."

As the undergraduate continued to talk, the graduate showed considerable interest and continued to ask for more details. As time passed, their conversation became more relaxed and more focused upon the specific issues and concerns.

The graduate student was *listening* and he invited the undergraduate to "say more." In so doing he was also saying, "You are a person, you count. I'm going to pay attention to you and maybe I can help." Through responding in this way he did help. And as the conversation came to an end the undergraduate was heard thanking the graduate for "listening to his problems."

In this chapter, the listener is viewed as an *active communicator* — a person who not only attends to speaker messages but also mediates them and reacts with responses that *make a difference*. Therefore, while we consider the traditional problems of attending and retaining we also focus on listener *strategies* that redirect and guide the exchanges between a speaker and a listener.

A MODEL OF LISTENING AND RESPONDING

A model of the communication process should recognize the *dynamic interaction* and *interdependence* that characterize all forms of human communication. An appreciation of this interaction and interdependence among speakers and listeners is more likely if we consider the *roles* of speakers and listeners — that is, what speakers and listeners do and how they affect each other.

SPEAKER AND LISTENER ROLES

Essentially, a speaker functions as an *initiator*: A speaker introduces a given issue or topic or describes his feelings about something. By introducing statements, the speaker has the effect of *directing* the course of speech communication; that is, he directs the listener to particular ideas or topics. The speaker may add further direction through such statements as "What do you think about that?" "How do you feel about that?" "Do you agree?" "Do you have any questions?"

A listener functions as a *mediator* — by mediating the initiator's comments. Mediation includes more than the traditional notions of attending and retaining. It includes all phases of human message processing such as perceiving, interpreting, analyzing, synthesizing, and evaluating. Mediation also includes the listener's codification and evaluation of potential overt responses. Thus, while the listener usually follows the speaker's lead, at least to the extent of attending to some of the speaker's verbal and nonverbal behaviors, he or she also is involved in other covert mediation behaviors that include some or all of the following:

Interpreting meaning:	What does the speaker mean?
Interpreting motives:	What does the speaker want?
Response consideration:	What are the implications of responding in that way?
Response selection:	Decision making.
Response formulation:	Message development.

The listener reacts privately or covertly to the extent that his reactions are not perceptible to the speaker, and he reacts both cognitively (with thought) and affectively (with feeling).

In effect, the listener's role is terminated when he communicates an overt message. At that point, he assumes the role of initiator, and his statements (verbal or nonverbal) direct the course of subsequent interactions. His messages might reinforce the direction introduced by the first speaker, modify that direction, or encourage a new one. In some cases, it is difficult to recognize the moment at which the listener has assumed the role of initiator. If the listener merely smiles, or frowns, or yawns, or assumes a different posture while another is speaking, he may be initiating a nonverbal message that serves to redirect the course of future exchanges. The essential process of speaker-listener interaction is summarized in the following model.

A MODEL OF SPEAKER — LISTENER INTERACTION

Covert Mediation Activities:

Overt Message Activities:

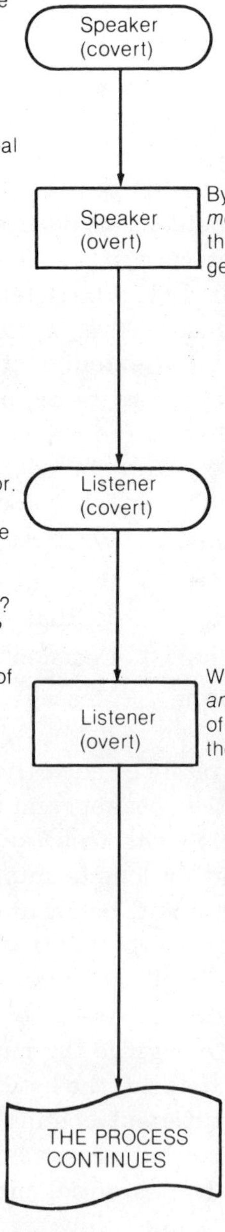

An individual is stimulated by some event in the environment or within his own skin.

(The individual can respond to this stimulus condition with a communicative behavior; a verbal or nonverbal message.)

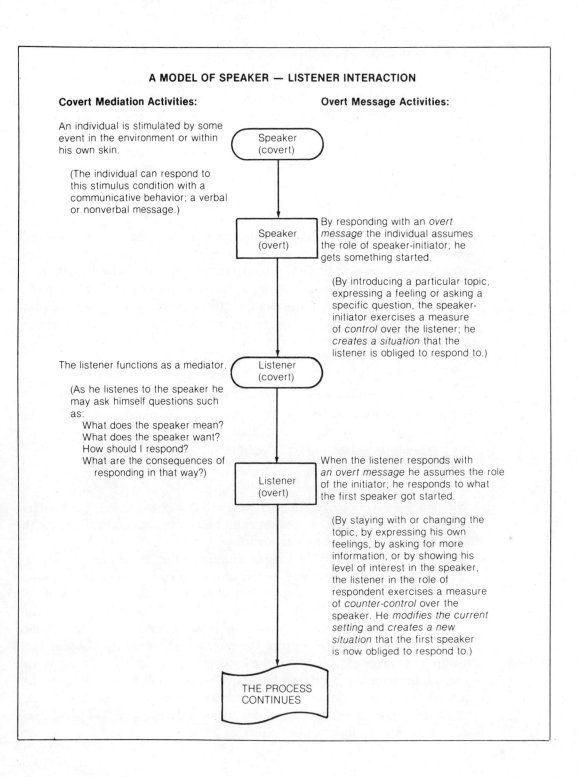

By responding with an *overt message* the individual assumes the role of speaker-initiator; he gets something started.

(By introducing a particular topic, expressing a feeling or asking a specific question, the speaker-initiator exercises a measure of *control* over the listener; he *creates a situation* that the listener is obliged to respond to.)

The listener functions as a mediator.

(As he listenes to the speaker he may ask himself questions such as:

What does the speaker mean?
What does the speaker want?
How should I respond?
What are the consequences of responding in that way?)

When the listener responds with *an overt message* he assumes the role of the initiator; he responds to what the first speaker got started.

(By staying with or changing the topic, by expressing his own feelings, by asking for more information, or by showing his level of interest in the speaker, the listener in the role of respondent exercises a measure of *counter-control* over the speaker. He *modifies the current setting* and *creates a new situation* that the first speaker is now obliged to respond to.)

SPEAKER-LISTENER INTERACTION

Speakers and listeners *interact* by exchanging the roles of initiator and mediator. In the dyad, the roles of initiator and mediator move back and forth between two participants. In small groups, the roles may move among several participants, with one or more people assuming the role of initiator at any given moment. In the public speaking setting characterized by the more formal roles of speaker and audience, the dominant initiator is the public speaker, and members of the audience are cast primarily in the role of silent mediators. Even during a formal speech, however, an audience usually provides considerable nonverbal feedback, which can take the form of initiator messages that influence the speaker's performance. In addition, on many occasions a formal speech is followed by a question and answer session, thus allowing for the exchange of initiator and mediator roles.

THE NATURE OF LISTENER-RESPONDENT BEHAVIORS

All forms of human communication — the basic means by which people affect each other — are characterized by dynamic interaction and interdependence. As we have seen, the speaker-listener dichotomy is misleading if we view the listener only as a passive receiver and retainer of messages. The listener is an active monitor and processor of speaker messages, and frequently shifts to the role of initiator by responding with verbal and nonverbal messages that can be as important, if not more so, than those of the original speaker. For these reasons, the *quality* or *effectiveness* of listening and responding is an essential issue in human communication. In this section, we summarize the nature of the listener's *attending* and *responding* behaviors and the motivation they require. Skills and strategies that can be employed to make these behaviors more effective are the subject of a later section.

SELECTIVE ATTENTION

Listeners are bombarded with a multitude of speaker messages, and it is inconceivable that a listener could or should try to identify and retain a sizable percentage of them. As a matter of fact, much of what we hear is of limited or even negative value, and the more quickly discarded, the better. Effective attending then requires *selective listening*. To gain the most from our listening experiences, we must selectively focus on messages that can make an important difference. Practical skills for selective listening include (1) listening for main ideas, and (2) effective note-taking.

Most speaker messages focus on a few main ideas, which, in turn, are clarified or developed through a larger number of supporting statements. The listener who recognizes this fact can begin to develop habits of listening for main ideas. When the listener can identify and understand a speaker's central ideas, he will usually find that only casual attention must be directed to the many statements used to clarify and elaborate those ideas. At the same time, when a listener senses that he has only a vague understanding of one of the speaker's main ideas, he can direct particular attention to the examples and other supporting materials designed to clarify or develop the implications of that idea. In any case, most of a speaker's essential meanings are usually captured in a few key statements; by learning to "zero in" on such statements, the listener can usually discover the essential content of a speaker's messages.

With classroom lectures or extended public speeches, a listener can be exposed to a large quantity of speaker messages. In these cases, effective note-taking can help the listener retain the speaker's main ideas. Like selective listening, effective note-taking usually focuses on the speaker's key ideas, permitting the listener to capture brief summaries that can be readily deciphered when the speech is over. A common mistake to be avoided is to try to record too much information. A listener can become so involved in the writing of details that he misses the speaker's main ideas. Since notes taken during an extended speech may be unorganized and sketchy, it is also helpful to rewrite and reorganize them while listener recall is still fresh. A listener will usually do most of his forgetting during the first twenty-four hours, so notes should be rewritten and clarified as soon after the speech as possible.

Selective listening is possible only to the extent that a listener has clarified his goals. Through goal clarification, a listener can recognize speaker messages that pertain to his goals and can direct his energies toward information that will facilitate goal achievement. By contrast, the person who has not clarified his goals has a limited basis for selective listening and is more susceptible to "distraction" messages that can waste his time and energies.

We do not suggest that a listener's goals should be too narrowly defined. If an individual's patterns of listening are too selective, he can run the danger of ignoring vitally important messages simply because they do not pertain to his narrow goals. In general, each individual must find his own style of selectively attending to messages. Like many other aspects of communication behavior, listening is a personal matter, and a person's style of listening will depend in part on his personal goals and values.

RESPONDING

The nature of appropriate and effective listener responding will vary with the listener's goals and the nature of a communication setting. Some listening and responding behaviors are more appropriate in *people-oriented* settings, while others are more appropriate in *task-oriented* settings. In the next section, we describe the basic characteristics of people- and task-oriented settings and then proceed to specific strategies that facilitate listening and responding in each of these settings.

PEOPLE-ORIENTED AND TASK-ORIENTED COMMUNICATION

People-oriented communication focuses on a communicator as a person — his or her feelings and concerns, and the quality of personal relationship between the speaker and listener. It is not concerned with the analysis of an "outside" issue or topic, unless that issue or topic bears directly on the immediate personal interests of the communicators.

Task-oriented communication, on the other hand, is directed toward a careful, detached analysis and evaluation of information that pertains to the issue or topic under consideration. Task-oriented communication does not negate the importance of the feelings and personal concerns of communicators; it simply focuses on a different direction. To be effective, task orientation may require the postponement of personal considerations until sufficient energies are directed toward task accomplishment.

Some communication events are structured primarily to serve the purposes of people-oriented communication, while others are designed primarily to serve the purposes of task-oriented communication. A visit to a hospitalized friend is usually weighted toward people-oriented communication. Most likely, the central purpose of this visit is to communicate concern for the patient as a person. The focus of this exchange is likely to be on the feelings and well-being of the patient, and comments that pertain to outside tasks are probably inappropriate. In contrast, the serving of a subpoena to appear in court is an intensely task-

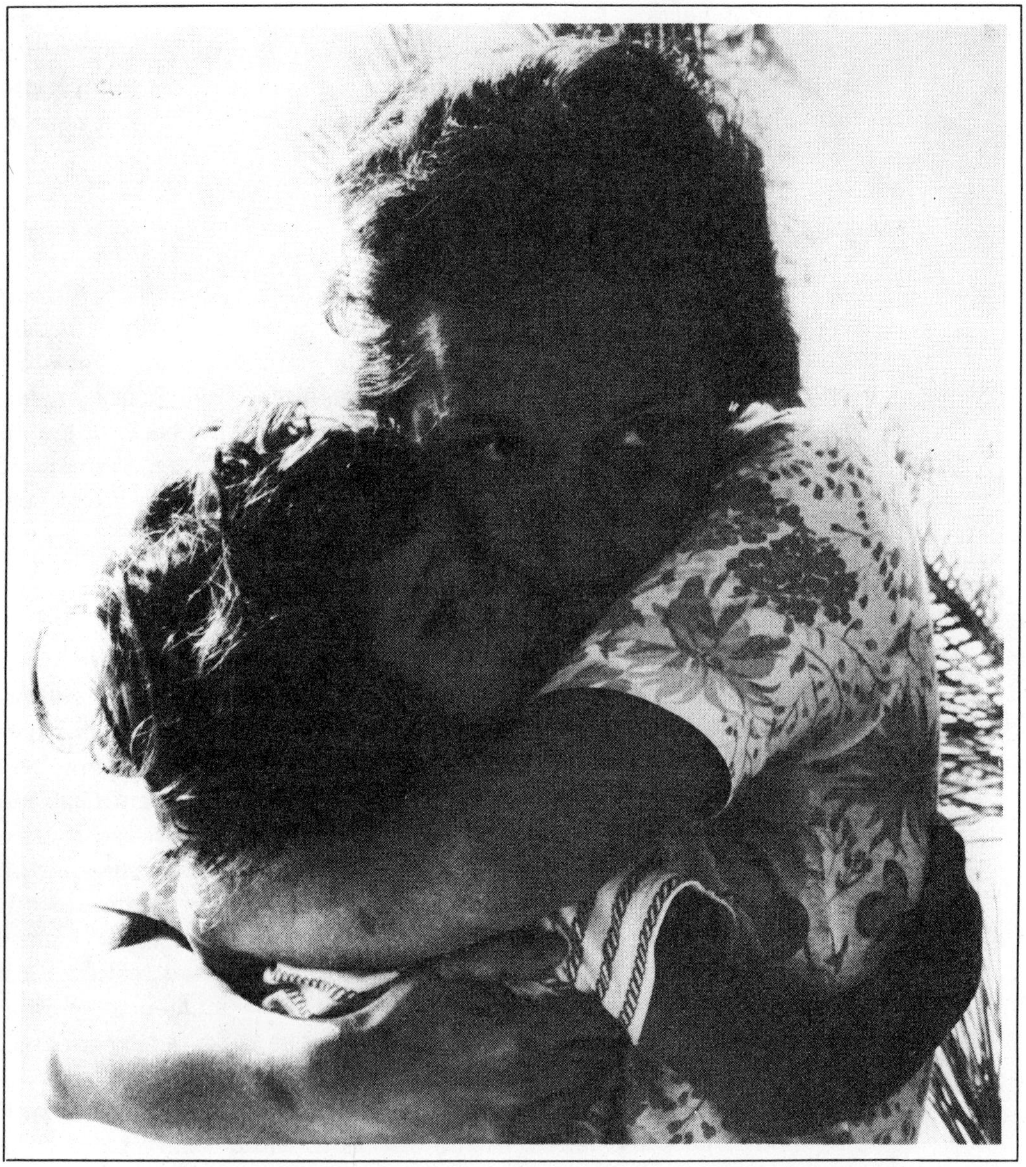

oriented communication event. In this case, the server's purpose is to gain the correct identity of the person to be served and to place the subpoena in his hand. It is doubtful that the exchange would include serious consideration for the person's feelings about being served.

In many communication settings, the direction of the exchange will fluctuate between people-oriented and task-oriented considerations. For example, a discussion between a car salesman and a customer might focus on specific performance aspects of the car and related topics such as the price of financing, the payment schedule, and the like. The discussion might also shift, however, to the customer's feelings about the car—its size, color, and comfort features, for example.

A total emphasis on people-oriented communication can preclude progress on an outside task, while a total emphasis on task-oriented communication can preclude the consideration of individual feelings and needs. In particular, progress on some outside task may require that adequate consideration be given to the more important personal feelings and concerns that surface during the discussion of that task. Total disregard for the feelings of individual communicators can be an important factor limiting task accomplishment.

LISTENING AND RESPONDING IN PEOPLE-ORIENTED SETTINGS

People-oriented settings function primarily by focusing on the feelings and personal concerns of the participants. They provide important opportunities to "sort out" our feelings and concerns and to receive useful feedback from others.

People-oriented communication can and usually does make a difference to the participants, for this is the setting in which we typically receive *confirmation* and *support* for many of our expressed feelings and attitudes or *disconfirmation* and *lack of support*. In effect, people develop hypotheses, or tentative conclusions, about themselves and others, and through communication gain feedback that tends to confirm or deny these hypotheses. If our encounters support our ideas about self and others, those ideas are likely to become more firmly established. If our encounters contradict ideas about self and others, we are more likely to modify those ideas or to substitute new ones.

Typically, then, the person who listens and responds in people-oriented settings will confirm or support the speaker's messages or disconfirm or deny those messages. Accordingly, supportive and non-supportive messages are the central ingredient in most people-oriented settings; their nature and effects must be understood if one is to listen and respond effectively.

TYPES OF SUPPORTIVE MESSAGES

Communicator messages that tend to confirm our hypotheses about self, others, and our relationships may be termed *supportive messages*. Generally, supportive messages include all statements — both nonverbal and verbal — that recognize the legitimacy of a person, including his ideas and feelings. Supportive messages also can communicate our interest in the other person as a unique individual and our willingness to become involved with that person's ideas and feelings.

At the nonverbal level, we might communicate our regard for another person through the way we manage space (finding him a chair when he enters a crowded room), or by the ways we manage time (being prompt for an appointment), or through physical proximity (sitting near the other person), or tactile contact (shaking hands).

At the verbal level we can evidence support with a wide variety of verbal comments. Even a routine comment such as "Hello, how are you?" recognizes the communicator as a person and demonstrates at least moderate concern for his well-being. At a more serious level, supportive interest or a willingness to become involved in the concerns of the other person can be communicated through *understanding responses*, which evidence an ability to verbalize the essence of what the other person has said; or *elaboration responses*, which evidence an ability to see the implications of another's statements.

Although supportive statements will frequently include understanding, elaborative, and even sympathy responses, supportive communication does not require total agreement with the other person's statements or point of view. For example, when it appears that a friend is misinformed or is entertaining an ill-conceived strategy, concerned disagreement might be the most honest response and the most constructive in terms of the friend's needs and goals. The concern itself is likely to communicate regard for the communicator as a person and provide an acceptable basis for constructive disagreement.

FOUR THEMES IN SUPPORTIVE MESSAGES

In her exciting and provocative research on confirming and disconfirming communication, Evelyn Sieburg (1974, 6–9) identifies four themes that seem to describe essential aspects of supportive communication:

1. It is more confirming to be recognized as an existing human agent than to be treated as nonexistent.
2. It is more confirming to be responded to relevantly than irrelevantly or tangentially.
3. It is more confirming to have one's emotional expressions accepted than to have [them] interpreted, evaluated or denied.
4. Personal response is more confirming than impersonal response.

Sieburg's first theme underlines the notion that the initial step in supportive communication is the simple act of recognizing the existence of the other person. Although this point may seem obvious, we should consider that individuals in contemporary societies spend much of their life in relatively large, complex organizations where it is possible to remain almost completely unnoticed. Even where people have opportunities for communication, many lack the basic communication skills that facilitate contact with others. Interpersonal communication is perhaps the most rewarding of all human experiences. How human would we be without our contacts with other people?

Sieburg's second theme focuses on the *quality* of interpersonal recognition. A listener demonstrates supportive communication through recognition of another person, but he evidences a higher quality of support when dealing directly with the other person's feelings or ideas. When a listener introduces irrelevant or tangential messages, he is saying, in effect, "Your ideas and feelings do not deserve my serious consideration." In a recent article it was noted that many so-called dialogs are actually "duologs." That is, the exchange consists of each individual pursuing his own ideas and feelings while remaining oblivious to the comments of the other person ("The art of not listening," *Time*, Jan. 24, 1969). A duolog may be compared to the "communication" between two TV sets turned on and facing each other.

Sieburg's third theme suggests that there are preferred ways of *dealing directly* with another's ideas or feelings. Acceptance can be evidenced through comments such as "I see how you feel" or "I can understand your concern." Specifically, it is more supportive to accept the other person's ideas and feelings than to interpret, evaluate, or deny them. According to Sieburg (8, 9), pseudoconfirming responses include:

You don't really mean that. (denial)

You're only saying that because you're angry—you'll get over it. (interpretation)

Forget it, you'll be ok tomorrow. (minimizing his feelings)

Everybody feels that way sometime. (discounting)

Finally, Sieburg's fourth theme suggests that communication can be more or less supportive depending on the extent to which it is *personal* as opposed to *ritualistic*. In Sieburg's words (9), "a person is more confirmed when he feels that others are willing to be involved with him as a unique person, not just as an organization role (supervisor, file clerk, executive, etc.)."

NONSUPPORTIVE MESSAGES

While supportive messages tend to confirm our hypotheses about self and others, nonsupportive messages tend to deny these hypotheses. Individuals evaluate communication experiences in highly unique ways, however, and those who are especially self-critical might emphasize the disappointing aspects of their experiences, while others seem capable of maintaining highly exaggerated evaluations of self and others — even in the presence of overwhelming evidence to the contrary. Nevertheless, most of us sense communication experiences that *threaten* our preferred hypotheses, and, many times, our pattern of reactions to these threats is similar. This pattern usually includes *defensive* and sometimes *amplified* communication, which is eventually followed by reevaluation and "salvaging" behavior.

DEFENSIVE COMMUNICATION

Defensive communication is *protective* communication directed toward the preservation of preferred hypotheses about self and others. When nonsupportive messages attack, question, or in some way threaten our preferred hypotheses, our repertoire of defensive strategies and messages is called into play.

Initial defensive responses frequently take the form of amplification. *Amplified* responses are those that are stronger, more intense, or more "magnified" than our typical responses. Raising the pitch and volume of speech is a typical form of amplification; a more extreme form could include the use of strong or harsh language. Amplification sometimes also includes a strong restatement of the central issues a communicator wishes to preserve. Dance and Larson (1976, 87) note that amplification is likely to occur as a ". . . consequence of explicit or implicit rejection wherein an individual increases his efforts to project an aspect of self which has been denied by others. It is an attempt to reinstate an aspect of self that has been challenged."

Through amplification an individual can communicate his resistance to the threatening messages. In turn, this resistance may result in reevaluations and message modification on the part of the threatening communicator, or perhaps a cessation of the threatening messages. However, when amplification does not reduce the threatening messages, it may be followed by an attack on the credibility of those who initiate the threatening messages. In effect, such an attack is one of the final means by which preferred concepts can be defended and retained. At this point, of course, attacks usually generate counterattacks, and all parties to the confrontation can feed this exchange to the point of mutual destruction. This destruction cycle can be reversed, but probably only through the introduction of supportive messages that minimize the effects of the threatening messages and redirect the exchange toward a mutual concern for the disputants as legitimate people.

SALVAGING RESPONSES

Our final response to threatening communication usually includes some form of "salvaging." As a result of nonsupportive communication, we may find it necessary to reevaluate and modify or abandon some of our preferred concepts about self or others. We may find that some of our preferred concepts simply won't hold up when put to the test of actual communication experiences, but we nevertheless are likely to salvage as much of our original viewpoint as we can. The making of "tradeoffs" is one way we can salvage as much as possible (Dance and Larson, 1976, 87):

> . . . for some individuals, engaging in communication with others has resulted in the loss of "exciting" as an aspect of self, but an unexpected gain, that of being "comfortable and easy to live with." Some individuals have lost "creative" but have gained "diligent." Some have lost "bright" but have gained "level-headed." And fortunately, some have been able to salvage aspects of self that they initially did not consider parts of their self-image.

In effect, then, nonsupportive and threatening communication may lead us to modify or abandon some of our preferred concepts. At the same time, however, the maintenance of an adequate concept of self and others is possible through tradeoffs and substitutions.

The revision of preferred concepts through "reality testing" and reevaluation is probably one of the most fundamental processes contributing to growth and maturity. The adoption of more realistic concepts should better equip an individual for future communication exchanges. Nonsupportive communication is detrimental when it leaves the communicator with major feelings of inadequacy or when it raises doubts about viable concepts that deserve preservation, but it can also provide the stimulus for needed reevaluation and constructive development of more reliable concepts of self and others.

LISTENING AND RESPONDING IN TASK-ORIENTED SETTINGS

Effective task-oriented strategies contribute directly toward task achievement. They include approaches and techniques that facilitate the careful and objective analysis of information that pertains to the issue or topic under consideration. It should be noted, however, that while some people-oriented strategies pertain solely to the recognition of a communicator as a person, *all* task-oriented strategies can be employed in people-oriented discussions where the resolution of a personal problem is viewed as a task.

In task groups, an effective listener is one who actively evaluates speaker messages in terms of their contributions toward task achievement and who formulates and delivers messages that provide needed information or serve to keep the exchanges moving in the direction of constructive task accomplishment. There are several mediating activities through which the effective listener can contribute to task achievement. These activities include: (1) the clarification of specific tasks to be achieved, (2) the evaluation of messages that pertain to the task, and (3) the encoding of statements that can be employed to keep exchanges moving in the direction of defined tasks.

CLARIFICATION OF TASK

Communicators who participate in a task-oriented exchange should devote initial energies toward a clarification of the task under consideration. Once the task is clearly understood, speakers are more likely to design messages that contribute to that task, and the listeners are more likely to recognize and respond to messages that bear directly on the stated task. Experience has shown that a public speaker has clarified his task when he can write a single relatively short sentence that captures the purpose of his public speech. Individuals interacting in a dyad or small group have clarified their task when the participants can agree on a single relatively short sentence that captures the central purpose of their interaction.

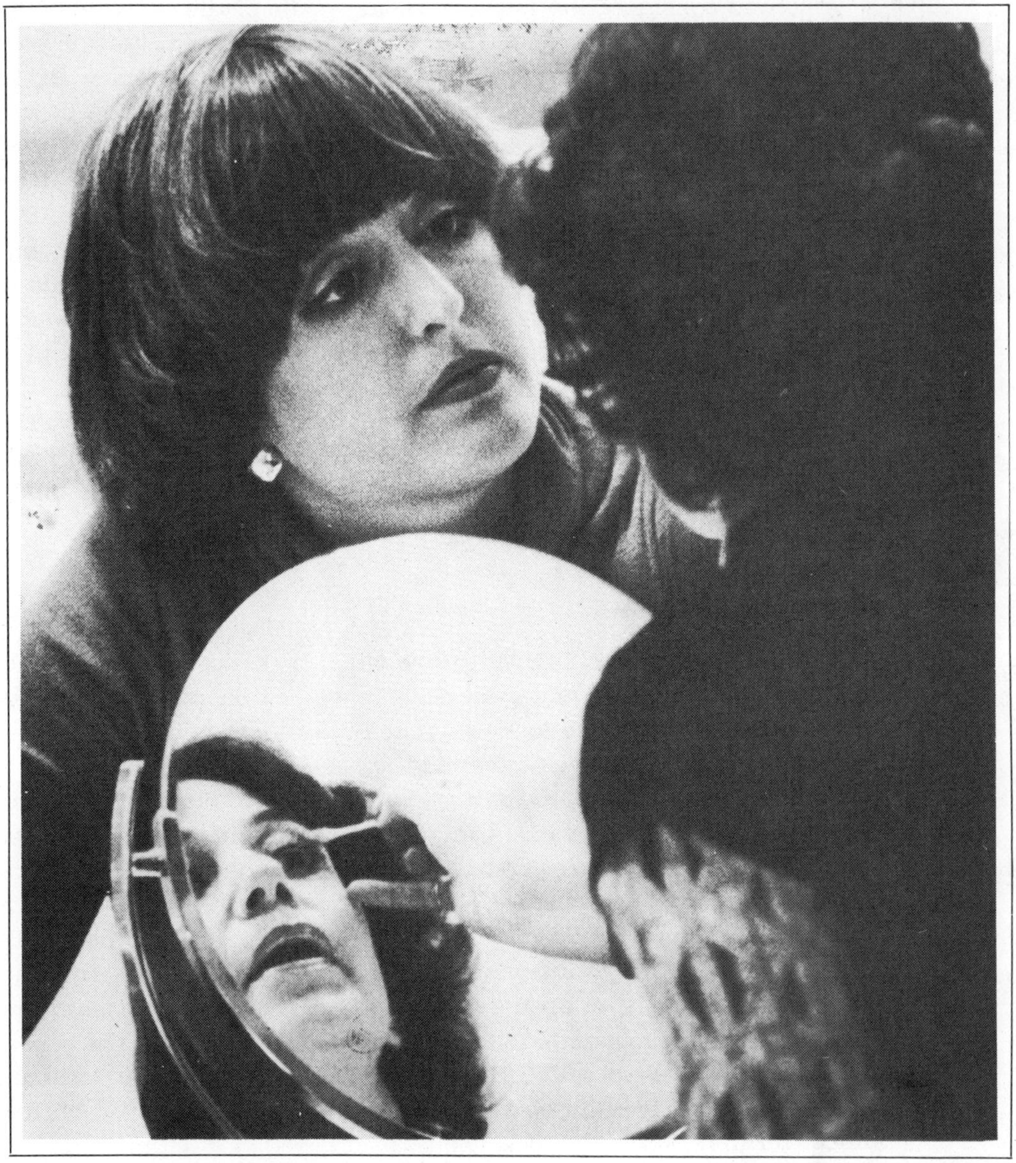

A second consideration is the personal goals of the individual communicators. Individuals usually have motives or incentives for participation in communication events. These motives can vary from a general interest in social interaction to a very specific interest in some aspect of task outcome. If a participant's interests are of a social nature, he may be inclined to "explore" the task, showing only a limited interest in actual task achievement or specific task outcomes. However, if an individual has a particular interest in task achievement or outcomes, his efforts may be far more directive. These efforts might include the initiation of messages that lead participants in desired directions or the use of supportive statements that encourage others who are contributing to preferred goals. To the extent that we are aware of the motives of participants, we are more likely to understand and correctly evaluate the nature of their participation. Motives, of course, are unobservable and can only be inferred. Accordingly, the process of "attributing motives" to others should proceed with considerable care.

PROBING LANGUAGE

A listener employs probing language when he seeks additional information, whether relatively general or specific. He can gain general information through use of "open-ended questions" and specific information through use of "closed-ended questions."

Open-ended questions provide the initiator with a strategy for gaining general information as a basis for the more specific exchanges that follow. Such questions are very general in nature and allow the respondent a considerable amount of latitude. For example, when presented with the question "How do you feel about starting college next fall?" an individual is free to answer in a large number of ways. In effect, when a listener asks an open-ended question, he exercises a minimum of control over the respondent. His question might influence the general direction of the conversation through the introduction of a particular topic, but the terms of an open-ended question can be satisfied with an almost infinite number of possible answers.

The open-ended question generates relatively free communication on a particular topic, and through such questions a listener can gain a considerable amount of information that can be utilized as a basis for future exchanges. For example, open-ended questions are frequently employed in the clinical setting to encourage an individual to talk about his problems so that the therapist can better identify and deal with them. In the deliberative group, open-ended questions can be employed to gain a sense of other participants' feelings about problems and their proposed solutions. At the negotiation table or in a debate setting, a listener might employ open-ended questions to discover more about his opponent's thinking on a particular issue. A member of an audience might direct an open-ended question to a public speaker to achieve a similar purpose.

Closed-ended questions provide the initiator with a strategy for gaining specific information. A listener can gain specific information through the use of closed-ended questions, which are very specific and tend to limit possible answers. For example, the question "Have you stopped beating your wife?" offers a person little latitude in his response. In effect, when a listener asks a closed-ended question, he exercises considerable control over the respondent. With the closed-ended question, the listener not only introduces the topic to be discussed, but also indicates the precise nature of the response desired. In the clinical setting a therapist might use the closed-ended question to learn of a person's precise feelings about a specific event. In a deliberative group, questions can be used to gain explicit responses on specific aspects of problems or solutions under consideration. In negotiation, debate, and public address settings, closed-ended questions can be employed to encourage a direct response to a particular issue.

The closed-ended question also provides an effective tactic for dealing with ambiguous or overly general comments. Through the skillful use of a series of closed-ended questions, a listener may direct another individual toward the more explicit expressions needed to achieve progress toward task achievement.

SUMMARY LANGUAGE

We have seen that individuals find it more confirming to be understood and accepted than to be denied, interpreted, minimized, or discounted. The simple paraphrasing of another's comments can communicate both understanding and acceptance. The listener can also use summary language to achieve a number of task-oriented purposes. In both people- and task-oriented settings, for example, the use of summary statements can provide a measure of communication fidelity and allow for the correction of errors. Through listener summaries the speaker has a chance to detect and correct for misunderstandings.

We know that individuals assign different meanings to the same set of speaker messages. Accordingly, the more effective listener is sensitive to the fact that messages received cannot be equated with messages sent. To avoid misunderstanding, the listener is well advised to check his interpretation of important messages against the intended meanings of the speaker. Clearly, the correction of errors is easier in a dyad or small group than in public speaking or larger group settings where two-way exchange is limited. As a general rule, however, the more important the message, the more important it is for the listener to check for accurate understanding before acting on that message. Without this kind of listener effort, the listener is too often misled and the speaker misrepresented.

Another common problem in most task-oriented settings is the tendency of some members to go off on a tangent unrelated to the immediate task. Through the use of summary statements, a listener can remind participants of the task at hand and thereby encourage more relevant comments. Summary statements also permit a listener to identify the essential points in a participant's comments and put those comments in perspective so they may be viewed in terms of the agreed-upon task.

The listener can also employ summary statements to identify specific points of agreement or disagreement. By summarizing different points of view one can clarify the degree of agreement or disagreement on a given issue. Once this clarification is achieved, all participants have a better opportunity to direct their energies toward task achievement.

In brief, a listener can employ summary language to achieve a number of goals that contribute to task achievement:

To determine communication fidelity and allow for the correction of errors

To remind participants of the task at hand and thereby encourage more task-related comments

To identify essential facts or points of view and relate them to the task

To clarify areas of agreement and disagreement

JUDGMENTAL LANGUAGE

Judgmental language includes all statements in which a communicator expresses his opinions as to the "rightness" or "wrongness" of something. Unfortunately, most people rely too heavily on judgmental language and tend to introduce judgments prior to adequate understanding or sufficient deliberation. The main problem with judgmental language is that it tends to generate defensiveness and inhibits or stops the more careful deliberative processes necessary for task achievement.

Once judgmental responses are introduced, they tend to generate additional judgmental statements. For example, if a speaker is presenting ideas on a particular socioeconomic issue and the listener responds with "That sounds like a communistic point of view," the speaker will likely feel threatened and turn his attention to a defense of his own position or perhaps a judgmental counterattack.

To avoid the barriers that result from the judgmental response, Carl Rogers (1961) advocates a simple technique that emphasizes the use of summary language. Rogers' technique requires the listener to repeat to the speaker's satisfaction the essence of what the speaker has said. The listener might introduce this summary with a comment like "If I am hearing you correctly, you are saying . . ." or "What I hear you saying is that. . . ." In the listener's attempt to summarize the essence of what the speaker has said, the speaker also is provided an opportunity to detect misunderstanding and to correct errors. Through this process, much of the potential misunderstanding and breakdown that results from premature judgments can be avoided. According to Rogers, in many cases, the listener discovers that once he or she understands the speaker's comments, he or she will be in agreement.

Clearly, not all human conflict is a result of communication breakdowns. Individuals hold different values, and quite often the conflict can be traced to these differing points of view. Nevertheless, it is also apparent that many of our conflicts result from impulsive judgmental statements that occur prior to any real understanding, and use of Rogers' technique can help to reduce inappropriate and unnecessary evaluative language. Eventually, of course, the nature of many communication encounters requires that we move in the direction of judgments, decisions, and the selection of a course of action. Even in these cases, however, it is likely that our tasks are more achievable if judgments are delayed until important issues and evidence have received mutual understanding and adequate consideration.

LISTENER ADAPTABILITY

Listener adaptability may be defined as the listener's total capacity for managing communication encounters while assuming the role of a listener. In general, we can say that listener adaptability is the product of *motivation*, *perceptiveness*, *strategies*, and *skills*.

As noted, effective listening is hard work. The more skilled listener should see a greater return on his or her investment, but even the skilled listener must invest a considerable amount of effort to develop and maintain effective communication with valued others. *Motivation*, then, is an indispensable prerequisite to listening adaptability. Indeed, it is a basic factor in all listening activities.

Useful skills and strategies can contribute significantly to more productive listening behavior. Nevertheless, it is doubtful that a person can become an effective listener simply through the mastery of skills and tactics. Effective listening requires a considerable amount of listener energy, and the more motivated the listener, the more likely he will put forth the needed effort. It may be that the TV era has given many listeners a false sense of importance. Since the survival of the TV industry requires a large number of willing listeners, major efforts are directed toward meeting the listener on his terms – catering to listener interests, values, and concerns in every conceivable way. To achieve listener satisfaction, important compromises are common. For example, substantive thought is frequently sacrificed for programming that provides popular interest and entertainment.

In many speech situations, however, listener satisfaction is not the primary goal. In many cases, a speaker cannot act with responsibility unless he explores complex ideas that some listeners will find difficult or advocates a position that some listeners may find unacceptable. Clearly, effective communication is more likely when the speaker's performance is intelligible, communicative, and, when possible, interesting and entertaining. But effective communication also places a good deal of the responsibility on the listener. Effective speaking is hard work, but so is effective listening. Effective listening frequently requires considerable effort for an understanding of difficult topics, as well as considerable tolerance when topics are controversial. A speech can be far more demanding, frustrating, or anxiety-producing for its audience than a television program; fortunately, however, it can also be far more provocative and enlightening and, in the long run, more substantive and rewarding.

Listener adaptability also requires *perceptiveness*. An effective listener must be able to "read the grid" – that is, answer the question "What's going on here?" Reading the grid requires useful concepts that help identify what's going on. For example, the concepts of people-oriented communication and task-oriented communication can help a listener distinguish between two unique forms of human communication – one focusing on a communicator as a person and directing special attention to his needs, concerns, and personal feelings, and another focusing on the messages and procedures that directly contribute to the accomplishment of a specific task.

Listener *strategies* contribute to communicator adaptability by answering the question "How can I cope with or manage this situation?" For example, selective listening can help direct us to information that pertains to our more important goals. The use of supportive and confirming techniques can provide strategic approaches to the management of people-oriented communication. Other techniques such as probing, summary, and judgmental language, when used appropriately, can provide adaptive strategies that contribute directly to effective task accomplishment.

Finally, listener adaptability requires communication *skills*. Motivation, perceptiveness, and a repertory of communication strategies can equip a listener to function with *awareness*, but to perform as an adaptive, articulate participant in dyads, small groups, and public speaking settings, the listener must develop effective skills in message analysis, development, and delivery.

SUMMARY

Traditionally, the speaker has been defined as an individual who transmits messages, and the listener has been defined as a person who attends to and tries to retain speaker messages. As we have seen, however, speech communication is a dynamic exchange of initiator and mediator roles. An initiator is defined as a person who transmits an idea or feeling; a mediator is a person who processes initiator messages and formulates responses to those messages.

Listener mediation can be more effective if it selectively focuses on the speaker's main ideas. Additionally, the listener should distinguish between people-oriented and task-oriented settings and adopt response strategies that are appropriate to each of these settings.

People-oriented communication focuses on a communicator as a person; the central topic is the feelings and concerns of the communicators and the quality of relationship between speaker and listener. *Task-oriented* communication focuses on a topic or issue apart from the personal feelings that the communicator may have about that issue.

Listening strategies in people-oriented settings usually involve the use of supportive or nonsupportive responses. In task-oriented settings, the listener usually attempts to clarify the task and apply various language strategies that help relate speaker contributions to task achievement.

Finally, listener-respondent adaptability requires sufficient motivation to listen, perceptiveness, communication strategies, and communication skills.

QUESTIONS

1. In what sense is listening more than just hearing and remembering?
2. How does selective listening differ from other forms of listening?
3. Under what circumstances can probing strategies facilitate a communicator's listening goals?
4. What are the similarities and differences between people-oriented and task-oriented communication?
5. What conditions tend to generate defensive communication? Describe some forms of defensive communication.
6. What are the differences between supportive and nonsupportive messages? Give examples of each.

SUGGESTED READINGS

Dance, Frank E. X., and Carl Larson. *The functions of human communication*. New York: Holt, 1976.

Scheidel, Thomas M. *Speech communication and human interaction*. 2nd ed. Glenview, Ill.: Scott, Foresman, 1976.

Sieburg, Evelyn. "Confirming and disconforming organizational communication." In J. Owen, P. Page, G. Zimmerman, eds., *Communication in organizations*. St. Paul, Minn.: West, 1976.

Wilmot, William. *Dyadic communication: a transactional perspective*. Reading, Mass.: Addison-Wesley, 1975.

5

ONE-TO-ONE COMMUNICATION: THE DYAD

PREVIEW

For hundreds of years, speech education has centered on a speaker-audience (one-to-many) communication model as students learned to prepare and deliver public speeches. The audience was viewed as a mass of humanity with certain general characteristics, and the speaker learned to develop a message with these general factors in mind.

Today speech education is increasingly concerned with the uniqueness of each individual in the communication event, regardless of the total number of participants in that event. We have begun to use the term *dyad*, or *one-to-one communication*, as the basis for understanding the communication process.

The dyad is not simply useful as a theoretical model. It is also a fact of our everyday interaction. We communicate with *one* other person much more often than with small groups or larger audiences. Hence, an excellent public speaker may be significantly handicapped as a communicator if he or she cannot also interact productively with another person. We think it is crucially important for speech communication students to develop awareness of and skill in dyadic transactions. Such competence is the basis for meaningful human relationships.

OBJECTIVES

To increase awareness of the enormous complexity of one-to-one communication

To identify common barriers to shared meaning in the dyad

To enhance the development of skills in dyadic communication

To increase awareness of special characteristics and problems in a formal dyad, the interview

FIVE The basic unit of interpersonal communication is the *dyad*, which we shall define as *communicative interaction between two people.* The dyad is the building block of which all other forms of human interaction are composed. That is, when more than two people are involved in a communicative encounter like a small group meeting or a public speech, the situation really involves a series of dyads. For example, in a classroom setting, a professor does not simply lecture to a nondescript blob of humanity called a *student audience.* Rather, he is involved in a series of dyads between himself and each student in the class. He "comes across" or "relates" to each student in separate and unique ways. The students themselves, to the extent that they are consciously aware of others, have a variety of dyadic relationships as well.

Though one-to-one communication is easy to identify and observe, it is highly complex. The first four chapters have outlined some of the factors that affect two people when they interact. In this chapter, we explore some typical dyadic situations, important variables that affect these encounters, and suggestions for improving the transactions. The concluding section addresses a special kind of dyad, one that most of us need to understand much better — the interview.

GOALS OF DYADIC COMMUNICATION

Dyadic interaction, although it is usually informal and spontaneous, can nonetheless be considered as a goal-directed communication behavior. Personal objectives usually lie at the root of dyadic development. One may be "I want to end this relationship as soon as possible," or it may be "I want this relationship to develop and continue; it is very meaningful to me." It is useful, therefore, to examine some of the common objectives of one-to-one communication as a first step toward understanding how and why we interact with others.

TO EXCHANGE AFFECTION

Our first major interpersonal relationship as infants is usually with a parent who introduces us to the experience of human affection. We now know that this type of dyadic interaction — giving and receiving love — is crucial to healthy child development. And, of course, we all can personally claim a continuing need to give and receive love throughout our lives.

TO BE SOCIABLE

Sometimes we simply want to appear cordial, congenial, friendly. We interact with one another as if to say, "You're here, I'm here, the situation is casual and nonthreatening, so let's just relax and chat with each other." The interaction may take the form of *ritual communication* in which the conversation may be fairly shallow and include conventional verbal sequences like "Hi, how are you?" "Fine, and you?" "Real good. What's happening?" "Oh, not much. What do you think of this weather we've been having?" Many social situations such as chance meetings on campus, cocktail parties, or friendly phone conversations do not foster communication with great substance; rather, they prompt us to use socially acceptable message behavior.

TO COMPLETE A TASK

We may form a dyad as a means to accomplish tasks. Our relationships in organizations frequently take this form. We associate with another simply because our job requires it. While such associations may be friendly, they are not always so. Yet they usually continue because people subordinate personal feelings to the task-completion goal.

TO SHARE IDEAS AND INFORMATION

We like to find out what others think and know, and we like even better to tell them what we know. When we hear gossip or inside information, we want to tell someone. When we need crucial information, we seek people out. We hate to be left out. Even when information is unimportant, our basic humanness compels us to form dyads to share it.

TO TEACH AND LEARN

Teaching involves a special type of shared information in a somewhat formal dyad with one person in the active role of instructor and the other as a comparatively passive learner. As with task goals, the teacher-learner dyad may be enhanced by interpersonal liking, but it does not depend on it. Rather, these dyads develop (often with little freedom of choice) because of special skills of one person and special needs of another.

TO PERSUADE

Dyads to persuade typically form because the persuader seeks out the person to be persuaded. The door-to-door vendor, the phone call to ask a favor, and the political candidate talking with a voter are common examples. One seeks the compliance of the other. Some dyads become coercive as the persuader goes beyond the bounds of cooperative behavior and uses threats or force to gain agreement. Perhaps it is this fear of coercion, of being compelled to do something against our best interests, that makes us wary of any dyad with obvious persuasive intent.

TO HEAL

Sometimes we participate in dyads for therapeutic reasons. We try to comfort those who experience personal crises, and we initiate dyads when we need someone to soothe us. The objective is to use *inter*personal communication to make someone well *intra*personally. Therapy dyads may be formal and long range, as with a psychiatric counseling program; or they may be informal and brief, as with a father consoling his dejected son who has just lost a Little League game. Though healing objectives are usually applauded, the therapy dyad can encounter problems (1) if the person habitually seeks therapy not because he needs it but because he wants attention from others, (2) when a person imposes his desire to help and advise on another who does not want it, and (3) when a person providing therapy is not competent to do so.

TO RESOLVE CONFLICT

An important objective of some dyads is to resolve competing or incompatible objectives through communication. The conflict may not be actual fighting but rather a difference of opinion, disagreement, or argument. Even bargaining can be thought of as a kind of conflict. When a buyer and seller reach agreement, the dyad objectives have been realized. Typical conflict-resolution dyads include: husband and wife trying to make up after a bitter argument; a representative from management and one from labor negotiating a contract; and a supervisor talking to an employee who has been antagonizing others. We are not claiming here that interpersonal conflict is always bad. People do tend to perceive it as harmful, counterproductive, or at least uncomfortable, however, and often turn to dyadic communication as a tool for resolution.

TO RELEASE STRONG EMOTION

When we feel anger, frustration, deep sorrow, elation, amazement, hatred, or any other overwhelming emotion, we may use the dyad as a source of release. Though we may also want to convey information or to seek comfort or approval, the act of unloading our feelings on another ("I hate him!" "Isn't that a fantastic sunset?" "We won!" "I'm so upset I could explode!") may fulfill our primary goal of getting something off our chest.

TO GAIN PLEASURE FROM INTERACTION

Human beings are affiliative, social animals. In addition to wanting love and affection, we often interact simply to enjoy the company of another. A chat over coffee, a round of golf together, a relaxing lunch date, a friendly conversation between business colleagues — these are some of the dyads that form because it is pleasant to talk to someone. Such dyads address no specific task, no agenda, no deep personal problems. We engage in them for the inherent rewards of the process itself, simply because we are the communicating animal.

The goals of dyadic communication often overlap. For example, when a task objective is combined with the enjoyment of affiliation, is the task accomplished any better or any differently? To what extent is the healer in a dyad also a persuader or a teacher? Dyadic goals may be unstated, subconscious, multidimensional, and even contradictory. Certainly, they are not always desirable or productive, but they are real and are at the heart of our interest in participating regularly in one-to-one communication. They also exert important influences on our interactions in the broader communication settings of the small group and larger audiences.

DIMENSIONS OF DYADIC COMMUNICATION

A dyad begins, obviously, with the conscious awareness of another person. For a variety of reasons we notice another human being and make some sort of verbal or nonverbal contact. The dyadic communication event begins, in other words, when two people perceive each other's presence and behavior and begin to give meanings to those behaviors. As we shall see, the seemingly simple act of one person's noticing and talking to another is, in fact, one of enormous complexity.

Why the dyad develops and is maintained in particular ways is the subject of entire courses on dyads. This question also is analyzed in some of the suggested readings at the end of this chapter. It is possible that the "why" of any relationship can never be known with certainty. For example, think of a personal relationship that involved intimate behavior, affection, and the feeling of attraction and love. Why did it begin? Because the other person was good looking? Fun to be with? Drove a nice car? Had interesting friends? Paid attention to you and made you happy? Had similar ideas and background? Or did the relationship develop because of a kind of unknowable chemistry between two people, a spontaneous attraction that could not be rationally explained or dissected? What difference does it make, anyway? We may agree with the standard movie line, "I don't know why our relationship happened and I don't care. All I know is that it *did* happen and here we are and that's the important thing." The "why" of some formal dyads is much easier to discern. You were hired for a job, and another person was your work partner; you enrolled in a speech class, and this person happened to be the instructor; you wanted a new car, and this person sold you one. Even here, however, the *quality* of that relationship depends on a unique mix of interpersonal factors.

INTERACTION VARIABLES

Even the simplest form of human interaction, the dyad, is enormously complex. Laing et al. (1966) note that, realistically, a dyad involves *six* people, not just two. Those six people who affect the communication event are:

1. Who I think I am.
2. Who I think you are.
3. What I think you think of me.
4. Who you think you are.
5. Who you think I am.
6. What you think I think of you.

These perceptions of ourselves and of each other clearly will intervene in our communicative interactions. For example, suppose that I am your boss in a company. Suppose I think I am competent, fair, and friendly and that I assume you feel the same about me. I also assume that you are enthusiastic about working for me. But what if you actually hate your job? What if you think I'm incompetent and pushy and that I don't like you as an employee? Such a dyad would undoubtedly confront several problems in an attempt to develop shared meanings.

The unique perspectives that each of us brings to a communicative encounter are shaped by *interaction variables*, the myriad elements that fluctuate in a particular dyad and help determine its outcome. Several of these variables can be identified. The following list is far from inclusive, but it gives us a glimpse into the complexity of communicative behavior.

Language How do language choices, verbal message behaviors, affect the interaction process?

Perception What verbal and nonverbal messages are the communicators perceiving through their five senses? Of all the things potentially perceivable, what things does each person selectively attend to?

Emotion How does each member of the dyad feel at any particular moment?

Attraction To what extent does each person like or feel affection toward the other member of the dyad? Are they drawn toward or repelled by each other?

Goals What objectives are the participants trying to achieve through dyadic communication?

Background What is the history of this relationship? What have the interactants experienced together?

Conflict Does any disagreement or hostility exist between the communicators? Are they trying to achieve incompatible objectives?

Role What role is each person playing? What expectations does each person have of the appropriate behavior of self and the other person?

Frequency/Time How frequently do members of this dyad communicate with each other? How long will this particular communication event last?

Culture What are the cultural backgrounds of the participants?

Environment What are the unique elements of the surrounding environment in which the dyad interacts? What outside events, conditions, or people affect or define this situation?

What other variables of dyadic interaction might be added to this list?

ACTION, INTERACTION, TRANSACTION

In his book *Bridges, Not Walls*, John Stewart identifies three perspectives on communication: communication as *action*, communication as *interaction*, and communication as *transaction*. Conceived as action, communication is simply the presentation of a message to stimulate a listener or audience. It is something the source does *to* the receiver. Considered as *interaction*, communication is two-way in the sense that source and listener exchange roles frequently and exert reciprocal influence on one another by alternately presenting messages to stimulate the other. Considered as *transaction*, communication is a process involving both action and interaction, but in which the reciprocal influence that occurs is intimately tied up with the very nature of the communicators themselves. The transactional perspective recognizes at least two important characteristics of human communication that are left unrecognized by the action and interaction points of view: (1) in every human communication event, the persons themselves are part of the subject matter of the messages exchanged, and (2) the participants are changed — for better or for worse — in the process of interpersonal communication.

We've included diagrams to show the distinction between the *action* and *interaction* perspectives. We leave it to you, the reader, to produce a similar diagram depicting the transactional perspective.

BARRIERS TO EFFECTIVE DYADIC COMMUNICATION

Awareness of dyad complexity is essential to effective communication. If we are sensitive to potential problems, we will be less surprised or frustrated when they occur. In this section, we discuss some of the more common barriers that may impede effective communication. Given the diversity of interaction variables noted in the preceding section, the potential for countless obstacles exists in any relationship. Here, however, we are interested in *quality* dyads: two people who attempt to establish *shared meanings* through *open, cooperative communication* so as to achieve *productive and meaningful relationships.*

COMPETING OBJECTIVES

One of the most obvious barriers to meaningful communication is *competing objectives.* In the mind of each participant, dyadic relationships may develop for quite different reasons. This difference need not be a barrier, but it can be. Suppose a young man and woman begin dating regularly. She wants a congenial companion and good times. He wants a serious, long-term, romantic involvement. As they continue to date, each thinks the other obviously shares the same goals. Since they never discuss their authentic feelings about the relationship, communication

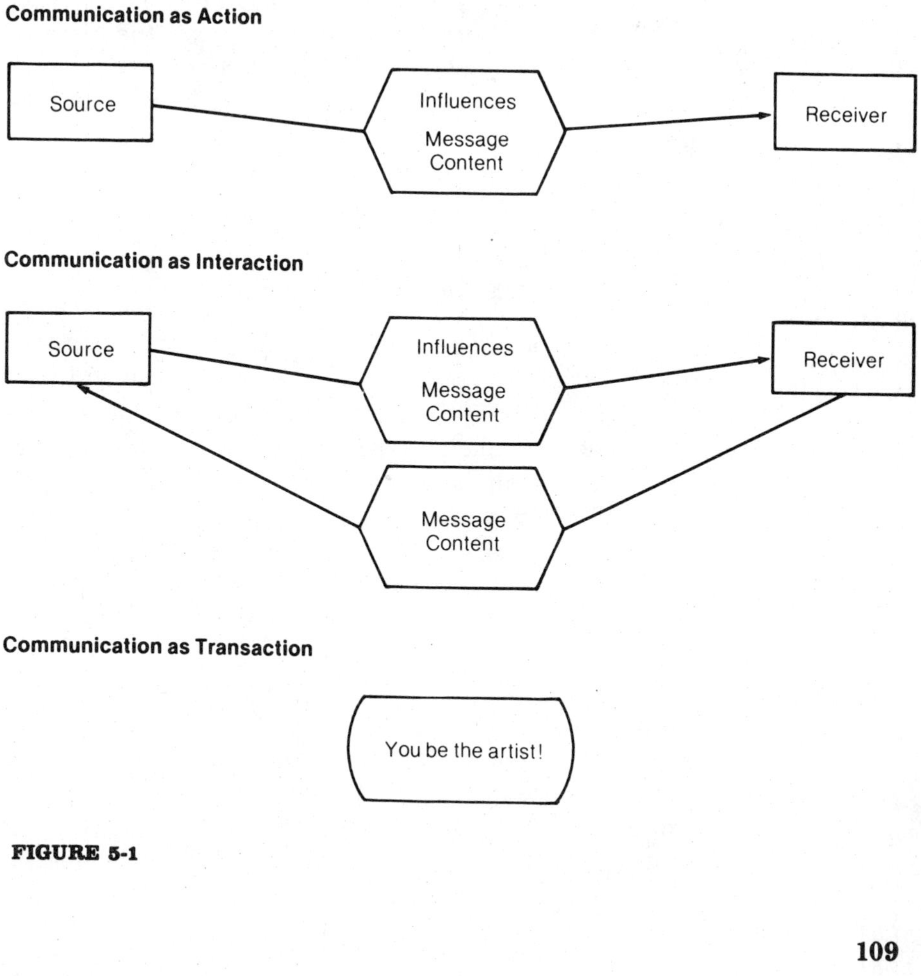

FIGURE 5-1

between them is frequently awkward and superficial. Until either or both are willing to confront and modify objectives, the relationship may remain clouded by communication behaviors that continually run at cross-purposes. What conflicting objectives might impede communication in the following dyads: husband-wife, parent-child, boss-employee, coach-athlete, teacher-student, salesclerk-customer?

INTERPERSONAL DIFFERENCES

Another barrier is raised by *significant interpersonal differences.* Any dyad will exhibit some differences between people, but sometimes they are enormous. A few years ago, a college basketball coach in a small town in the Southwest recruited Black players from urban areas in the East. When the players arrived, they found an all-white, conservative, and somewhat intolerant community. Though successful on the court, the players eventually left in disillusionment. Differences in cultural backgrounds, lifestyles, and attitudes gave them no opportunity to form meaningful dyads. It is often said that "opposites attract," and perhaps they do. We believe, however, that when differences between people become too pronounced we lose any common assumptions concerning appropriate behavior. Members of such a dyad cannot make enough accommodation to permit a cooperative relationship.

SELF-CENTEREDNESS

A third barrier is *self-centeredness.* Self-centered people will participate in a dyad merely for personal gain, without regard for the well-being of another — and perhaps at the other's expense. Self-centeredness typically means an insensitivity to others' feelings, a failure to read interpersonal cues, an attempt to control or dominate by strategic manipulation or deception, an unwillingness to compromise, and an "I" orientation. The self-centered person may use fear appeals, flattery, lies, threats, promises, or insults as messages to confuse, cajole, or distort. He may withhold messages that would otherwise clarify meanings, and he may refuse any interaction that does not enhance his personal goals. Though self-centeredness may not always be consciously manipulative or malicious, it nevertheless obstructs the open sharing of information that is crucial to productive dyads. In *Man, the Manipulator*, Shostrom (1967) shows how common are our attempts to control other people. We seek to dominate and do so through communication behavior. Not all messages designed to control others are

necessarily bad, but attempts to cancel out the other person's interests and input lead to a one-sided relationship. When *both* participants behave egotistically, shared meanings and productive outcomes are unlikely indeed.

DESTRUCTIVE EMOTIONS

A related barrier is the broad category of *destructive emotions.* Hate, hostility, anger, resentment, fear, sorrow, and suspicion may impede open communication. Of course, we all feel these emotions, and it often is useful to describe them to others when they occur. We should not feel guilty about them. They are not immoral; they are nothing to be ashamed of. When our destructive emotions are covered by a veneer of *deceptive messages*, however — when they motivate *unproductive behavior* toward another person — the dyad may suffer.

Probably the greatest barrier to openness is suspicion. A key point in the little book *Why Am I Afraid to Tell You Who I Am?* (Powell, 1969) is that we avoid being honest with others because we are suspicious that they might use that information to hurt us. Our ideas and feelings become ammunition that can be used against us. So we remain detached in dyadic encounters; we don't want to achieve shared meanings. Further, emotions like fear and hate are often considered socially unacceptable so we hide them with deceptive messages. On the other side of the coin, sometimes *exhibiting* our intense emotions with verbal attacks like name calling, accusations, angry challenges and criticism, and threats can permanently damage a relationship.

PERCEPTION

Perceptual problems make up a broad category based on the ways in which we see or experience the environment. Perception is not simply the receiving of input through our sensory organs; it also includes our selection and interpretation of that input. One's own perspective is always unique. We cannot climb behind the eyes of someone else and see the world as he or she does. Hence, when two people see a particular event and then talk about it (like a controversial new movie), their differing perceptions are likely to impose a barrier to shared impressions about the event.

Perhaps the greatest single perceptual barrier is *stereotyping*—the tendency to label and categorize people according to obvious but incomplete and misleading characteristics. We are stereotyping, for example, if we perceive a muscular athlete and think "dumb jock," or a male with long hair and think "hippie," or a Chicano with heavy Spanish accent and think "lazy wetback," or a person in a police or military uniform and think "fascist." Since we cannot possibly be aware of all the events and environmental characteristics around us, we must selectively perceive only a portion of those stimuli. The labels we place on people cue us on *what to look for* ("He's a used car salesman." "Oh, yes, I can tell by his shifty eyes.") and then influence our eventual interaction with them.

In turn, the label we create itself leads to equally stereotyped communication behavior. We tend to show hostility toward people with negative labels and affection toward those with positive labels. Too often, furthermore, we let our perception—and our communication behavior—be governed by labels that others place on people. For example, how would you interact with a new acquaintance if someone told you:

She is a prostitute
a professor
a minister
a narcotics agent
a millionaire
terminally ill
a recording star

He is a homosexual
a weight lifter
a corporate executive
a heroin addict
a cop
an epileptic
mentally retarded
a social worker

Since stereotypes are based on limited information, they are often grossly inaccurate, meaning that the dyad proceeds on faulty perceptions and with inappropriate behavior.

LANGUAGE

Another barrier is *language.* The obvious problem of two people who speak totally *different* languages is sometimes less serious than people who use the *same* language symbols in different ways. Dyad participants who speak different languages are aware of the barrier and are prepared to make special accommodations (an interpreter, sign language, slower and more repetitious speech) in an effort to develop shared meanings. Participants who speak the same language, on the other hand, may be unaware of the different meanings each is ascribing to words. A TV public service ad about drug abuse claimed, "Parents of America! If you think 'horse' is a four-legged mammal that eats hay; if you think 'coke' is a popular soft drink; if you think 'hash' is a meat and potato dish; if you think 'uppers' are false teeth—you are in trouble!" Many dyads face similar problems of language differences.

PAST EXPERIENCE

Past experience with another may pose a barrier to future interaction, especially if that history has been generally negative. For example, consider the nature of communication between:

two people who just broke up a long romance and who must interact regularly in their jobs

a son, after flunking out of college, returning home to a father who had to borrow money to pay his tuition

a formerly married couple appearing together in court to agree on a final divorce settlement

a student who serves on a college committee with a professor who failed him in a class

a friend whom you once trusted with an important secret and who later divulged that private information to others

While past communicative involvement can help us know better how to relate to a person, it can also impede progress toward open, honest, meaningful interaction.

RESPONSE REPERTORY

Whenever we interact with another, we have a choice of messages we can send. This set of choices is our *response repertory*. A *limited* repertory can be a difficult barrier. For example, suppose a person has learned only one way to respond to criticism—with anger and hostile counterattack. That person is probably less proficient in dyadic communication than the person who also knows how to respond congenially and appreciatively to helpful criticism.

IMPROVED DYADIC COMMUNICATION

Productive dyadic communication does not come naturally. It requires careful attention and often enormous energy to maintain a relationship. Notice the really significant dyads in your life. You must regularly take time to *notice* the other person, to *exchange* information, to *resolve* differences, to *do* things together. Each person has an upper limit on the number of healthy dyads that can be maintained. What can we do to improve communication within these important relationships? The following suggestions cannot ensure communicative success in dyadic encounters, but they can help bridge the gaps between people.

USE INTROSPECTION—"KNOW THYSELF"

Have you ever surprised yourself by something you said? "Now *why* did I say *that*?" Perhaps we spend too little time asking such questions as: "Who am I? What do I want to achieve? What do I feel? What are my needs? Why do I do what I do?" We cannot communicate well with others until we first communicate well with ourselves and understand the meanings of our own verbal and nonverbal behavior.

ANALYZE DYADIC RELATIONSHIPS

Just as we must think about our own behavior, we must think about the interdependent behaviors—the transactions—with others. We can analyze a dyadic relationship regardless of whether the other member of the dyad participates. Return again to the lists of goals and variables in earlier sections. In each category, think about how these factors affect a particular relationship. Use pen and paper, if necessary, to identify and consider various elements in the relationship. Give particular attention to typical communication patterns between you and another. What are their characteristics? What are common topics discussed? In what ways has message behavior changed as the relationship developed?

Most dyads develop spontaneously. Even some long-term, intimate relationships (like a marriage) are never subjected to conscious scrutiny; what happens to them occurs purely by chance. Since we have so much of ourselves invested in these dyads, since our lives often depend on their quality, isn't it appropriate for us to think about them candidly?

TALK ABOUT THE RELATIONSHIP WITH THE OTHER MEMBER OF THE DYAD

Especially when the interaction appears unproductive or antagonistic, we might suspend messages on issues or topics and instead discuss *process*, the nature of our communication with each other. For example, "Whenever we talk about politics we always seem to become angry. Why is this? Should we just avoid the subject or should we try to find the reason for our anger?" Or "We've been dating now for over a year. Where is our relationship going? Are we happy about each other or do we want some changes?"

In fact, some people avoid talking about their dyadic communication because it might uncover threatening information; it might rock the boat; it might produce an unpleasant emotional scene; it might even destroy the relationship. True enough, though perhaps these outcomes are precisely what the dyad needs. More often, we suspect, such open intervention into the dyadic process can stop a snowballing or spiraling level of discomfort or conflict by forcing participants to think through the bases for their problems. Such analyses may be stormy, but they may conclude with mutual relief that each understands the relationship better. They are certainly better than suffering in silence through a long, uncomfortable, meaningless relationship.

USE SELF-DISCLOSURE

A more specific application of the previous suggestion is *self-disclosure*, the communication of personal or private information to another person, information that another would probably not be able to know unless the initiator revealed it. If I tell you my age, where I live, my profession, and what kind of car I drive, that would not be self-disclosure. The information, though personal, can be verified easily without my telling it. But if I tell you that I am afraid, or that I really enjoy your company, or that I don't like certain people, or that I crave affection, or that I am a cautious and somewhat shy person, or that I've had various tragic or happy experiences, or that I have certain political and religious views—then I am self-disclosing. You might learn these things on your own through long, patient observation and haphazard guesswork. However, you can know them for certain only if I tell you.

Communication in some dyads is hampered because we simply do not know enough about the other person to have a guide for our behavior. We say things that mislead or antagonize partly because we cannot judge what is meaningful or appropriate to another. We guess and we make mistakes. Over time, of course, we naturally pick up information about how the other person thinks, and we learn to predict the other's response in certain situations. But honest self-disclosure can strip away much of the ambiguous content of interpersonal messages; it can speed up the slow process of getting to know each other. The result may be more sensitive behavior toward another person. With self-disclosure comes increased *empathy*—the ability to understand, identify with, appreciate, or put oneself in the position of another. Empathic relationships are characterized by messages that suggest genuine concern for each other's interests and feelings.

In spite of all the benefits of self-disclosure, we seldom use it as a tool to improve dyads. Why?—because it involves *risk*. The unproductive emotion of suspicion is inversely related to our willingness to trust others to treat personal information with respect and to refrain from using it against us. The greater the suspicion, the less we risk. Some people go a lifetime playing it safe, "close to the vest," arguing that to be open is to be vulnerable. Yet they also miss the invigorating potential of revealing one's inner self to another and the rewarding relationships that often result. The possibility of "getting burned" once or twice is, we believe, far outweighed by the potential of self-disclosure to make dyads more meaningful and productive.

We do not suggest using this communication style to unload regularly on anyone we meet, as a strategy to get sympathy and attention. Nor do we suggest that *all* our personal attitudes, feelings, past experiences, motives, or ideas should be divulged. We all have a hidden area in our consciousness, things that remain private throughout our lives. But when those hidden elements are highly relevant to the way we perceive and behave toward others, then self-disclosure may be desirable. One person must take the first step toward openness and trust, and that requires both courage and a sincere commitment to a healthy relationship.

SEEK FEEDBACK

Feedback is inevitable in the communication process. We send and receive information simultaneously. Feedback may be incomplete, however, so we should actively seek it and not be satisfied that it will occur naturally. An essential dyadic goal, therefore, is *perception checking*, assuring that each understands the way the other perceives reality, the environment, personal behavior, and the meaning of messages. Questions like the following are useful: "What do you understand about what I'm saying?" "You seem upset; am I right?" "How do you see my role in our relationship?" "How can I help you understand me better?" Because we assume that our messages are understood, we usually avoid soliciting feedback. Furthermore, feedback may be negative and threatening.

"Helen, how long have I been sitting here without my newspaper?"

Why ask for trouble? Again, we see the spectre of risk. Nevertheless, like self-disclosure, perception checking and honest exposure to feelings, even if they involve confrontation, are crucially important to authentic communication.

PRACTICE VARIED RESPONSE OPTIONS

By expanding the different ways in which we can react to the behavior of others, by increasing our response repertory, we can better match one of those options to each unique communication event we encounter. You'll recall that Chapter Four provides more information on this suggestion.

ALTER THE COMMUNICATION ENVIRONMENT

As noted in Chapter Three, behavioral and attitude changes sometimes evolve from alterations in space, objects, time, movement, and other environmental factors. Some dyads can be improved by a change of scenery. Two people arguing in a conference room begin to relax over a cup of coffee in a nearby restaurant. A married couple hassled by job and family problems is rejuvenated by a quiet dinner out or a short vacation. Two people ask others to leave a crowded office so they can better discuss a complicated issue. A casual lounge area in a professor's office induces a student to be more open and relaxed.

Of course, some dyadic communication problems are not directly related to the environment. If you and I hate each other and feel we have nothing in common but must interact regularly in our job, installing Muzak or redecorating the office or adding a coffee klatch will not improve our communication. Environmental changes should not be viewed as a panacea for all dyadic problems. Nevertheless, it is reasonable to ask whether the communication setting is optimum.

PARTICIPATE IN COMMUNICATION TRAINING

You may become more productive in dyadic encounters if you participate in an advanced interpersonal communication class that involves simulation exercises, discussion about dyadic problems, and appropriate reading materials. Organizations sometimes sponsor training workshops or ongoing programs to improve the interpersonal competence of their members. Private training programs like the National Training Laboratory (NTL) in Bethel, Maine, seek intensive focus on interpersonal awareness, growth, and sensitive communication. The growing popularity of communication training is encouraging, for it suggests a growing awareness of communication problems and the tools available to solve them.

SEEK THIRD-PARTY INTERVENTION

When members of a dyad fail to develop productive communication strategies and the relationship continues to deteriorate, a useful option is a third party who can intervene to help both members develop more objective insights about their problems. The marriage counselor is a good example of a third party to a dyad. Unfortunately, some third parties *impose* a resolution on dyadic conflicts rather than facilitating mutual problem solving. For example, when two conflicting employees go to the boss for consultation, that supervisor may order the disputants to behave differently toward each other, or may side with one member and tell the other to "shape up." Such solutions are short range at best because neither party is truly motivated, at the feeling level, to improve relations. Similarly, a parent is too often tempted to impose a settlement in a quarrel between two children simply because getting them to talk out their problems takes too much time and energy. It is easier to be dictatorial than accommodating. The third-party role is most useful when both parties have tried and failed to improve their interaction, and when a trusted, sensitive, and willing person can be found to intervene.

A SPECIAL DYAD: THE INTERVIEW

Most everyday dyads develop spontaneously and are fairly casual and unstructured. A special type of dyad, the interview, is usually more formal and structured—both in content and in its setting. Huseman et al. (1976, 153) give the following definition of an interview: "goal-directed communicative behavior between or among two or more individuals who, through direct, structured interaction in a given environment, exchange information." Though this definition implies that an interview may include more than two people (as, for example, a three-member interview with a grade-school teacher and two parents), most of these communication events are dyadic. In this section, we examine interviews separately because they are common and important events in the lives of most people. It is important to remember, however, that the interview is subject to all the variables and problems of dyadic communication discussed in earlier sections. And the central objective —shared meaning—remains the same.

TYPES OF INTERVIEWS

Formal dyads vary significantly in their specific purposes. Listed below are some common types.

The *employment interview*, also termed a *selection* or *hiring* interview, is probably the most common type. Job applicants usually have to go through at least one and sometimes several interviews before they can be hired. The interviewer seeks specific information about the interviewee and also evaluates more subjectively his or her manner and appearance. The applicant in turn attempts to present that information in the best possible light and to learn more about the potential employer and job opening.

The *performance appraisal* interview brings together a supervisor and subordinate to discuss past performance in an organization and plans for future performance goals. Like the employment interview, performance appraisal sessions are uneven dyads in terms of relative power; the supervisor clearly is dominant and usually controls the communicative transaction. It can also be a threatening dyad with the supervisor occasionally having to criticize the employee's performance and the latter responding defensively. Some more progressive organizations try to make the performance appraisal session a positive event, with the two participants attempting to focus on *future* performance standards and less on rehashing past problems. In some cases, the interview is a mere formality, a meeting to explain the contents of official written evaluations.

The *news interview* is usually conducted by the press or other public information agency. Interviewees include anyone with special or newsworthy information. The interview may be essentially unplanned, as in an eyewitness account of a traffic accident, or very carefully orchestrated, as with a TV news program like "Meet the Press" or some staged political press conferences. A common problem with the news interview is that limited air time or newspaper space usually forces the interviewer to condense the information gleaned from the interview and use only short and sometimes misleading excerpts in a televised or printed message.

Briefing and debriefing essentially involve giving instructions and getting feedback. In a briefing dyad, the person conducting the inter-

view imparts information for a job or assignment; in the subsequent debriefing, that same person asks for information on how the instructions were carried out. The briefing/debriefing interview is a useful supplement to written memos and reports because it permits elaboration and clarification in a face-to-face dialog.

The *research interview* is designed to collect information through a set of questions structured to support conclusions. Public opinion polls rely heavily on the research interview as do many laboratory studies. Organizations sometimes use this type of dyad to find out about employee attitudes and company problems. A person preparing a research paper or public speech may use this type of interview as he would a library, to obtain authoritative information from experts.

Counseling and correctional interviews are designed to change attitudes or behaviors or to resolve conflicts. Job, marriage, and psychological counseling sessions are examples. In an organization, interview objectives may range from clarifying information to issuing reprimands to terminating an employee. The real artistry needed to draw out information from reluctant interviewees suggests that interviewers should have special training for their role.

The *grievance interview* involves a complaint by the interviewee about a matter over which the interviewer has some control. For example, the complainant might be an employees' representative who describes poor working conditions to a supervisor. Should that supervisor appear insensitive to the grievance or react defensively about the complaints, this interview may actually increase the antagonism instead of resolving disputes. For legal reasons, many grievance interviews now include taped or written records of what transpired, a strategy that may further stifle open, candid information exchange.

The *exit interview* occurs between a representative of an organization and someone who is voluntarily leaving that organization. Often overlooked, this type of interview can help an organization identify possible problems in its operations because the employee can provide insights about why he is leaving—what caused him to seek work elsewhere. The event can be unproductive, however, if the employee is bitter about leaving and burns some bridges with this last opportunity to unload pent-up hostility against his employers.

The *sales interview* is an attempt to persuade someone to buy a product or service. If possible, the interview should also maintain good public relations for the salesperson and the product. These dyads may involve high-powered sales representatives and corporate executives or simple door-to-door campaigns. Because of the potential personal gain for the initiator of the dyad, the persuader, this type of interview is prone to incomplete or deceptive messages by unscrupulous communicators. Potential buyers may become wary, and the entire interview may be conducted in an atmosphere of suspicion and distrust.

INTERVIEW PLANNING

Because most interviews are less spontaneous than informal dyads, there is usually some time for preparation and planning. In fact, the communication event begins when the interview participants begin to think about the approaching interaction, sometimes long before they see one another and begin to speak.

There are two important questions for both parties. "What is the purpose of the interview?" "What sorts of information must be exchanged?" In a recent job interview, the employer became so engrossed in telling the applicant about the company and locale that he never achieved his main objective—finding out how the interviewee could respond to tough questions. The interview was a pleasant communicative experience, but little relevant information was exchanged.

Once the purpose of the interview is established, all other plans follow from it. The interviewer will often prepare questions that will elicit information in support of the interview objectives. This plan may be a formal questionnaire or interview schedule (some organizations use a standard question form or guide for all hiring interviews) or it may simply be a list of key topics. The interviewee may try to predict some of the questions likely to be asked, the topics on which he should be informed. The interviewer should also devise some unobtrusive yet accurate method of recording information.

Sometimes we are not careful enough in selecting the people to participate in interviews. For example, an executive who has no training or experience in interviewing may fall into the role quite by accident and know little of the company's expectations for new employees. He may select the wrong people to interview and be inefficient in the actual dyadic transaction. He may get the wrong information and not know how to evaluate it properly. In press interviews, organizations may select a person to answer questions who has a good grasp of the information but cannot communicate it well. Progressive organizations recognize the importance of interviews and develop specific teams to handle employment interviews, job counseling, research, briefings, and press conferences.

Environmental factors like personal appearance, setting, and time limits should also be considered ahead of time. Why is this office or conference room appropriate for the event? Why not a coffee shop or lounge? Why thirty minutes? Why not five minutes or an hour? What outside events like a phone call or knock on the door might interrupt progress? How should the participants be dressed? Why? In most dyads, the participants have some control over the environment; in the planned interview, that environmental manipulation may be the key to productive communication.

DURING THE INTERVIEW

In most interviews, the *opening phase* is crucial since it sets the tone for the rest of the event. If the dyad involves a distinct power or status differential (as in employment, grievance, appraisal, and counseling interviews), it may be necessary for the interviewer to set the interviewee at ease so that subsequent interaction may be more open and relaxed. A few moments spent in casual "break the ice" conversation may be a time-saving investment compared to the "get right down to business" style that stifles personal contact and the free flow of information. Also important is a clear understanding by both parties about the specific objectives of the interview. What does each expect to accomplish? Ulterior motives, innuendos, and subtle strategies usually breed suspicion and restricted exchange of information. Confused objectives also waste time and leave the dyad partners groping for appropriate messages.

The *middle phase* is the heart of the interview, the time in which both parties attempt to achieve their goals. The productivity of this phase depends on two elements: structure and questioning techniques. *Structure* means the organizational plan for approaching various topics. For example, in a structured or directive job interview, the questioner might ask first about the applicant's credentials, then go on to more general discussion of ideas and goals, and finally move to answering questions about the company. Interviews can also be fairly unstructured or nondirective in that the interviewer lets the discussion proceed spontaneously. Counseling and correctional interviews often take this form, though both participants should nevertheless remain aware of process as well as information content, regularly reminding themselves of where they are in terms of achieving their objectives.

Questioning techniques refer to the types of questions selected to elicit particular kinds of information. Brooks (1974) suggests five basic types of questions, which are paraphrased below:

1. *Open questions* ask for an answer of more than a few words and give the respondent some leeway as to the kinds of information to be included.
   "What do you think about this problem?"
   "What would you hope to accomplish in this job?"
   "Why do you feel that way?"
2. *Closed questions* demand a very specific response, usually requiring only a few words, like yes or no or specific data.
   "Do you have a college degree?"
   "Where have you previously worked and for how long?"
   "Are you Republican, Democrat, or independent?"
3. *Mirror questions* simply rephrase a previous answer so as to get more extensive information. It says, in effect, "Tell me more."
   "You say you think you can help this company?"
   "You have some experience, then, in this kind of work?"
4. *Probing questions*, like mirror questions, attempt to elicit more information from the respondent or the reasons behind particular opinions and feelings. Probes are the short "why's" and "how's" or utterances like "uh-huh" or "Oh?" that encourage the respondent to keep talking. Silence can also be a probe as the interviewee feels he should keep talking rather than let the conversation stop.
5. *Leading questions* tend to direct the respondent toward a specific answer the interviewer is looking for. It is asked in such a way as to suggest an expected or appropriate response.
   "You aren't advocating government intervention, are you?"
   "Would you say you have significant experience for this job?"
   "What do you think of this stupid policy?"

The style of questioning behavior can affect the interview outcome. Open, mirror, and probing questions will mean a much longer interview, one that is usually less structured, since the respondent has much greater freedom to elaborate and move in new directions. Closed questions are efficient for obtaining specific factual data in a short time (as in some job interviews or public opinion surveys) but can also seriously restrict the amount and depth of information. The limited information from closed questions can be deceptive. Leading questions should be avoided. They are prohibited in the courtroom, rejected by careful researchers, and they run counter to the real goals of the interview—to obtain complete, unbiased information.

The *concluding phase* brings the interview to a close. A simple summary is a good technique. In hiring, counseling, or grievance interviews, the interviewer should very specifically indicate what will happen next, such as "We will call you within a week to let you know our decision" or "I'll take your complaint to the board and get back to you in writing." As in any conversation, many interviews may conclude with some casual, nonsubstantive remarks that reaffirm the interpersonal relationship that has developed during the interview.

POST-INTERVIEW CONSIDERATIONS

The communication event has not necessarily ended when the dyad breaks up physically, because the participants may still be responding to what took place. It is essential to have some reliable way of organizing, evaluating, and using the interview information. What do we know now that we didn't know before? Opinions? Problems? Factual data? Personal traits? Comments like "She seemed poised and intelligent" or "He's a real nice guy" may be relevant, but unless they are accompanied by more specific information, the post-interview analysis may show that the dyad was a waste of time. If interview information is to be used to make decisions, select an employee, implement a policy, or form a conclusion, it should be supplemented and compared with other kinds of information like written materials, direct observations, and personal experience.

GENERAL SUGGESTIONS

Interviews vary widely; even job interviews differ greatly from one organization to the next. However, we can generalize about some problems to avoid.

In many interviews, the questioner *talks more* than the respondent. His questions are long and involved, and he makes elaborate replies to the interviewee's responses. Unless the interview is clearly intended as an open dialog for sharing information, the interviewer should ask brief questions and avoid lengthy comment.

In most cases, avoid the unstructured interview. According to Mayfield (1964) and Carlson et al. (1971), studies generally show that the more structured (planned) interview is more likely to produce the information sought and to ensure reliable interpretation of that information. Use pre-interview time to develop a careful plan. Try to strike a balance, however, so that this procedure does not result in a rigid and unadaptable interview.

Avoid prejudging another person or information. The purpose of the interview should be to get more accurate information than other communication formats can provide. Prejudgment causes us to perceive selectively only that information that confirms our judgment. Though some initial impressions are inevitable, we need to get the information *first* and then evaluate it.

Avoid the communication barriers of rank, status, and power. We communicate more freely and accurately with peers than we do with superiors because our equals do not pose a threat. If the interviewee fears punishment for inappropriate messages, the interview may become a series of less-than-authentic messages designed to please a superior. The individual in the superior role therefore should try to encourage the relaxed climate that will encourage candor. He or she should be cordial and cooperative, recognizing that in addition to playing particular roles in the interview setting, the participants are also *people* with many similarities, people who can share not only information but an interpersonal relationship as well.

CHECKLIST FOR THE JOB APPLICANT

Perhaps your most immediate concern with interviewing is its role in helping you to land a good job. The following checklist utilizes some of the material in previous sections. It suggests some strategies for the individual seeking employment.

Obtain Information about the Interview Process How long will it last? What types of questions are usually asked? Can you find out the name and some details about the interviewer? Does the interview come early or late in the hiring process? If early, the interview may determine whether your application will be taken seriously. If it occurs later in the hiring process, perhaps you have already gotten favorable evaluation from your written credentials and, as one of the final candidates, will be interviewed in depth.

Anticipate Possible Questions Questions on previous work experience, reasons for interest in this job, and types of skills that could be brought to this job are quite common. The interviewee should perhaps

be ready to answer the question "Why should we hire you rather than someone else?" Bone up on possible substantive information that one should know to do the job well—materials learned in a training program, a college class, or previous work experience, for example.

Develop Verbal and Nonverbal Communication Strategies Should speech delivery be conversational or fairly formal? What will be considered appropriate dress for the occasion? Will interaction be highly structured (speak only when asked a question) or spontaneous (interact casually and openly as in a friendly conversation)? For some jobs, like receptionist, teacher, public information officer, counselor, bank teller, and others that involve frequent interaction with the public, you may be expected to exhibit the same kind of interpersonal style and competence *in the interview* that will be expected in the job itself. Thus, communication style is crucial and should be given prior thought.

Listen Carefully to Questions Do not assume that the interviewer is a skilled communicator. The questions may be muddled and awkward. Do not answer any question that you do not fully understand. Follow a confusing question with a specific question of your own: "Are you asking me to describe what I would do if . . .?"

Answer Questions Fully but Succinctly Though a question like "Have you had previous experience?" could technically be answered with a simple yes, the interviewer obviously expects you to elaborate. Avoid long-winded, rambling replies, however, and keep the initial question always in mind. Interviewers become impatient with irrelevant responses.

Always Plan Three or Four Questions about the Job Opening The interviewer may say, "Do you have anything you'd like to know about us?" The quality of your questions indicates to the interviewer the kind of employee you will become and may help determine whether you get the job. For example, do not ask "How soon could I expect paid vacations?" or "Are there any fringe benefits not listed in the job announcement?" Such questions may be important to you, but they also imply that you have only shallow interest in the job itself. Furthermore, you can obtain such information through other sources before or after the interview. Instead, prepare more substantive questions that indicate your interest in the actual work to be performed. "Do you provide opportunities for me to learn new types of jobs or skills?" "Do employees have any input, any participation, in determining how to get the job done?" "What will be the company's major goals and problems in the next few years?"

Be Frank about Your Strengths and Assets Do not brag, of course, but do not let modesty prohibit you from describing fully your accomplishments and abilities. Volunteer information about important personal assets if the interviewer neglects to ask.

Have Written Support Information Available during the Interview A neat file folder with documents like transcripts, letters of reference, and resumes is a useful device. Never force the employer to write or phone for such documents. Comments like "You can contact my college registrar for a transcript" or "If you call Mrs. Thompson, she will vouch for me" will limit your chances, especially if another applicant has such information in hand. Written support materials communicate nonverbally as well as verbally. They say "I am a thorough person who believes in careful preparation."

Clarify What Comes Next in the Application Process Do not lose a good job because you were not aware of the company's hiring process —for example, that a final application form had to be completed before you could be hired or that letters of reference had to be received by a particular date.

SUMMARY

The dyad is the basic unit of interpersonal communication. Human beings are goal-directed, and they form dyads to achieve some of their diverse goals. One way to improve dyads is to recognize those reasons for communicating with another person.

While we can rarely know precisely why a dyad began, we can watch it develop and identify and observe the variables or factors that intervene to affect the quality of the relationship. These variables include language, perceptual, cultural, and role differences; attraction, feelings, past and present experiences with each other; and environmental factors.

Communication barriers like incompatible objectives, interpersonal differences, self-centeredness, emotional and perceptual problems, and language differences can be overcome if either or both dyad members will make conscious attempts to become aware, to understand themselves and their relationship, to talk about the dyad, to self-disclose and seek feedback, and in some cases to seek outside help in third parties or training programs.

Finally, the interview, although a dyad in every sense of the term, includes some special concerns because it is usually highly structured. Interview types are varied, but all can profit from careful planning, from sensitive and goal-directed communication during the interview, and from objective post-interview analysis. The successful interview provides information exchange in a way that other communication media and formats cannot, and the development of interview skills should be an important goal of students in speech communication.

QUESTIONS

1. How do personal goals or objectives affect the development of dyads? How might communication behavior differ according to one's goals?
2. What are some of the characteristics of good dyadic communication? Of bad dyadic communication? By observing the message behavior between two people, how can we tell the difference between effective and ineffective communication transactions?
3. What are some verbal and nonverbal characteristics of an interviewee that would tend to lead to a favorable evaluation in a job interview? What characteristics might prompt a negative assessment? To what extent are these factors situational—that is, dependent on the particular type of job, type of interviewer, and surrounding environment?
4. To what extent can *one* member of a dyad improve the communication process without the help of the other member? Is there anything one person can do if the other will not cooperate completely?
5. What are some of the different types of interviews? What are some of the communication problems that could develop in each type?

SUGGESTED READINGS

Bach, George R., and Peter Wyden. *The intimate enemy*. New York: Avon, 1968.

Berne, Eric. *Games people play*. New York: Grove Press, 1964.

Giffin, Kim, and Bobby R. Patton. *Personal communication in human relations*. Columbus, Ohio: Charles E. Merrill, 1974.

Harris, Thomas A. *I'm OK—you're OK*. New York: Harper & Row, 1967.

Jourard, Sidney. *The transparent self*. New York: Van Nostrand, 1964.

Morris, Desmond. *Intimate behavior*. New York: Bantam, 1971.

Powell, John. *Why am I afraid to tell you who I am?* Chicago: Argus Communications, 1969.

Rogers, Carl R. *On becoming a person*. Boston: Houghton Mifflin, 1961.

Stewart, John, ed. *Bridges, not walls*. Reading, Mass.: Addison-Wesley, 1973.

Wilmot, William. *Dyadic communication: a transactional perspective*. Reading, Mass.: Addison-Wesley, 1975.

6

SMALL-GROUP COMMUNICATION

PREVIEW

Most of us communicate regularly in small group settings. In these groups we try to solve problems, maintain and nourish friendships, and learn more about the world and about ourselves. If interpersonal communication in these groups is effective, our participation is highly rewarding, and the group is productive. But if communication is ineffective, we may not only fail to achieve group goals, but our personal satisfaction and growth may also be impeded.

Of special concern is our society's growing dependence on the small group to solve its problems. Planning, decision making, task achievement, problem solving, conflict resolution, research—these are some of the important activities that we must do well if we are to survive. Increasingly, we are turning away from both the single, powerful individual and the broad democratic input to fulfill these functions. Instead, we are turning to the small group. Chances are that most of us will regularly participate in work teams. For both personal and societal reasons, our groups must work well for us. Thus, it is important for students in speech communication to learn more about how small groups work and how they can be more productive group members.

OBJECTIVES

To discuss major characteristics of a small group and how these elements affect the group process

To describe the process by which groups make decisions

To enhance the development of practical communication skills for the improvement of leadership and participation in small groups

SIX The logical extension of one-to-one interaction is communication in the small group. A *group* may be broadly defined as a discrete or specific collection of people who interact with a common interest in making decisions, completing tasks, achieving objectives, and receiving rewards. A *small group* is one in which direct interpersonal relationships among all group members are possible. Rice (1965, 11–12) suggests that a small group may also be called "primary" or "face-to-face." While the size of small groups will vary across cultures, Rice points out that "the relationships that have to be sustained in groups with more than 12 to 15 members become so complex that the group tends to split into subgroups." He concludes that, in general, a *small* group becomes *large* at the point where "face-to-face relationships are no longer possible."

Students may wonder why a separate chapter on small-group communication is necessary if one understands the basic communication process and the components of and barriers to effective interpersonal communication, and if one develops skills in face-to-face interaction. If a small group is simply people talking to people, why not simply apply the same kinds of communication principles we use for analyzing everyday casual interaction? It is true that some people who have developed personal communication skills are more effective than others in small groups. However, the small-group situation not only *modifies* the ways in which we interact with others but also adds *new components* that will affect the quality of communication. We shall examine some of these new dimensions in this chapter.

An even more important reason for studying small-group communication is that our society is becoming increasingly small-group oriented. Most of us engage in regular and extensive participation in groups in our homes, occupations, and social lives. The family is a type of small group. So is the subcommittee in a governmental organization, a management team in a business, a bridge club, a basketball team, a therapy group, a bull session, or an airline flight crew. We are members of literally hundreds of small groups throughout our lives, and the rewards we receive depend largely on the quality of interaction within those groups. When a family breaks up, a business goes bankrupt, an athletic team loses, or a friendly meeting degenerates to name calling and fighting, we become aware of how *counter*productive small-group experiences can be. When small groups succeed, our participation can be enormously satisfying. When viewed in this light, small-group interaction takes on a new importance—one that justifies not only discussion in a separate chapter, as here, but entire courses and books that focus solely on small-group communication.

GENERAL CHARACTERISTICS OF SMALL GROUPS

Several principles are common to all small-group situations, characteristics that we should expect to encounter each time we engage in group communication.

GROUPS HAVE BOTH "TASK" AND "MAINTENANCE" FUNCTIONS

Two interwoven yet identifiable events occur in small-group encounters. Group members exchange information designed to *move them toward a work or task objective*; and they interact in ways intended to *preserve the group as a social unit.* The former is the *task* function, and the latter, the *maintenance* function. Both functions must be fulfilled if the group is to survive and be productive. The task dimension is also termed the *content* side of work groups, while *process* often denotes the maintenance side of work-group effort.

The perceptive observer of small-group communication can identify messages intended for either function. Progress on the task is furthered by comments like:

"I think we've identified the problem; now let's discuss some possible solutions."

"The caterer will charge us $6.50 per serving."

"Does anyone have more information on that point?"

"I think we should summarize what we've decided so far."

"That proposal just won't work, and I'll tell you why."

These remarks obviously relate to the group's substantive objectives, to "getting the job done."

In contrast, maintenance messages are illustrated by the following:

"John, you haven't said anything yet. Would you like to comment?"

"It's natural for us to disagree, but I don't think we should resort to name calling."

"Hey, that was some party we had last night, wasn't it?"
"Before we begin, why don't we each introduce ourselves."
"We seem to be getting tired. Let's take a ten-minute break."

Maintenance communication thus suggests awareness of group members as unique people and of the quality of their interpersonal transactions.

We cannot ignore either dimension, and all group members should try to remain perceptive of both. People differ, however, in their own orientation. In most groups, we are likely to find some members who seem preoccupied with content—task achievement and decision-making efficiency. The more process-oriented members seem especially aware of how the group is developing as a social unit and how each person feels at any particular moment. We believe that having both types in the group is useful and that the ideal is to have people who are continually aware of both the task and the maintenance functions.

GROUP MEMBERS ARE LINKED BY VERBAL AND NONVERBAL COMMUNICATION

This fairly obvious characteristic may be overlooked as group members become actively involved in the content level of decision making. Yet the quality of these linkages and transactions does much to determine group productivity. Why might a group fail to meet its goals? It may be due to insufficient information, time constraints, highly complex and complicated issues, lack of participant expertise, personal animosities, and many other factors. Continually, however, we observe groups whose inherently achievable goals are never attained because the communication process is counterproductive.

Typical problems include misperception and misinterpretation, the inability to achieve shared meanings. Group members may never truly comprehend the viewpoints of others, particularly on complex and controversial topics. Instead, they may be too concerned with advocating their own ideas to really listen to and seek clarification from those with opposing positions. Nonverbally, they may become antagonized by frowns, grimaces, shaking of the head, defiant body posture, angry vocal inflections, sighs of impatience or boredom, or any other indicators of hostility or frustration. In contrast, comments or nods of agreement, smiles, enthusiasm, friendly banter, expressions of satisfaction or consensus, accurate restatement of the ideas of others, and other positive indicators of group harmony suggest a quite different communication climate. We are *not* claiming that interpersonal conflict in groups is necessarily bad; we are, rather, establishing the centrality of communication variables in determining the interaction climate and achieving objectives.

The communication relationships in small groups remain dyadic. All the variables that operate in one-to-one communication are relevant to small groups. Every group member hears and sees verbal and nonverbal responses of every other group member, and each person takes meaning from those behaviors. For example, think of a small group in which you have recently participated. Notice how different your relationship and interaction was with each person. You may have given much importance to the comments of one person because his ideas made sense to you, while virtually ignoring the messages of another who appeared uninformed or foolish. You probably felt rapport with some and alienated from others. Your comments, though heard by all, may have been directed at a single participant. Thus, though you were involved in a group process, your communicative relationships were dyadic. If there were, say, six people in the group, you were simultaneously involved in five dyads.

As groups increase in size, the number of dyadic communication channels increases dramatically. To illustrate,look what happens when a three-person group acquires a fourth member:

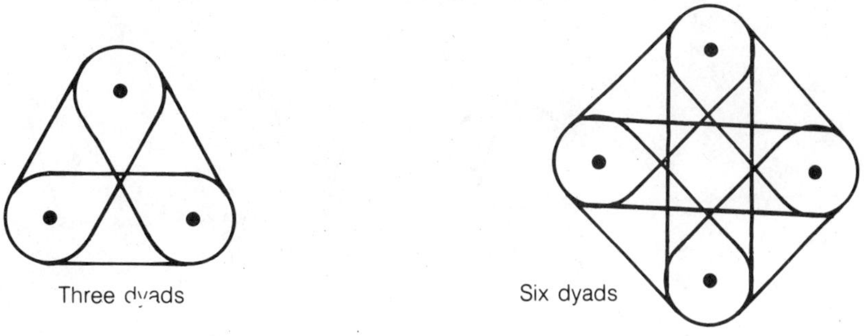

FIGURE 6-1

Keep this in mind when making decisions about group membership. The presence or absence of even one group member exerts a profound influence on the potential communication dynamics of groups.

In general, the task and maintenance functions discussed earlier depend heavily on sensitive and skillful interpersonal communication. And the personal rewards to group members come not simply from achieving objectives but from sharing in a pleasant communication event.

GROUP COMMUNICATION OFTEN IS CONTROLLED BY NETWORKS

Sometimes small-group communication is controlled or channeled by explicit or implicit *networks* of communication channels or paths that group members utilize (Figure 6-2). For example, in some groups all comments are directed at the leader, who controls the interaction and calls on specific people to speak (Figure 6-2*a*). In other groups, the networks are more extensive, and a member may talk to any other member or to the group as a whole (Figure 6-2*b*). One dyad may dominate other parts of the communication network, as when an argument breaks out between two people and the other members silently observe the interchange as if they were at a tennis match (Figure 6-2*c*). Finally, the network sometimes excludes a particular member from active verbal (but not nonverbal) participation. That person becomes virtually isolated from the rest of the group; he or she does not speak and has no comments directed toward him or her (Figure 6-2*d*).

Probably the most divisive network is that resulting from the appearance of subgroups, whose members interact as much within that

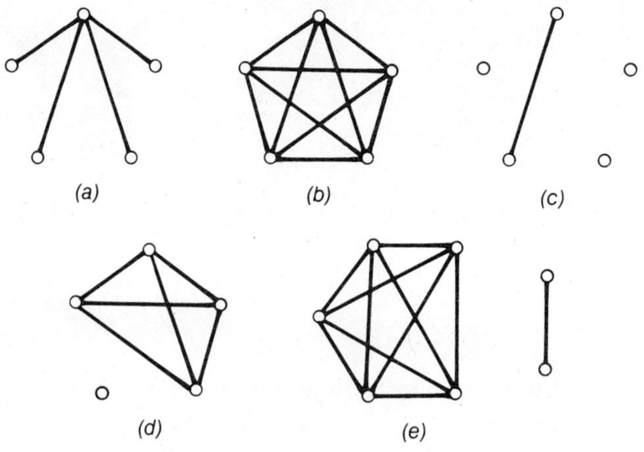

FIGURE 6-2

subgroup as with the total group. An example might be a group of seven people, five of them interacting on the task and two carrying on a side-conversation dyad (Figure 6-2*e*). This dyad may return periodically to the general discussion, but too often it remains passive and outside the mainstream of group communication.

SMALL GROUPS DEVELOP A UNIQUE CULTURE

As a group gradually acquires a history, collective experiences prompt the emergence of general group characteristics. These elements can be clearly identified, though they often remain unstated.

One element of group culture is called *norms*, a set of standards or guidelines for acceptable kinds of behavior in a given situation. Every culture has its norms, and one of the objectives of educating our children is to reveal these appropriate or *normative* behaviors. Similarly, group members establish norms and gradually educate each other as to their description, significance, and penalties for violation. The standards may be explicit, and some group leaders prefer a kind of *contracting* early in group development. "Let's decide on a smoking policy." "Everyone should be here on time, and we will end on time." "One person should talk at a time; I'll call on people who raise their hands." Other norms are merely implied: "We don't use profanity because several people find it offensive." "We call everyone by his first name." "If someone resorts to name calling or other personal attacks, the group will side with the victim and reprimand the guilty party." In most groups, a member could, if asked, write down a fairly elaborate set of implicit group norms. Because such standards are rarely codified, however, new members in an ongoing group must spend some time trying to discern the acceptable behaviors.

Another element of group culture is *cohesiveness*: "a process in which group members are attracted to each other, motivated to remain together, and share a common perspective of the group's activity" (Applbaum et al., 1974, 161). Cohesiveness varies within and between groups. In the early development of most groups it is minimal, evolving slowly in some associations (a business conference of people with different backgrounds and interests, for example) and very rapidly in others (such as a dormitory social committee). Obviously, interpersonal communication is a key factor in building cohesion, and groups that are preoccupied with task functions may not interact enough on the maintenance level to create a common interest in meeting and sharing. While intragroup conflict is inevitable and sometimes productive, if un-

POLICE
DO NOT CROSS

resolved it may destroy whatever cohesiveness previous group interaction may have built.

Still another element of group culture is the *belief-attitude-value structure.* Beliefs are judgments about what is real or unreal, true or false. Values are beliefs about good and bad, desirable and undesirable, right and wrong, beautiful and ugly. Attitudes are systems of beliefs that apply to one central object of judgment or topic. These systems or clusters of beliefs invariably include value-type beliefs, and thus represent not just what we believe to be the facts about some topic, but our likes and dislikes about the topic as well. Together they make up assumptions or givens that guide future decisions. If a work group is to establish a new policy, for example, it must first factually identify the problem and describe the environment in which any new policy must function. The group must develop beliefs about what is real in that environment. Group members also express personal feelings about that real world and about proposed policies (attitudes), and they assess behaviors, programs, ideas, people, and objects in terms of their relative goodness, or value.

While the group agreement on a belief-attitude-value structure may not be perfect, some general consensus is necessary, for this structure becomes the basis for eventual decision making. The group culture is polarized, for example, if half the group *likes economic growth*, believes it is inevitable, and thinks it is good, while the other half *fears growth*, thinks it hurts people, and claims that it is possible to curtail it. How productive would the group process be under these polarized conditions? If we think of groups in which we regularly participate, we may begin to identify those basic assumptions that we share with all the other members.

Shared experiences make up another important group culture dimension. In-jokes, interpersonal conflicts, crisis situations, shared information, group activities, and many other elements of an "insider" perspective become part of each member's understanding of the group experience. Outsiders can only know of these events second hand, but for insiders, the feeling of "we've been through this together" is a potent unifying force. Group culture is strengthened whenever members pause to recall and rehash these events, almost as larger national or ethnic cultures develop a folklore that is regularly retold or reenacted.

Status and power frequently develop in group culture, especially if the group is continuing. *Status* is the importance of a person in the group as ascribed by other members. Some people obviously develop status as the culture develops, and the group may use overt or subtle devices to indicate that position—special titles, rights and privileges, central seating and larger chair, expanded responsibilities and authority.

Power, which is akin to influence, is the ability of a person to reward or punish others as a means of manipulating their behavior. Small group literature is filled with research that firmly establishes the importance of power in group culture (Jacobson, 1972). How might one acquire and use power in small groups? What rewards could be granted or penalties inflicted? An example might be someone who has the resources (knowledge, money, meeting facilities, equipment) necessary to sustain the group and threatens to withdraw those resources if others do not conform to his wishes. Perhaps the power source can promote the cooperative group member and fire the hostile one. Or perhaps someone is an especially adept and witty debater who can intimidate or embarrass anyone who disagrees with her. For whatever reason, power and status relationships inevitably develop, and they clearly affect the ways in which people communicate in the small group.

Overall, the term *identity* best explains the concept of group culture. We seek to identify with others on common ground. Members learn to answer the question "Who are we?" in similar ways. "We are a team of professionals tackling a tough problem." "We are a competent staff of coaches trying to develop a winning team." "We are a group of concerned citizens trying to raise money for our candidate." Without group culture, there can be no group identity, only individual identities. Perhaps the cultural element is the key to distinguishing whether a particular event is simply "several individuals talking" or truly "small-group communication."

A GROUP IS CHARACTERIZED BY ROLE BEHAVIOR

Roles of group members typically become a significant factor in group communication and productivity. However, this factor could just as easily be considered an important subcategory of group culture discussed above.

Before defining roles, we first introduce the premise that *any group participant has a potentially large and varied behavioral repertory*. That is, he or she has a *choice* of several possible actions and messages at any moment. Admittedly, some of these choices are bad ones, like walking angrily out of the room, jumping up and down, or pouring coffee on another member. But behavioral options, some appropriate and some not, nevertheless exist for every group member.

We are especially interested in *communication behavior repertories*. In developing a method for studying small-group communication, Robert Bales (1950) outlines several behavioral categories that can be identified. The following summary of those message behaviors suggests a fairly complete small-group communication repertory. The first six responses involve what Bales calls the "social emotional area," roughly similar to what we term the *maintenance* function:

Solidarity Helping, rewarding, showing appreciation, raising the status of another

Antagonism Punishing, criticizing, attacking, deflating the status of another

Tension release Laughing, joking, showing satisfaction

Showing tension Asking for help, expressing worry, withdrawing

Agreement Showing acceptance, understanding, concurrence, willingness to comply

Disagreement Rejecting, opposing, refuting

The next six responses in Bales' repertory deal more directly with the *task* function:

Giving suggestions Directing, offering options, proposing, recommending

Seeking suggestions Collecting information, seeking solutions or options

Giving opinions Evaluating, analyzing, judging, expressing feelings

Seeking opinions Collecting ideas and points of view, seeking options, assessing feelings of others

Giving orientation Repeating, clarifying, explaining, informing, instructing

Seeking orientation Seeking repetition, background information, instruction, clarification

It is not difficult to think of messages that illustrate each of these categories. For example, "What do you think we should do, John?" asks for an opinion. "I think we can be proud of what we accomplished today" shows solidarity. "So far, we have come up with three proposals" provides orientation. The communication choices that group members make are the most perceivable indicator of the role they are playing. *Roles* may be considered similar to parts played by actors in a drama. They are made up of a set of expected or predictable behaviors that "fit" with the general category that defines or describes the person. We can easily think of a variety of behaviors that seem typical of people whom we have seen in such roles as *tough guy*, *old maid*, *minister*, *villain*, *fashion model*, or *intellectual*.

We play many roles in our lifetime, and sometimes several each day. Since a small group quickly develops a culture, it shares with larger social groups the common trait of specific and complex role development. Group members not only identify others by their unique features —name, age, background, physical characteristics—but also by more general categories like *quiet*, *assertive*, *obnoxious*, *phony*, *intelligent*, *unhappy*. When this process occurs, role development has begun.

Importantly, role development is a process that will occur above and beyond prescribed or planned group behaviors—that is, it occurs naturally. In one of the best textbooks on small-group communication, Bormann (1969) describes some of the characteristics of *leaderless group discussions* (LGDs) that were observed in studies at the University of Minnesota. Two important conclusions were: (1) members began specializing and acquiring status and esteem as the group got going; and (2) their role development did not take place *independently* but rather in the context of joint group consensus. Role emergence and specialization occur when key task or maintenance functions are identified (like gathering information, resolving differences, keeping the group on the track). Then, various group members are given either positive reinforcement or negative feedback as they attempt to fulfill these group functions. Role emergence is thus a trial-and-error process, often a very subtle rendering of group consensus about who should perform various tasks. An example might be two people who purport to be authorities on the discussion topic. One person is authentic; his comments gain immediate group approval and appreciation with reactions that say, in effect, "tell us more." The other is a phony. His information does not jibe with general group knowledge; it is either disputed or ignored. Soon the group expert has emerged, and the impostor has withdrawn to a different role through group consensus.

Role development and definition occur primarily through communication. By the selection of different mixes of the message repertory discussed earlier, we gradually take our places in the group culture. The most common role in groups is *leader*. We shall discuss it later in more depth; for now, notice how we tend to ascribe traits like confidence, poise, assertiveness, knowledgeability, status, and power to that role category. We also can predict certain behaviors from people in such official roles as *recording secretary*, *parliamentarian*, *treasurer*, and *social chairman*.

Many small-group roles are unofficial but still very real to group members. The effective group participant learns to watch and listen for behaviors that signal these roles. The following are only a few of the many that have been suggested in small-group literature:

The Authority People in authority roles enjoy dominating the content level of group decision making. They are opinionated, purport to be well informed, and become judgmental of others. They participate frequently and have something to say on nearly every issue. They may be dogmatic and intolerant of opposing viewpoints.

The Facilitator Facilitators are process oriented. They are especially aware of the feelings of others and are adept at reading both nonverbal and verbal feedback of group members. Facilitators attempt to provide full participation, ensure fairness, protect group members who are attacked, perceive group tension or fatigue, and develop strategies for enhancing interpersonal relationships.

The Compromiser/Harmonizer Closely related to facilitators, compromisers try to resolve conflict at both the substantive and interpersonal levels. They do not feel comfortable with conflicting points of view or with rigid positions; hence, they urge a give-and-take posture as a group norm and regularly suggest points of agreement and possible compromise positions.

The Efficiency Expert Efficiency experts are very task oriented. They want to ensure that the group achieves its stated objectives with acceptable results and in the allotted time. They remind the group of the topic under discussion, make lists of group conclusions or decisions, summarize key points, and keep an eye on the clock.

The Antagonist Often in the aggressor's role, antagonists are typically judgmental, combative, and assertive. They enjoy the lively verbal game of attack and defense and view differences of opinion among participants as a win-lose situation, often turning a cooperative problem-solving venture into a competitive game. A potentially valuable antagonist role is that of the *devil's advocate*, who purposely argues a contrary position simply to assure that the group has considered all alternatives and can defend the eventual decision.

The Comedian Some group participants view wit and humor as a fundamental part of group experience. They tell jokes, laugh, make what they believe to be humorous side comments, and generally seek an atmosphere of convivial mirth. Comedians want the group experience to be a fun time. Some people are singularly unfunny and become obnoxious, but occasional humorous communication can be a welcome release from the tension of difficult group situations.

The Socializer Somewhat similar to comedians are the socializers, who view the group experience primarily as a chance to share casual and relaxing conversation with friends. Their messages usually express interest in what others have been doing as well as relate personal experiences and sundry gossip. Socializers are outgoing and expressive and are especially interested in perpetuating the group as a social unit, even after the group task has been achieved.

The Digressor Digressors enjoy expounding and elaborating. They may try to tie marginally related personal experiences to discussion topics. Their messages are usually lengthy and poorly organized. Most important, their comments may evoke responses by other group members, pulling the discussion even farther off the track.

The Intellectual/Philosopher Some group participants have a penchant for the abstract or theoretical. Their comments on relatively matter-of-fact topics often show deeper analysis or a search for meanings. They tend to generalize and try to discover new, more profound ways of phrasing group conclusions.

The Grouch Occasionally groups are shackled with malcontents who, like the angry Muppet in the garbage can on television's *Sesame Street*, do not attempt to hide their foul mood. Their negative attitudes, their "nay-saying" responses to group decisions, often dishearten other participants and deflate group morale. Their messages are usually judgmental, clearly implying the errors of others. The skeptical, cynical verbal communication of grouches is usually accompanied by ample nonverbal cues like frowns, sighs, vocal inflections, and negative body postures.

The Quiet One The larger the group, the greater the likelihood that some members will show minimal verbal participation. More verbal members may find these more silent members quite threatening. Although reticent members may be genuinely interested, we may interpret their silence to mean shyness, arrogance, hostility, stupidity, or disinterest. Verbal members, even if their opinions conflict with our own, still may seem more trustworthy, less suspicious, because we know where they stand. But the quiet ones may remain a mystery. They do not seem to contribute to either the task or maintenance function. Realistically, however, we all know of groups in which more constructive outcomes might have occurred had more members more frequently chosen to play the silent role!

Role development may be elaborate, varied, and subtle. The roles we have discussed are obviously the extremes, and they do not necessarily develop with such clear and uniform definition. Group members may play composites of several roles, as with a socializer who also facilitates or the digressor who philosophizes, and two or more group members may play similar roles, as with the troublesome situation of two or three task achievers having to interact with four or five socializers.

What additions to our list might be appropriate? What modifications? Which roles, if fully developed, are in inherent conflict with other roles? Are most of these roles constructive or destructive? What situations might modify their positive or negative influence? *What communication behaviors (messages) tend to indicate particular roles?* These are just a few of the questions that group participants should regularly attempt to answer.

SMALL GROUPS ARE DYNAMIC

A fairly obvious point, clearly suggested by the discussion of culture and role development, is that groups change over time. Still, we are tempted to look at familiar faces in a familiar setting with familiar tasks and procedures and assume that it is the same group we left after the previous meeting. Some cultural constants remain, of course, but the group has been modified by many intervening events. We often experience an exhilarating, meaningful group session and seek to renew that experience. Eagerly anticipating the same feelings, we may be disappointed when the next meeting fails to fulfill our expectations.

What has happened? Why can't we return to the exciting group we remember? For one thing, group membership may change. With a new member, we may be more guarded and reserved in our interaction. Or an old member may be absent, leaving us without a strong leader or tension reliever or information source. The unique blend of roles that prompted an exciting group chemistry no longer exists.

Second, the group may be affected by intragroup experiences. Perhaps the meeting begins with a comment that starts a bitter argument or insults a group member. Perhaps a usually optimistic, cheerful member expresses anger or discouragement. The communication events within the group change its basic character.

Third, extragroup experiences may affect certain members. A personal crisis or tragedy, an outside argument with another group member, or an encounter with new information that the old group did not have ("I talked to the boss, and he said he would never approve our proposal") are some of the extragroup experiences that can change the behavior of individual members. In other words, people are different because of what they have experienced since they last met.

Finally, the larger environment may change significantly. We often hear of business or government committees that try to solve problems that no longer exist. Similarly, the dynamic environment may render irrelevant the task of a small group, or environmental changes may add urgency to group deliberations or modify the kinds of things the group must do. In turn, the necessary changes in tasks, roles, and procedures will significantly alter group process.

Members of small groups are often like the college student who goes home for spring vacation and seeks out her old high school friends; because she and her companions have changed so much, however, she finds the interaction depressingly shallow and unrewarding. The perceptive group member will be alert to the internal and external factors that change group experience and notice the verbal and nonverbal behaviors that signal basic changes in group culture. The naive group member, on the other hand, will continually search for "the way it used to be," unable to adapt to the inevitable shifts in group dynamics.

PARTICIPANTS SEEK BOTH INDIVIDUAL AND GROUP GOALS

It would be nice to think of a small-group effort in which each person contributed in a totally cooperative and selfless manner, cheerfully sacrificing personal interests and comfort for the good of the group. Athletic coaches, business executives, club presidents, and the like frequently use the team approach as an appeal to people to act unselfishly.

We believe it is naive to think that such a perfect condition is possible in group processes. The fact is that whenever we participate in a group, we bring personal objectives with us. These goals may be quite subtle or fairly obvious; they may enhance or compete with group interests and objectives. But personal goals, in some form, will always be a factor in the group experience.

What are some of those personal goals? The list below suggests only a few:

> I want to be confirmed as a human being; I want people to like me and recognize me.
>
> I want people to think that I'm intelligent.

I want to convince others of my point of view; I want them to follow my advice.

I want to avoid criticism or ridicule.

I want to make new friends; I want to profit socially from the group experience.

I want to acquire new information or skills that will help me in my everyday life.

I want the group to be a sounding board for my ideas; I want reliable feedback.

I want to tell others what I know and what I've done; I want to impress them.

I want to get revenge against someone who criticized my ideas and embarrassed me.

I want to criticize someone or something outside the group; I want to let off steam with the group members as my captive audience.

I want to make this group experience as brief and painless as possible; I want to get it over with.

I want to avoid interpersonal conflict and maintain harmony among participants at all times.

I want the group to do what I say.

I want to tell the group about my problems and have them give me comfort, support, and solace.

Obviously, these personal goals may impede group progress. Suppose the group goal is to obtain as much information on a public issue as is possible in a short time. The person who wants to talk about his problems, dominate the discussion, attack others, make new friends, or philosophize may detract from this fairly explicit goal. Sometimes a frank discussion of personal objectives—a kind of self-disclosure—can make all participants more aware of the kinds of behaviors that may destroy or disrupt a group's progress. Self-analysis by each member of personal interests and motives can also focus on potential conflicts between individual and group goals.

GROUP MEMBERS ARE INTERDEPENDENT WITH EACH OTHER AND WITH THE LARGER ENVIRONMENT

Recent interest in environmental ecology has heightened our awareness of the interrelationships of all living things. Organisms behave in relation to other organisms, not independently. We are all *interdependent*. The behavior of one affects, and is affected by, the behavior of another.

Interdependence is enormously important in relation to small-group interaction. Fisher (1974) focuses heavily on this concept, suggesting that an individual behavior or *act* is not the key to understanding group behavior; rather, the crucial component is the contiguous or sequential behaviors of two or more people—the *interact*. A comment by A is the act, but B's response to A forms the interact. Then A's response to B completes the *double interact*. The focus on interaction forces us to explore the process of interaction between people and between messages rather than simply to concentrate on a single group member or message in isolation. For example, if A makes a comment that appears to be hostile and inflammatory, the statement becomes counterproductive only if B responds in equally negative ways. If B chooses to respond less antagonistically and more positively, however, the initial comment might not cause serious problems. Hence, the consequence of the single message, whether friendly or hostile, depends on subsequent messages—the interactions that result.

Another implication of interdependence is personal responsibility. Whether we decide to say something or to say nothing affects in part the eventual interaction. Since we are presumably responsible for personal decisions that affect other people, we are therefore at least partially responsible for what happens in the group. Put differently, all group members are collectively responsible for group interaction and outcomes. We argue that a person cannot realistically say "The group has failed in its objectives because Bill and Susan are always arguing" or "It's not my fault that the group degenerated into petty quarrels and bickering; I didn't say a word all day." Appropriate comments might have stopped either conflict and smoothed the ruffled feathers; the person who chose not to intervene was partially to blame for the negative group outcome.

In addition to the interdependence of its members, the group as a whole is interdependent with the outside environment, with the larger communication system. Group members should be aware of the effects of that system on group process, as well as aware of the effects that group decisions could have on the environment. The failure of many well-intended programs developed in a small group is frequently due to unexpected clashes between the program and elements in the larger system.

DIFFERENCES BETWEEN SMALL GROUPS

Obviously groups vary in their objectives and composition. They can nevertheless be categorized on the basis of important distinctions in terms of origin, structure, membership, and orientation.

HISTORY

Is the group *zero-history* or *continuing*? If the group is brand new—if the particular mix of people has never come together before—there is no "history" on which to base their behavior. Group members cannot recall past experiences that can guide their interaction. They must start from scratch. Hence, they begin with "zero-history." The continuing group, on the other hand, does have a history of interaction. Although not all group members will have participated equally in that history and although each person will recall and interpret the history in different ways, their collective past will help guide group behavior. They will tend to conform to the established procedures of the group, for they cannot arbitrarily wipe out the past or behave as if the group had never been together before.

DURATION

Is the group *ad hoc* or *permanent*? *Ad hoc* means "for this special purpose." The term implies that the group was formed to achieve a specific, usually short-range, objective and should disband as soon as that objective is achieved or when it is obvious that it cannot be achieved. In contrast, the permanent group remains operative regardless of the types of problems or tasks that will confront it. This does not mean that the permanent group has no specific purpose. However, when the group achieves a particular goal or finishes a task, it continues to function by taking on new but related work.

A common problem with permanent groups is that they may outlive their usefulness. Because of a rapidly changing environment, the kinds of problems they were set up to solve no longer exist. Hence, the group members may struggle to find new tasks to accomplish, not because such work is necessary, but because the group does not want to disband! Such groups are typical in large bureaucracies, but most of us have been in permanent groups that should not have continued to exist.

A related problem is the ad hoc group that tries to become permanent because the members enjoy the interaction. They feel a sense of accomplishment in completing their "one-time-only" task so they try to convince outsiders that the group should continue. As a result, the real advantage of the *ad hoc* group—specific and adaptive focus on a unique problem—may be lost to a formality or rigidity that makes the group inappropriate to deal with new and quite different problems. Further, the membership mix may no longer include the skills needed for the new problem. Hence, new tasks should be handled by new ad hoc groups.

STRUCTURE

Is the group *structured* or *unstructured*? In the structured group, the roles of each member, the procedures by which the group moves through its business, and group goals and tasks are all well developed and formalized. Members know specifically what is expected of them as well as what topics will be discussed. Examples of the structured group are a corporate board of directors, a student council meeting, or a military court-martial.

An unstructured group flows freely from topic to topic, procedures are only vaguely and indirectly defined, and personal roles vary as the interaction progresses. Unlike a more structured group, the unstructured group may have only casual awareness of a task or objective. Time constraints are fairly unimportant. When participants tire of the interaction, they simply adjourn. An example might be a group of students who meet in the coffee shop after every class to relax, converse, and simply enjoy the company of peers.

Obviously, *structure* is a relative term. Structured groups always are somewhat spontaneous, and unstructured ones inevitably develop various stated or implicit group rules and expectations. But relative structure is nonetheless an important dimension. Some people want to know precisely how the group will proceed; others feel uncomfortable and stifled by rigid group norms and procedures. Degree of structure is one of the first decisions any group must make.

A common misconception about task groups is that the more structured the group, the more efficient it will be. Actually, strict rules and procedures may impede progress toward the goals. Members must wade through rigid agendas, tight parliamentary procedure, and restricted communication patterns. They cannot move easily from less important to more crucial items because the rules do not permit it. Thus, small groups are susceptible to the same stifling red tape that paralyzes

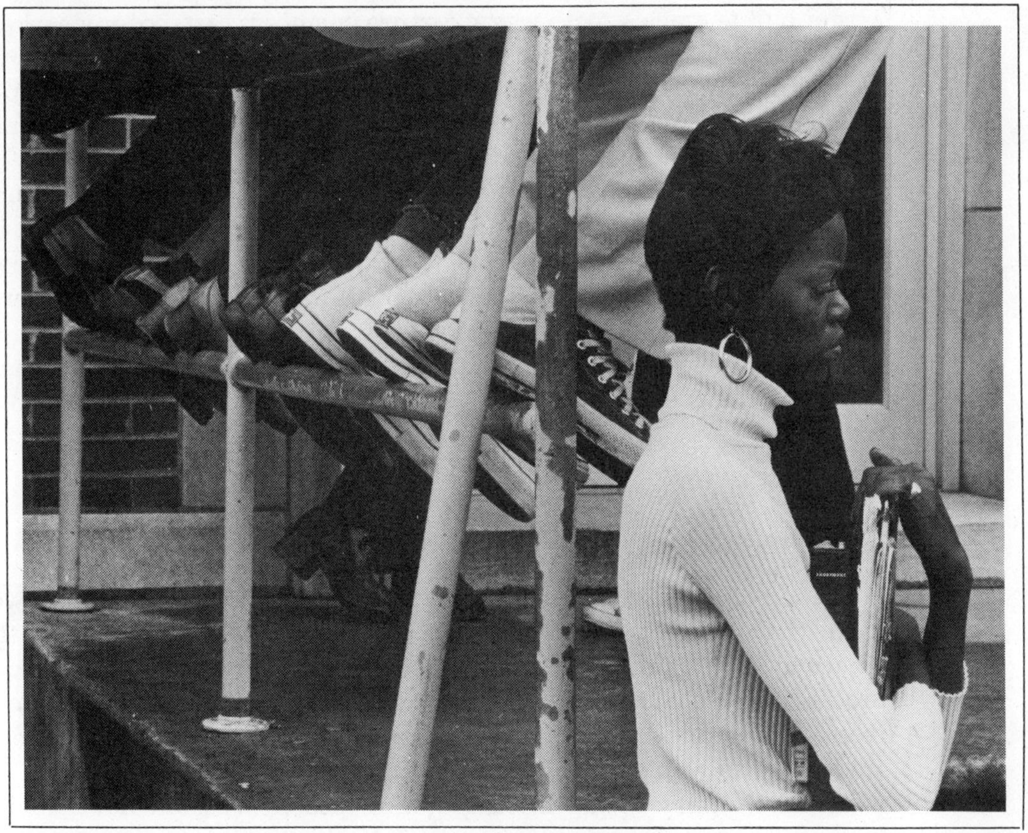

larger bureaucracies. With less structure, members can recognize when the decision-making process is lagging and can increase productivity simply by offering informal suggestions that the others accept. The group may then move quickly to a decision without procedural constraints.

Structure is not *inevitably* counterproductive, but when any structural element is proposed, group members should always ask what it is meant to achieve: "Who will be the leader?" "How long shall we discuss this?" "Shall we prepare an agenda?" "Shall we vote on it?" "Do we want group bylaws?" Too often we adopt group procedures simply because we are accustomed to them. And we must conclude, like the familiar poster in the executive's office, "There's no reason for it; it's just our policy!"

MEMBER MOTIVATION

Is the group membership *voluntary* or *involuntary*? By *voluntary*, we mean that group members perceive or feel a need to assemble with others to solve a problem or complete a task. They welcome the group process because it represents a way of achieving personal objectives and receiving personal rewards. An example is a college study group, a few students who want to pool their information before a big exam.

An involuntary group is composed of people who did not initiate their own group membership; someone else (or the circumstances of the moment) required that they participate. This does not suggest that involuntary participants are dragged kicking and screaming into the group or that they remain resentful and uncooperative during group interaction. It does suggest, however, that members may have to work harder to sustain enthusiasm and build commitment to the group task. Examples of involuntary groups include a management team assigned by top management to make policy recommendations, a subcommittee appointed by a club president to plan a fund-raising project, or speech fundamentals students whose instructor divides them into small groups and assigns a specific project.

Our relative voluntariness fluctuates through time. Sometimes we are motivated to meet and participate; at other times we would rather abandon the group. The perceptive group member is not only aware of personal motives but regularly assesses the temperament of the group. The leader of an involuntary group should always supply members with good reasons for participating.

ORIENTATION

Is the small group *externally* or *internally* oriented? If a group tends toward external orientation, tasks or objectives relate primarily to achieving some impact on the outside environment. This does not mean that group members will be personally unaffected by their decisions. It means that their reasons for meeting are based on outside needs. For example, an externally oriented group might be concerned with developing a new product for a company, organizing a political campaign, or preparing a convention program. Most of our group affiliations, although they may provide significant personal rewards, are based on external factors.

In contrast, an *internally* oriented group focuses on personal rewards, development, or change for group participants. Such groups are usually termed *learning*, *growth*, or *therapeutic* groups. Members want to learn more about themselves, develop greater awareness of the world around them by sharing group experiences, or even try to solve personal problems through the supportiveness of other group members. Internal groups may also complete specific tasks, however, as with the six students who met and planned a fishing expedition in which only they would participate. Internal groups may be called self-centered because outsiders are linked only indirectly to group outcomes.

The inherent conflict between individual and group goals is examined in a later section. For now, we should note that in externally oriented groups, problems may arise when a participant is preoccupied with an internal justification for meeting and impedes progress on the group task. In general, groups should remain aware of their relative internal or external objectives.

DECISION MAKING IN SMALL GROUPS

We have explored several characteristics of small groups. Since we are concerned in this chapter primarily with work groups, we need to examine the ways in which they typically achieve their tasks—the way they make decisions. Sometimes the decision will be a *conclusion* about what the information shows, as, for example, an interpretation of experimental data by a team of scientists. The task may involve *problem solving*, as with the strategy developed by a legislative committee to curb pollution. Such decisions are integral parts of the construction of programs to accomplish specific objectives.

PHASES OF GROUP DECISION MAKING

Decision making is sometimes haphazard and unpredictable and, therefore, difficult to analyze. Fisher's important study (1974) of small groups helps describe a typical process of decision emergence. From an analysis of both the message acts and interacts, Fisher develops a process based on four phases: orientation, conflict, emergence, and reinforcement. While Fisher makes no claim that the four phases apply uniformly to all groups, his study gives us some confidence that we can learn to observe and understand the ways in which groups use communication to accomplish tasks in fairly predictable ways.

During the *orientation* phase, group members search for ideas, directions, and purposes. Many ambiguous comments and expressions of agreement suggest that the members are still uncertain of their roles and want to feel out the situation with more tentative points of view. In the *conflict* phase, issues become identified, and people state positions that others strongly support or dispute. Dissent, controversy, and polarization are frequent. Opinions are stated frequently and without the ambiguity of phase 1. In phase 3, the *emergence* phase, conflict decreases gradually and comments become somewhat more ambiguous and tentative, less dogmatic or absolute, as the group moves toward consensus. Phase 2 statements like "That idea is totally unacceptable" might become, in phase 3, "Perhaps we shouldn't totally rule out that idea." Group members whose attitudes are changing slowly toward the emerging decision probably use ambiguous statements as a kind of "modified dissent." Finally, phase 4 is characterized by *reinforcement* as argument virtually disappears and comments favoring the emergent solution increase. Vague comments diminish, and specific positive reinforcement becomes a device for showing unity behind the group decision.

We are reluctant to prescribe a rigid step-by-step sequence for group decision making, though such sequences have been proposed. The basis for many of these systems is Dewey's (1910) "reflective thinking" model, which suggests how disciplined minds actually solve problems. Dewey's five steps include:

1. Feeling a difficulty, being aware that something is wrong
2. Locating and defining the problem
3. Suggesting possible solutions
4. Developing, elaborating, and finding information on the suggested solutions

5. Continued testing, observing, evaluating of solutions, leading to rejection of all solutions but one

Similar processes, usually more prescriptive than Dewey's, have been developed in current literature. For example, in a popular textbook on group discussion, Brilhart (1974, 110–111) suggests specific patterns for group problem solving, as in the following series of questions:

What is the nature of the problem facing us?
What might be done to solve the problem?
By what specific criteria shall we judge among our possible solutions?
What are the relative merits of our possible solutions?
How shall we put our decision into effect?

Each question—or stage in the problem-solving process—can include several subquestions, which the group leader may use as a general outline for the problem-solving effort. Ross (1974, 323) introduces a four-step agenda as paraphrased below:

Definition and limitation of the problem
Analysis of the problem, its type and causes
Establishment of criteria for assessing solutions
Evaluation and selection of the best solution

It is probably unrealistic to expect group communication to progress neatly from step to step, but it clearly is useful for both leader and participants to have a general strategy clearly in mind. We suspect that regardless of planned agendas, participants will regularly digress, over-elaborate, move out of sequence, and develop ideas irrelevant to the specific discussion topic. For example, a group might become preoccupied with an intriguing new program, enthusiastically discussing its merits, until one person interjects, "Hey, wait a minute. There are other ways to solve the problem, and I think we need to look at them." Another participant might complain, "By now we should be discussing some possible solutions, but we still can't agree on our goals!" Nevertheless, we know that unsystematic groups are often just as productive as more structured ones.

ESSENTIAL ELEMENTS OF GROUP DECISION MAKING

A general set of requirements for group decision making is explained below. While these elements need not develop in sequence, they are essential for productive group achievement, and all depend on verbal communication. The group leader, discussed in the next section, is usually the most significant determinant of how these four interrelated elements are developed.

Objectives Though groups sometimes flounder aimlessly on a variety of topics, eventually they must answer the questions "What do we want to happen? What are we trying to do or achieve? Why are we here?" Goal setting may become the most difficult and lengthy decision the group must reach or it may be brief and perfunctory. Objectives may not even be stated openly if, for example, the group meets regularly and its purpose is patently obvious. Without some general sense of objectives, however, good decisions are unlikely.

Procedure Admittedly, many groups or committees become prisoners of procedure. They get bogged down in strict agendas and rigid parliamentary rules when spontaneous group interaction might lead to a quicker and better solution. Some structuring of group interaction is necessary, however, if only in the form of a simple statement: "Today let's decide what kinds of information we need; then we'll discuss how we can get it." Or the procedure may involve a carefully structured set of rules like those that govern such arenas of decision as courtrooms or legislatures. A middle ground might be the step-by-step guidance provided by a meeting agenda.

The more specific and rigid the procedures, the more limited the appropriate content of any message. "I think we should still be discussing our objectives; your comments about the problem can be presented later." While less rigidity may allow group members wider latitude in the kinds of messages they may communicate, it may also create uncertainties about how they should contribute. "May I tell you what I think we should decide or should that wait until later?" Even leaderless groups will develop some procedural guidelines, in part because such guidelines suggest appropriate kinds of input.

Information Processing Good decision making depends on good information. A crucial advantage of group over individual decision making is the potential for pooling information and submitting it to group evaluation. The group must seek, gather, sort, combine, modify, and evaluate information. While insufficient information may lead to faulty decisions, an excess of information can cause difficulties as well. An individual may experience *information overload*—too much data to process neatly and meaningfully. The same problem may develop in groups, suggesting that one of the most important decisions the group must make is to answer the questions "When do we have enough good information? When will further input simply confuse the issues and delay a decision?"

The Decision The group must arrive at a decision. An obvious point? Yes, but one that is sometimes forgotten. This writer once sat on a university committee that had met several times annually for several years. We had a title and a purpose, a chairman and recording secretary, regular meeting times, and a rough agenda. But we never *decided* anything substantive. We shared an enormous amount of information, analyzed and evaluated it, wrote and distributed reports on our deliberations, commiserated about the difficulty and complexity of the issues involved, argued about potential policies we might suggest, and regularly revised our discussion topics, focus, and procedures. But we never decided on any new policies or alteration of old ones. The committee still exists, continues to meet, and still has not decided anything, except perhaps deciding not to decide!

Work groups meet because they want to accomplish something. The constraints of time or the urgency of the moment may force the emergence of decisions. With complex tasks and ample time, however, we may forget our ultimate purpose—to arrive at a conclusion, to achieve an objective, to make a decision. In a courtroom, when a jury cannot decide after a reasonable time, it becomes a hung jury and ceases deliberations. In some cases, when indecisive groups flounder, members may not admit their inability to get closure on their ascribed tasks, and they continue to wallow in uncertainty.

LEADERSHIP IN SMALL GROUPS

How does a person become a leader of a group? What are the objectives and duties of leadership? What styles of leadership generally emerge? What suggestions can improve group leadership? These are some of the questions we shall answer in this section.

GROUP LEADERS

Any group leader should ask, "How did I get here? What is my legitimacy? How will the selection process affect my relationship with the group?" Groups usually acquire leaders in one of three ways. First, the leader is assigned or elected by outsiders or is self-appointed. Examples might be a supervisor who asks an employee to head a management team or a legislature that elects someone to chair a subcommittee. In such cases, the group members have no say as to who will lead them. They also have no doubt as to who has the right to lead, for legitimacy is established immediately. However, the appointed leader must maintain that legitimacy through effective performance of leadership tasks.

Second, the leader is selected through formal group procedures as the group begins its discussions. Perhaps annual elections determine the group moderator or perhaps a casual suggestion that someone would make a good leader prompts a show of support to establish legitimacy. Thus, the group quickly assures that someone will assume responsibility for coordinating group effort, and the person chosen is secure in knowing that the role resulted from group confidence in his or her abilities. If the selected leader fails, of course, the group must face the awkward task of replacing someone whom they initially supported.

Third, the leader emerges. From the Minnesota Studies on group discussion, Bormann (1969, 207–216) notes that leaderless groups usually develop structure and roles spontaneously. Through the "method of residues," the group eliminates various people from consideration until only one person remains as the emergent leader. Sometimes groups have to select from two or three contenders for the leadership role. While the eventual leader may know that his special skills, knowledge, or interpersonal style may be deemed effective by the group, he should also recognize that some group members, especially any who also wanted to be leader, may be uncooperative and continue to harbor bad feelings.

LEADERSHIP GOALS

Leadership objectives vary with the type of group and task involved. Nevertheless, there are several goals, listed below, that are commonly suggested as relevant in work groups. Notice that some are task- or content-oriented, while others focus on group maintenance and interpersonal process. While reading each goal, try to think of the kinds of messages a group would use to achieve it.

45
45
26

To initiate discussion of the topic at hand

To help structure the group decision-making process, as through setting an agenda

To regulate participation, assuring that all can provide input and preventing some from monopolizing

To establish an appropriate physical environment through room preparation, chair and table arrangements, and provision of supplies

To develop appropriate communication climates: positive, cordial, relaxed, task-oriented, cooperative

To help manage or resolve interpersonal conflict

To restate and clarify ideas of participants

To keep the discussion relevant and productive

To provide summaries and closure on group conclusions

To bring the group to productive achievement of overall objectives

To develop plans and objectives for future meetings

To stimulate development of group culture: build rapport, commitment, cooperation

To distribute rewards and punishments, confirming positive contributions and criticizing negative ones

To integrate oneself into full-fledged group membership; to assure personal as well as leadership input

To foster group morale and enthusiasm for the task

To provide liaison between the group and the outside environment by representing group consensus and decisions to outsiders

What other objectives might be added to this list? Are some of these goals inappropriate for certain situations? How might goal setting vary according to particular types of group experience? In general, we believe that it is useful for the leader not only to think carefully about leadership objectives in advance of the meetings but also to *discuss with the group*, perhaps even negotiate with group members, the goals she or he hopes to accomplish.

LEADERSHIP STYLES

The goals listed above depend heavily on leadership style. The communication behavior of a small-group leader is also influenced by his or her leadership style.

A distinction is made among authoritarian, democratic, and laissez-faire leadership. *Authoritarians* use authority, power, rewards, and punishments to assure group compliance with their wishes. Their communication may consist of commands, opinion statements, evaluation and criticism of others, and dogmatic arguments. Interpersonal contact is distant and cold. Authoritarian motives include domination, power, and self-fulfillment. Task achievement is more important than people.

Democratic leaders attempt to distribute power more widely throughout the group, seeking greater input for each member. They stress a "we" orientation rather than the "I" approach of the authoritarian. Key terms are participation, reinforcement, persuasion, supportiveness, mutual responsibility, and trust. Communication is usually facilitative, with leader messages consisting of suggestions, questions, clarifications, and encouragement. Democratic leaders attempt to balance concern for the group tasks with concern for people in the group. Many comments are process- or maintenance-oriented, in essence asking "How are we doing?" and "How do we feel?"

Laissez-faire leaders essentially abandon their directive roles, letting the group progress as a spontaneous social unit. Their attitudes suggest indifference and nonresponsibility for group outcomes, and may be motivated out of disgust, hostility, or hurt feelings. ("It's obvious that you don't care what I think, so you all just go ahead and discuss without me.") Such passive leaders may have been appointed to their role, and because they are shy or unskilled in group processes, they may simply withdraw. The laissez-faire style may be motivated by a sincere belief that direction stifles creativity and that total spontaneity leads to the most productive group process. Whatever the reason, abdicated leadership usually leads to (1) a group that flounders aimlessly, or (2) assumption of leadership by a more dominant, task-oriented person. Passive leaders are silent most of the time, comment only when spoken to, and are noncommittal on group decisions. Fortunately, such leaders are rare.

The key element in leadership style is *control*, the degree to which the leader seeks to direct and regulate group interaction and outcomes. Ross (1974, 332) suggests the continuum in Figure 6-3 as a model for the varying levels of control. The authors generally support the midpoint on the continuum, the democratic style, though they agree with Fiedler (1965) that the optimum style depends in part on the type of task, its relative structure, and the comparative power and influence of the leader. In some cases, a more directive strategy of control might be appropriate. Still, leaders who are willing to treat others as legitimate

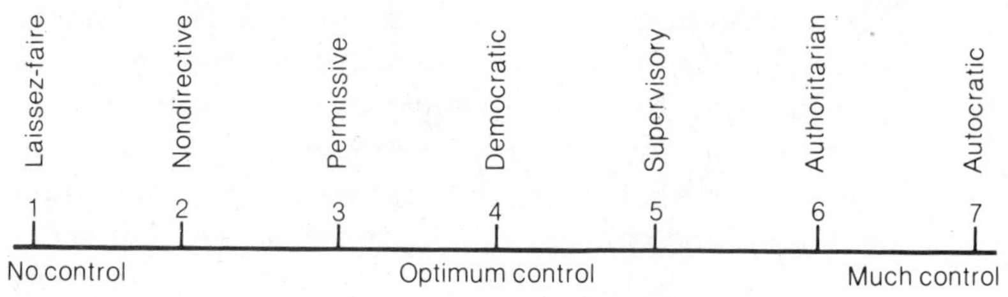

FIGURE 6-3

partners in the group process with equal rights to participate are probably the most effective leaders in most situations.

We suggest one addition to the concept of democratic leadership—a *consensus strategy*. Phillips (1966, 7–8) offers a good definition of consensus:

> The word "consensus" refers to the distinguishing feature of the small group, any group of two or more people who, for a given period of time, are concerned with a mutual goal and who devote their efforts during this time to the achievement of that goal. . . . Sometimes consensus is built on agreements about minor points over a period of time. Sometimes it is a major insight that suddenly reveals a solution that all members can accept. Consensus is the result of careful interpersonal communication in which members subordinate some of their personal feelings and desires to demonstrated facts or necessity. . . . The basic idea is that some personal preferences must be surrendered to the welfare of the group. The minority must not sulk in silent opposition. It must be reconciled. The final agreement must include the ideas of all.

Thus, consensus does not mean "majority." It means *total group agreement* on decisions. If a vote is necessary, then there are winners and losers, and the consensus strategy has failed. To achieve complete agreement, the leader may need to take more time arriving at group decisions, assuring that a cooperative, problem-solving attitude has been developed, that full discussion by all members on all important issues has been encouraged, and that all points of agreement and potential compromise have been explored. The democratic leader with a consensus strategy is quick to praise members with the courage to change their opinions and is himself open to accepting what he previously opposed. Some differences are irreconcilable, and no one should be forced to join the majority simply out of group pressure. Nevertheless, the consensus style is remarkably productive and can usually be developed by the perceptive, patient leader.

SUGGESTIONS FOR GROUP LEADERS

We have noted the several types of small groups and the many spontaneous ways in which individual roles and group culture develop. Because of these variations, because each situation, leader, and task is unique, we cannot develop a list of rules that applies generally to small-group communication events. On the other hand, development of leadership skills is possible if one is willing to adapt general principles to the unique group situation.

Below we try to make such an adaptation to a fairly common type of small-group situation – a zero-history group with an assigned leader, the group to meet periodically to gather information and solve a problem. We have provided general suggestions, not hard and fast rules. Feel free to dispute any suggestion and to consider situations when such behaviors would be inappropriate.

Before the first meeting

1. Review the time schedule, the topics or problems to be covered, and the background materials, if any, that apply to the group task.
2. Review the roster of group members, learning their names and pertinent biographical data.
3. Visit the room or area where the group will meet, and note potential problems like lighting, seating, and noise levels.

The first meeting

1. Arrive early enough to arrange the physical environment. Use a circular seating arrangement so that each person can see everyone else. Set up any necessary equipment or supplies.
2. Remain in the meeting location to greet arriving group members.
3. Select a seat in a noncentral position to help discourage participants from directing all their comments to you. Don't isolate yourself in a special chair, and don't always sit in the same chair each meeting.
4. Explain your role as group leader and how you would like to interact with the others. They should know what to expect of you.
5. Discuss the concept of *collective responsibility* for achieving group goals, that no one person should bear the burden, and that if the group is unproductive all should share the blame. Emphasize the active role that participants should take.
6. Negotiate ground rules for the meetings:
   avoiding personal attacks or innuendos

starting and ending on time
one person speaking at a time, with no side conversations
avoiding tendencies to monopolize
smoking policy
policy on breaks or recesses

Whatever the ground rules, they should result from group consensus rather than being imposed by the leader.

7. Negotiate group objectives; seek group participation in defining and limiting what the group wants to achieve.
8. Encourage an informal atmosphere. Use a casual, conversational speaking style. Suggest that the group operate on a first-name basis.
9. Do not forget the social or maintenance dimension of small groups. At this and all other meetings, encourage a few minutes of small talk on nontask topics.

All other meetings

1. In advance of each meeting, prepare at least a rough agenda, and seek agreement with the group on that agenda as the meeting begins. Be selective; it is better to discuss two or three items in depth than to be a slave to a lengthy agenda and discuss items sketchily.
2. Try to avoid defensive reactions to participants' suggestions that attempt to modify your ideas about group objectives or procedures.
3. Try to steer the group away from becoming a gripe session; suggest a more constructive problem-solving or task-oriented attitude.
4. If certain group members regularly look to you as the authority or final arbiter or ask you to clarify information and provide definitive statements on issues, try to *deflect* those questions to other group members. This may encourage participation and enhance the climate of *group* responsibility for effective results.
5. Respond selectively to group comments. Do not respond to every statement or group members will tend to direct all their remarks toward you.
6. Your substantive input (opinions, information, ideas) should be as relevant as anyone else's. Avoid dominating, but remember your dual leadership role as facilitator *and* participant. Leaders should not attempt to be neutral on all issues; nor should their points of view be communicated dogmatically.
7. Be sensitive to nonverbal cues about how well the discussion is going. Recognize, for example, people nervously shifting in their

chairs, or daydreaming, or their negative facial expressions, audible sighs, and avoidance of eye contact with the speaker. Make a visual survey every couple of minutes, watching especially for people trying to get a chance to speak.

8. Be sensitive to your personal nonverbal behavior, like frowning, avoiding eye contact, or looking at your watch as another is speaking.
9. Try to observe and analyze role development in group participants.
10. Do not let the group perpetuate misunderstandings. Seek clarification and elaboration. Encourage members to restate in their own words what they understand another member to have said.
11. Try to steer long, meandering digressions back on the track, but do not adhere slavishly to the suggested topic if the group is avidly pursuing an equally relevant item. Remember that groups rarely progress in a neat, linear fashion and that group consensus often emerges at the end of a so-called digression.
12. Keep track of time; help the group modify procedures if time becomes a factor.
13. Provide occasional summaries of what has been said and about where the group is in its progress toward a solution. Note points of stated or implied agreement.
14. Avoid voting to resolve disagreements.
15. Protect the individual group member — his or her right to be heard, to finish what is being said, to be free from personal attack, and to have ideas interpreted accurately.
16. Do not discourage humor; it can relieve tension and build rapport. But do not let the group degenerate into a joke-telling session.
17. Do not permit the group to sidestep awkward or sensitive information or issues if such content is crucial to the best possible solution. For example, if the group carefully avoids any criticism of a previous policy because a group member directed that policy, the leader may have to introduce (tactfully, yet clearly) the troublesome issue and seek responses.

Closure

1. Provide *closure* with a brief summary that suggests what has been accomplished and perhaps what issues remain. Give a sense of completion. You may want to ask a competent group member to provide the summary.
2. Suggest a time for the next meeting along with possible objectives or agenda items.

3. Be the last to leave; chat casually with members about any concerns that they did not want to discuss with the entire group.

In addition to these specific suggestions, we offer some comments on knotty problems that may arise regardless of the type of small group involved.

Discussion Monopolies If one person is monopolizing the discussion, reaffirm the ground rules. "Some of the participants haven't had a chance to speak yet." Seek responses from less vocal members. It may be necessary to talk to the monopolizer privately: "I appreciate your input, John, but I'm worried that some people aren't getting a chance to speak."

The Chronic Interrupter In the case of chronic interruptions, reaffirm your group's ground rules. "Let's permit people to finish their comments." Interrupt the interrupter. "Just a moment, Jane; I don't think Bill was finished." If the interrupter persists, a private talk may be necessary.

Private Conversation between Subgroups of Two or More People Stop side conversations by noting, for example, "I'm having trouble hearing. Let's try to have just one person talking at a time." If problems persist, manipulate the seating arrangement to split up the subgroup.

Silent Group Members If the quieter members of the group appear interested, watch for nonverbal indicators that they might want to speak, and call on them occasionally. Don't embarrass them with too frequent recognition. Show interest when reticent members are talking. If silent members appear uninterested or hostile, talk to them privately to get at the cause of their negative feelings.

Extended Argument between Two People When it is apparent that arguers are no longer giving new information but simply rehashing old data, ask for input from others. "I think Jane and Bill have given us the basis for both sides of the issue; now let's have the rest of you react to some of their ideas." Ask each disputant to rephrase the other's position. "Jane, before you reply to Bill, I'm wondering if you would tell us what you hear Bill saying. What do you think his argument is?" If more such dyadic arguments are likely, incorporate the debate format as a decision-making tool and set clear time limits.

Interpersonal Conflict If conflict within the group is issue-oriented, it can be a constructive way of getting at all aspects of the problem. In many cases it adds interest and can be encouraged. If conflict is people- or personality-oriented, on the other hand, in most cases it must be stopped, or it can destroy group cohesion. Remind members of ground rules—no personal attacks. Affirm the legitimacy of conflict. "It's natural for us to disagree on controversial problems, especially when we come from such different backgrounds." Talk about the disagreement and suggest some self-disclosure on why it may have developed. *Do not try to sweep it under the rug*. Talk it out—a slow, painful, yet crucial task for group maintenance.

A Lifeless Session with Bored, Unresponsive Members Talk out the apparent problem and make sure others share your perception. Remind the group that everyone shares responsibility for making the group a meaningful experience. Ask for suggestions. Do some self-analysis. Is part of the problem due to your own lack of enthusiasm? Analyze group members. Are the negative reactions of one or two opinion leaders casting gloom over the proceedings? Suggest a frank discussion on group goals, topics, and methods. Would other strategies, like debates or guest participants or the establishment of subgroups, enhance interest? Is this just a bad day in the life of a generally enthusiastic group? Should we adjourn early and try again next week? Has the group outlived its usefulness? These and similar questions prompt group participation in what is too often thought of as the leader's problem.

PARTICIPATION IN SMALL GROUPS

We conclude this chapter with some comments about productive group participation for leaders and nonleaders alike. The following suggestions may improve one's constructive contribution to group goals:

1. Be aware of personal motives and objectives. Assess the extent to which those personal perspectives may either help or impede group progress.
2. Assess the expectations of other group members toward you. What role do they expect you to play? Is such a role productive? Are you willing and able to fulfill those expectations?

3. Accept equal responsibility to intervene when the group encounters problems. Recognize the interdependence of participants and that your decision *not* to intervene is still a decision affecting group outcomes.
4. Develop nondefensive, nonjudgmental communication styles. Evaluate information and ideas, not people. Remember, too, that arguments against your ideas do not necessarily signal a personal attack.
5. Actively seek clarity in communication. Ask others to rephrase comments you do not understand, and seek feedback from others regarding your messages.
6. Remain sensitive to group process. Do not place on the leader the full responsibility to monitor the interacting task and maintenance functions.
7. Develop commitment to group goals. If you cannot conscientiously do this, it may be better to drop out of the group.
8. Confront group and task problems openly and honestly. Avoid deception or evasion. Do not pretend that important group or task problems do not exist.

SUMMARY

A student with a deep interest in small-group interaction should eventually take an entire course in the area. In this chapter, we have introduced some of the key concepts that would be studied in such a course.

A small group is a collection of people who interact to achieve specific objectives. Direct relationships among all members of a small group are possible. Small groups vary widely in their objectives and composition, but the zero-history work group having both task and maintenance functions is perhaps the most common type. Communication is the primary glue that holds group members together.

Small groups develop unique cultures with role development as one of the most crucial components. Cultural and role characteristics change over time, giving special meaning to the term *group dynamics* and suggesting that group members need to be continually aware of the current condition of their groups. They also must be cognizant of their interdependence (and mutual responsibility) with other group members and with the outside environment.

Group tasks are achieved through the process of decision making, for which several prescriptive procedures have been suggested. Four elements that must be present for good decision making are group objectives, group procedures, information processing, and the will to make the decision.

Group leadership is the key to effective group process. Leaders are either selected or emerge naturally; the group itself provides the eventual legitimacy for the leader's role. Several leadership styles are possible, ranging from the rigid control of the authoritarian to the abdication of control in the laissez faire style. We recommend a democratic style for most small groups with special emphasis on developing consensus decision making through patient, goal-oriented, participative interaction of all members.

Finally, this chapter suggests behaviors for both leaders and participants. Most of the suggestions are implemented through communication behavior, suggesting that message competence is a key to small-group productivity.

QUESTIONS

1. How do the following concepts affect group process or interaction?
   zero history
   involuntary group
   maintenance functions
   role behavior
   networks
   norms
   individual goals
2. Why is it appropriate that we study the communication process and dyads before we explore small-group communication?
3. Explain the relationship of dyads to small-group behavior.
4. Suggest some pros and cons of having a structured agenda for controlling the decision-making process in small groups.
5. Describe hypothetical situations in which a laissez-faire, a democratic, and an authoritarian leader might be the most productive.

SUGGESTED READINGS

Ardrey, Robert. *The social contract.* New York: Atheneum, 1970.

Bales, Robert F. *Interaction process analysis: a method for the study of small groups.* Reading, Mass.: Addison-Wesley, 1950.

Brilhart, John K. *Effective group discussion.* Dubuque, Iowa: Wm. C. Brown, 1974.

Burgoon, Michael, Judee Heston, and James McCroskey. *Small group communication: a functional approach.* New York: Holt, 1974.

Cathcart, Robert, and Larry Samovar. *Small group communication: a reader.* Dubuque, Iowa: Wm. C. Brown, 1974.

Fisher, B. Aubrey. *Small group decision making.* New York: McGraw-Hill, 1974.

Jacobson, W. D. *Power and interpersonal relations.* Belmont, Calif.: Wadsworth, 1972.

Phillips, Gerald. *Communication and the small group.* Indianapolis: Bobbs-Merrill, 1973.

Rogers, Carl. *On encounter groups.* New York: Harper & Row, 1970.

Zelko, Harold. *The business conference: leadership and participation.* New York: McGraw-Hill, 1969.

During a discussion in a speech class on contemporary public speaking, a skeptical student complained, "I don't see why people are concerned with public speaking nowadays. We don't have the great orators anymore, people are more interested in watching a ball game or a movie than going to hear a public speech, and we know that political campaigns now consist of sixty-second TV spots, not public speeches. I think the age of public speaking is just about over." The professor thought a moment and then replied, "You're entitled to your opinion, of course, but I think you are wrong. I think the age of public speaking is just beginning!"

We suspect that the professor was probably right. Why? For one thing, the TV medium and communication satellites now permit enormous exposure for a single public communication event. A public speaker can be seen and heard simultaneously by well over one *billion* people around the globe. On a regular basis, public officials, teachers, and business executives use public or closed-circuit TV to communicate with large audiences. The electronic media have replaced the print media as the source of news for most Americans, and the reporter who bangs out a news story on a typewriter is being slowly outnumbered by news announcers who are, above all, fluent public communicators.

In addition, more people today have the opportunity to speak publicly. The great orators of the past were almost all white males, most of whom had wealth and education. With the improved, widely available education of today, women and minorities are finding increasing opportunities to assume leadership positions that regularly put them in the speaker-to-audience setting. The number of situations in which public speaking is appropriate has also increased. Social movements and public demonstrations, labor union meetings, business conferences, public information and instruction programs, professional conventions, and service club programs are but a few of the arenas that increasingly demand effective presentational and persuasive speeches.

Although the public speech is unique among other communication settings, *it is still part of the interpersonal communication process.* We think that the person who is competent in the communication behaviors discussed in Part One, and who understands the communication process of which his or her speech is a part, will potentially be a better public communicator than the person who does not have those skills. We separate *public speaking* from *interpersonal communication* in this book partly for convenience and clarity and partly because speech communication classes often are similarly divided to permit special focus on particular interpersonal or public communication exercises and activities. However, we urge you to view this separation only as a convenient organizational tool. From the perspective of communication theory, everyday communicative interaction and the public speech are similar in most important respects.

PUBLIC COMMUNICATION

In Chapter Seven, we explore some of the strategies for developing and preparing a speech, a challenging artistic as well as practical enterprise. In Chapter Eight, we move on to strategies for delivery, for presenting the speech to an audience. We also look at that old bugaboo stage fright. Chapters Nine, Ten, and Eleven provide materials on informative and persuasive speaking. These chapters should be especially useful to students with experience in preparing and delivering speeches and who now need additional suggestions for improving their composition and delivery strategies and skills.

Finally, in Chapter Twelve, we consider some of the special problems of interaction between the speaker and the audience, as well as strategies for dealing with these problems.

Not only do we think that the age of public speaking is just beginning, we also claim that people who expect to be active participants in this society will inevitably find themselves having to speak to audiences. We are convinced that their success in these public communication events will substantially enhance their happiness and well-being.

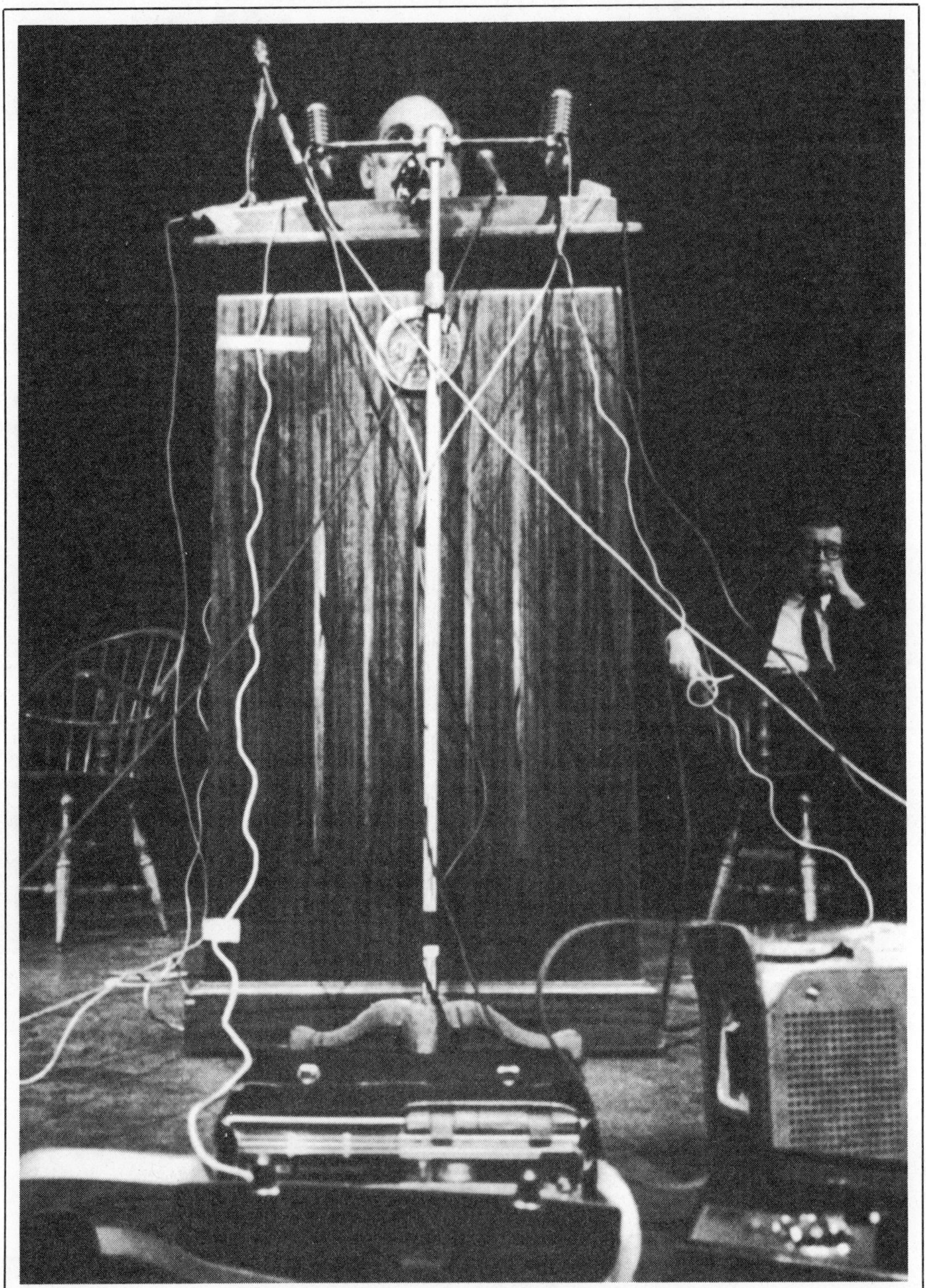

7

SPEECH DEVELOPMENT

PREVIEW

Public speaking continues to be one of the most important forms of human communication. Public speaking is characterized primarily by its one-to-many format. An inherent advantage of this format is the opportunity to deliver messages to a large number of people in a relatively short time span. At the same time, the one-to-many format limits interpersonal interaction and the clarification of misunderstandings through feedback. To compensate for these limitations, the public speaker has a special need for well-developed and well-organized messages. The speaker's ability to construct appropriate speeches can be markedly improved through the study and mastery of basic composition and stylistic techniques.

OBJECTIVES

To explore the nature of public speaking

To identify and describe the general purposes of speeches

To identify and describe five basic stages of speech development

To describe and illustrate basic patterns of speech organization

To describe and illustrate basic supporting materials that can be used to develop main ideas

To describe the four basic forms of speech preparation

SEVEN Public speaking enjoys the longest of all academic histories. The first textbook on public speaking was probably that of Kegemini and Ptahhotep of Egypt about 2600 B.C. Public speaking was one of the three academic areas included in the first formal curriculum of the Middle Ages. The *Trivium* of the Middle Ages included (1) rhetoric, the theory of speech composition and delivery; (2) grammar; and (3) logic. Later the *Trivium* was expanded to include the *Quadrivium*: (1) arithmetic, (2) astronomy, (3) geometry, and (4) music.

Public speaking continues to serve as one of our most important means of human communication. We employ public speaking for personal expression, to transmit information, to influence attitudes and behavior, to highlight ceremonial events, and to entertain. In recent years speech education has seen the development of new and meaningful courses in the areas of small-group and interpersonal communication. These courses have expanded the focus of speech communication and provide needed and useful communication training, but public speaking continues to play a central role in academic programs designed to facilitate the development of knowledge and skill in communication.

Although the various subdivisions of human communication tend to overlap in a number of important ways, we can observe differences in emphasis that distinguish public speaking from small-group activities. For example, small-group communication can be characterized by its one-to-one format, whereas public speaking gains much of its character from the one-to-many format. Both formats have inherent advantages and disadvantages. A major advantage of public speaking is that it provides the opportunity to reach a sizable audience in a small amount of time. In our modern era of electronic media this central advantage can be maximized to the point where one speaker can reach the greater part of a nation's population in a single speech. Many contemporary speakers reach a larger audience through one televised speech than speakers from earlier eras could have reached in a thousand years of continuous platform speaking.

A significant limitation of the one-to-many format is the restriction it places on human interaction and instant feedback. Whereas dyad and small-group formats tend to encourage instant exchange among the participants, public speaking usually requires a relatively formal presentation from one communicator to a larger audience. These generalizations cannot be applied, of course, to *all* public speaking and small-group activities. Speeches to small groups, for example, can allow for a considerable amount of audience participation immediately after, if not during, the formal presentation. In some small groups, on the other hand, we find that the board chairman or other group leader may provide little opportunity for group participation.

We need not try to achieve all communication goals within a single speech communication format, and occasionally we can combine formats to achieve different goals. For example, the public speech might be used to present new information or to stimulate audience awareness of a particular problem. Following the speech, small groups of five to seven people could explore the implications of the speaker's messages on a more personal and individual basis.

Speech communication is one of the primary means by which individuals achieve self-expression, develop, maintain, and change interpersonal relationships, and maintain or change our social order. In attempting to achieve these goals through speech communication, the communicator should consider the relative advantages and disadvantages of the various public speaking and small-group formats. The more experienced and perceptive communicator will ask: "Can our communication goals be achieved more effectively through a speech or through discussion and participation in a small-group format?" "Do we really need time-consuming exchange on this issue, or can the communication goal be effectively achieved through a well-organized and relatively brief public speech?"

TYPES OF SPEECHES

Most public speeches are designed to *inform*, to *persuade*, or to *provide ceremony*. Any given speech includes *all these elements* in some degree, but it is possible to identify the major emphasis of speeches in each category.

THE INFORMATIVE SPEECH

The essential purpose of an informative speech is to *provide information* to an audience. In most cases the purpose of an informative speech is to transmit *new* information to an audience; that is, the speech is designed to increase the audience's knowledge about some aspect of our world. However, the speaker's information can be *familiar* or *unfamiliar* to the audience.

The speaker may wish to convey familiar information when his essential purpose is to review and reinforce what the audience already knows. For example, a club president may review information that pertains to a particular issue before he asks the membership for a vote on that issue. In some cases, a speaker may wish to review familiar information as a means of preparing his audience for the new information he is about to introduce. Clearly, however, the presentation of familiar information is appropriate only for specific purposes, and most informative speeches will emphasize new information that will expand audience awareness.

THE PERSUASIVE SPEECH

The basic purpose of a persuasive speech is to *influence the attitudes*, *feelings*, or *behaviors* of the members of an audience. A persuasive speech can serve to *reinforce* and thereby strengthen current attitudes, feelings, and behaviors, or it can be designed to *change* attitudes, feelings, or behaviors.

A politician's speech to his party membership may be designed to reinforce and strengthen the party's point of view on some political issue. A church leader's presentation to the congregation may be designed to reinforce and strengthen particular beliefs already held by the members of that congregation. In both of these examples, the central purpose is to maintain and strengthen the status quo.

Other persuasive speeches are designed to change some aspect of the status quo. If a Democratic candidate is speaking to an audience composed mainly of registered Republicans, he may design a speech to change audience voting behavior. If a church leader is dissatisfied with certain of his congregation's behaviors, he may develop a speech designed to encourage a change in those behaviors.

THE CEREMONIAL SPEECH

In a wide variety of settings, social ceremonies are conducted with the assistance of special event speeches. These special events include: the introduction of a speaker, the presentation of gifts and awards, traditional ceremonies surrounding graduation, marriage, and death, and traditional ceremonies conducted within particular social institutions.

The usual purpose of a ceremonial speech is to *provide a meaningful experience*. Audience expectations, based on tradition, tend to determine the appropriateness of ceremonial speeches. Just as a person selects attire that is appropriate for a particular event, a speaker prepares for the social event by selecting customary speech materials. Of course, customs change over time, and the way we dress and the kinds of ceremonial speeches we give change with them. Also, originality and inventiveness can provide a refreshing departure from past customs. At the same time, too much departure can reduce the satisfaction that accompanies the familiar and predictable.

Ceremonial or special event speeches might also include the speech designed to entertain. In this case, however, we have little in the way of traditional standards for speech preparation and delivery. Usually, the important ingredient in the entertainment speech is the uniqueness and originality of the speaker's ideas and style.

Since ceremonial and entertaining speeches vary considerably among institutions and subcultures as well as with speaker uniqueness and originality, we have not attempted to deal with them in depth. Instead, this chapter focuses on the informative and persuasive speeches, which are the types of speeches delivered by most people on most occasions.

APPROACHING YOUR OWN SPEECH

Individuals who have little experience in speech preparation often find it difficult to choose a topic or get beyond the first sentence of a speech outline. Many approach speeches as though they were entering a wholly new world where all their previous knowledge, experiences, and common sense are irrelevant. These attitudes not only are unrealistic, but also can be a major obstacle to progress in developing speeches. Some of the following suggestions may help the speaker get off to a better start.

SPEAKER ATTITUDE

The novice public speaker does not approach the public speaking task wholly unprepared, nor need he be intimidated by it. Few of us have ever designed and constructed a house, but based on our current knowledge and skills most of us could design and build an acceptable one. At the same time, of course, we could build a better house if we gained more information on their design and construction, and learned more about available tools and building materials. Similarly, we have all had a considerable amount of experience with public speeches; we can all

POWELL
THE COMPLETE
ABSOLUTE
TRUTH

develop and deliver public speeches; and we can all learn to do these jobs better through additional knowledge and experience. In approaching the task of speech preparation, then, we first must *recognize the public speech as a familiar event* where past experiences and common sense remain as useful guides to the speaker.

SOURCES OF SPEECH MATERIALS

The basic ingredients of a speech are messages. Ideally, they are well-selected messages that carry similar meanings for both the speaker and the listeners. As noted in earlier chapters, speaker messages are both verbal and nonverbal. They include language statements in the form of words and sentences as well as nonverbal messages in the form of gestures, charts, pictures, and various physical relationships between the speaker and audience. In some cases a speaker's messages are the products of his own unique experience and insights. But to be well informed on a particular topic, it is usually necessary for the speaker to go beyond his or her own level of information and seek additional ideas and data from others.

The Speaker as a Source The speaker is a depository of experiences, ideas, information, attitudes, and unique ways of viewing the world. These resources should be used to the extent that they contribute to the purposes of a speech. For example, if the speaker's purpose is to achieve self-expression on a given issue, he might achieve his purpose by relying entirely on his own resources. If, however, the speaker's purpose is to inform his audience of the amount of heat energy that is lost through each square foot of window pane, his own knowledge may be wholly inadequate and he may need to discover and review the most recent data on this topic and utilize this information as the basis of his speech.

Others as a Source When the speaker concludes that personal resources are not the best available for accomplishing his purposes, he turns to others. In doing so, he must consider the expertise and reliability of these sources. Usually, the speaker will rely on people who, through training or experience, have demonstrated special knowledge concerning the speaker's topic.

Individuals who possess reliable, current, and specialized information are usually referred to as "experts" or "authorities." As we continue in our evolution toward a more complex society, individuals find it increasingly difficult to keep abreast of the most recent developments that bear on any given speech topic. Accordingly, the speaker must frequently turn to the experts and rely on the information that they can provide. Since it may be difficult to evaluate the accuracy of the information available from a single source, some measure of safety is assured if the speaker takes care in his selection of sources and checks the information of one against others.

The speaker can have many good reasons for incorporating outside source materials in his own speech: (1) quoted material may provide information or facts needed in the speech; (2) authoritative material may lend support to the messages of the speech; (3) literary statements from prose or poetry may give appropriate expression to the speaker's ideas or help to present them in a novel or interesting way. It is not only acceptable for speakers to employ quoted materials; in many cases it may be imperative! However, the speaker should recognize the ethical and legal obligation to identify the sources of quoted material used in a speech. The ethical question is rather straightforward: the person who created the original statements deserves the credit for those statements. The speaker who presents another's material as his or her own is engaged in an unfair and unnecessary deception.

The legal question is sometimes clear and sometimes not. If a speaker were to "borrow" someone's original poem and present it as his own, it is likely that the poem's author could bring a legal suit, provide evidence of authorship, and win damages from the speaker. At the least, he could cause the speaker a degree of discomfort and embarrassment. At the same time, some information has been well diffused throughout the community and is viewed as part of our public domain. Such information can be employed without credit to its creator.

Whether the question is one of ethics or law, the speaker can satisfy both considerations by providing (1) the name of the person who generated the statements, (2) the approximate date on which the statements were made, and (3) the medium through which the statements were presented. For example, "In a 1977 article by Dr. David Gibbon, published in the *Saturday Review*, the following information is revealed." Or, "During a recent interview conducted by a *Time* magazine staff writer, former Senator Mike Mansfield was reported to have made the following statement." Or, "A line from Shakespeare's King Lear makes the point quite clearly. . . ."

By using these kinds of statements to introduce quoted materials, the speaker accomplishes several goals. Most ethical and legal obligations are satisfied; the audience is given the opportunity to know and thereby evaluate sources; and a useful transitional statement is created that indicates the point at which original material stops and quoted material begins.

The novice speaker will wonder how much quoted material is appropriate. That's similar to the question "How long should a dog's tail be?" Just as the appropriate length of a dog's tail should depend on the dog, the amount of quoted material should depend on the speaker's purpose and the appropriateness of available materials for accomplishing his or her purpose.

In general, it is reasonable to expect a speaker to rely upon personal resources in choosing his or her purpose and in selecting, organizing, and developing ideas. Nevertheless, the speaker is well advised to incorporate direct quotations where they will provide additional credibility for the speaker's ideas or can enhance the speaker's style and rhetorical effect.

CREATING YOUR OWN SPEECH

This section suggests a general sequence of steps for creating and developing a well-organized and effective speech. You are encouraged to consider this general plan as long as you follow one hard and fast rule: *When you seem to have a good idea, write it down!* Ideas don't come along in a nice neat sequence. Even as you work on one section of a speech, ideas that pertain to other sections will come to mind. Accordingly, record ideas as they occur; eventually, you can work them into your speech if they seem to serve a useful purpose.

It is helpful to *record* your ideas, issues, pieces of evidence, or whatever on separate 3 × 5-inch or 5 × 8-inch index cards. Each card becomes a building block that can be arranged and rearranged among the others until the most desirable speech pattern is achieved. Eventually, the ordered set of index cards becomes a roughly composed speech, which can be condensed into fewer cards for the presentation of a shorter speech, or expanded for the presentation of a longer speech.

With these general thoughts in mind, we now turn to a simple five-stage sequence of speech development:

1. Develop a clear statement of your central purpose.
2. Identify major topics or arguments that relate to your purpose.
3. Determine an overall plan for organizing topics or main ideas.

4. Develop each main idea with supporting materials that clarify or substantiate those ideas.
5. Add an introduction and conclusion.

PREPARE A STATEMENT OF PURPOSE

The Mock Turtle advised Alice that "no wise fish would go anywhere without a *porpoise*. . . . Why, if a fish came to me, and told me he was going on a journey, I should say 'with what porpoise?' " It might also be said that no wise speaker would go anywhere without a *purpose*. If an individual came to one of your authors and said that he was going to give a speech, our first question would probably be, "What is your purpose?"

The importance of being able to state the specific purpose of a speech might appear obvious. Nevertheless, many novice speakers devote a good deal of energy to a speech before really understanding what they are trying to achieve. Before working on the speech, the speaker should be able to write a simple and direct statement identifying his major purpose. Frequently, the speaker will need to rewrite this statement a number of times before it accurately states what he wishes to achieve.

A common mistake is to develop a statement that is too long, too vague, and too general. Here are examples of such statements:

> The purpose of my speech is to *talk about* energy conservation.
>
> The purpose of my speech is to help *develop more understanding* of energy conservation.
>
> The purpose of my speech is to *develop more appreciation* of the energy-conservation problem.

These statements do little more than identify the general topic of the speech—that is, energy conservation. The fact is, several thousand different speeches could be written on the subject of energy conservation, each requiring a different direction and the selection and development of different types of materials. The speaker can greatly simplify the task by narrowing the range of possible subjects with a more specific statement of purpose. For example:

> The purpose of this speech is to identify and describe the best ways to achieve efficient use of kitchen applicances.
>
> The purpose of this speech is to describe specific ways to better insulate your home.

> The purpose of this speech is to describe alternative lifestyles that would result in less energy consumption.

By clarifying the purpose of a particular speech, the speaker helps focus on the particular direction he wishes to select and the particular kinds of materials needed to achieve his purpose. A speech should not be viewed as so many minutes filled with words. A given speech should have a specific purpose, and only those materials that contribute to that purpose should be reviewed for possible inclusion.

A clear statement of purpose helps the speaker clarify his intended direction, identify appropriate speech material, and avoid expensive false starts. Having served the speaker in these ways, however, the statement of purpose is not usually a part of the speaker's presentation. The purpose of a well-developed speech will be apparent to the audience; the speaker should not need to hang a sign on the speech to identify its direction.

IDENTIFY MAJOR TOPICS OR ISSUES

Once a speaker has clarified the direction of the speech, it is easy to develop a list of relevant subject areas and determine which topics make a substantial contribution to the purpose and which do not. Consider the following statement of purpose:

> The purpose of this speech is to describe specific ways to better insulate a home.

Topic areas related to this purpose include

1. Insulating the ceiling
2. Insulating the floors
3. Insulating the windows
4. Insulating the doors

If further examination indicates that these major topics adequately support the stated purpose, the speaker can turn his attention to the development of each topic area. To this end, the speaker first develops a list of subtopics that appear necessary for each major topic area. For example:

1. Insulating the ceiling
    a. Types of ceiling insulation

b. Cost-effectiveness of each type of insulation
c. Recommended amounts of insulation
d. Installation

The final selection of major topics and essential subtopics constitutes a basic outline of the speech. In some cases, the outline will follow a neat pattern of development; in others, the topics may need some reshuffling before they fall into a convenient pattern.

SELECT AN OVERALL PATTERN OF ORGANIZATION

The speaker is more likely to present his ideas in an orderly and coherent fashion if he can devise an overall design or pattern that provides a clean structure for his materials. Several overall designs can be useful in the preparation of informative or persuasive speeches. These include (1) the time pattern, (2) the topical pattern, (3) the logical pattern, and (4) the problem-solution pattern.

The Time Pattern In many cases, the events we describe in a speech can be ordered in a time sequence. This pattern of organization is particularly appropriate for (1) giving step-by-step instructions on how to perform a specific task or (2) describing a sequence of events that has led to a particular state of affairs. For example, we have followed this pattern in describing some of the important steps involved in writing a speech: first, writing a statement of purpose; second, identifying major topic areas needed to achieve the stated purpose; and third, developing a list of subtopics needed to explain, illustrate, and further develop the major topic areas.

Many of our speeches provide step-by-step instructions, and many others deal with events that occur in a time sequence. The time pattern, therefore, is useful for a wide range of public speeches. Fortunately, it also is one of the easiest ways of organizing speech materials.

The Topical Pattern A speaker's comments often can be developed under a few major topic areas. Suppose, for example, that the speaker is summarizing recent developments in our energy crisis. He might organize his materials around the topic of (1) political problems, (2) economic problems, and (3) social problems. By organizing speech materials under major topic areas the speaker is less likely to jump back and forth between ideas that pertain to the different topics.

Sequence is a factor in the topical pattern as well as in the time pattern noted above. The speaker discussing developments in the energy crisis, for example, should consider whether members of the audience may need information on political problems before they can fully appreciate information on economic and social problems. Experience and common sense will usually lead to an appropriate sequence for the ordering of speech topics.

The Logical Pattern The logical pattern employs a line of reasoning that includes two or more logically related statements. For example:

Statement 1 Evidence shows that men and women have similar abilities to perform many of the essential tasks that are common to our armed services.

Statement 2 Therefore, both men and women should have the opportunity to be admitted to our service academies and to receive academy training.

The organizing concept in many speeches is a line of reasoning. A speaker can bring order to his speech by developing materials around a sequence of *arguments* (contentions) that develop into a line of reasoning. A popular logical pattern consists of a series of *arguments*, each supported by items of *evidence*. Each argument advances the contention that something is true or that some condition exists, and items of evidence are employed to support each argument.

Various logical patterns are available, but their effective use usually requires some study of their structure and development. The use of logical argument is discussed in greater detail in Chapter Ten.

The Problem-Solution Pattern On the surface, the basic approach of the problem-solution pattern is quite simple: In the first part of the speech the speaker presents a problem, and in the second part he presents a solution to that problem. Nevertheless, a well-developed problem-solution pattern can be relatively complex and sophisticated.

In many cases, the problem part of the speech is actually an informative speech. In order for the speaker to *identify* and *delineate* the problem and to show the *magnitude* of the problem, he must provide the necessary information. The pattern used in this phase could follow any of the informative patterns. For example, he could trace the chronological development of the problem (time pattern), or he could discuss the various topics that shed light on the problem (topical pattern).

Occasionally, a thorough analysis of the problem will point to an almost inevitable solution. For example, if a speaker can show that the problem is the amount of heat loss in the home, and if he can further show that the problem can be easily and economically solved by placing insulation in the attic, the simple facts of the situation can point to the obvious solution. More frequently, however, a problem can be solved in a variety of ways. The variety of possible solutions combined with variations in audience attitudes, tastes, and values means that some measure of advocacy, or persuasion, is needed to gain support for a given solution. In effect, the solution phase is frequently a persuasive speech structured around a pattern of logical argument. Taken together, the arguments develop logically toward the speaker's preferred solution.

There are several essential ingredients in most problem-solution speeches:

1. The problem phase
  a. The problem phase should include a clear *description* of the *problem*; that is, the central concern of the speaker should be obvious to the audience.
  b. The speaker should provide information that documents the *importance* and *magnitude* of the problem.
  c. When possible, the problem phase should show *how the problem relates* to members of the audience.

2. The solution phase
  a. The speaker should provide a clear description of his or her solution including such major points as:
    (1) The *nature of the solution.*
    (2) The *estimated cost* of the solution in time and/or money.
    (3) How the solution can be *initiated and/or administered.*
  b. The speaker should be able to demonstrate the *relative advantages* of the solution—that it is both *practical* and *beneficial.*

The relative time spent on the problem or solution will vary with each speech. In general, when the problem is familiar to most members of the audience, the speaker can simply summarize it and use the greater portion of time to develop the needed solution. If, on the other hand, the audience is not aware of a problem or convinced of its importance, the speaker might devote most of the time to the problem and merely suggest the direction of possible solutions. In fact, simply gaining audience awareness of an important problem may be a major contribution, particularly if it is coupled with a clear, if brief, closing presentation on an appropriate solution.

DEVELOP SUPPORTING MATERIALS

Hammers and saws are useful tools. A hammer is useful if we want to pound something, and a saw is useful if we want to cut something; neither has much value, however, unless used for the proper purpose. There are several tools at the disposal of the speaker seeking to *clarify* or *substantiate* major points in a speech. An understanding of the alternative supportive techniques and the purposes they can serve will enhance the speaker's ability to prepare effective speeches. Specific techniques considered here are: (1) explanation, (2) example, (3) specific instance, (4) analogy, (5) restatement, (6) internal summary, and (7) statistics.

Explanation Explanation simply consists of verbal narrative or description, and it accounts for most of our simple and direct communication. The purpose of explanation is to transmit or exchange information. We employ words and sentences to tell someone about something, to show how something works, to give directions, and to define the way we are using a word or concept. For example, consider the use of explanation in the following statement:

> The rubber seal on a refrigerator door will tend to deteriorate over time. Eventually the seal does not do its job, and cold air escapes. To check to see if your refrigerator is properly sealed, do the following: Place a dollar bill at a point where the door closes against the refrigerator and close the door. Then with gentle jerks, try to pull the paper dollar from the door. If your refrigerator is properly sealed, you will meet with some resistance; a slight "tug" will be necessary to remove the dollar. Repeat this process at various points around the door. If you find spots where the dollar bill slips easily from the closed door, you should arrange to have the seal replaced.

Simple explanation, without further development, is frequently an adequate means of transmitting relatively simple messages about familiar objects. When the topic is less familiar or the subject more complex, explanations might require further clarification through visual demonstrations or other illustrative devices. For example, in explaining a method of spraying additional insulation into the attic, the speaker could use visual diagrams to help clarify critical steps in the spraying operation, or provide an actual demonstration.

The Example The example is probably one of the most useful tools of speech construction. Although most individuals are familiar with examples, many have not considered the essential nature of an example or developed a composition style that uses well-chosen examples appropriately.

An *example* may be viewed as a *specific sample* of a more general condition. The essential value of an example is that it gives precision to our messages. We frequently speak in general terms regarding an issue or topic, and the general nature of our messages results in vagueness and misunderstanding. A well-chosen example can *specify* and thereby *clarify* the meaning of a general statement. Consider the following generalization and how it is clarified through the details of an appropriate example:

> Generalization: *Many homeowners are terrible energy wasters.* Mr. Jones, for example, has no storm sashes on his windows, and he heats all rooms in his house even though three are rarely used. He has large cracks around exterior doors; the insulation in his attic and under the floors is minimal; and the temperature of his hot-water tank is set at such a high level that it is continuously heating the water.

Although we are all familiar with examples and use them regularly in our everyday conversations, the more experienced speaker does not use examples in a hit-or-miss fashion. Rather, she or he will review the speech with an eye for generalizations that are in need of further clarification and specificity.

Specific Instances Whereas an example serves as a representative sample, *specific instances* simply *identify* a *series of cases* or conditions by name or brief reference. For example, an individual presenting a speech on energy conservation might provide a series of specific instances to identify essential ways in which we can conserve energy in the home.

> The homeowner can turn the thermostat to 68 degrees.
> He can install storm sashes on all windows.
> He can check all doors to see that they are properly sealed.
> He can add insulation to ceilings and floors.
> He can check the water heater to make sure he is not heating the water to an unnecessarily high temperature.

If the homeowner is familiar with the specific instances mentioned, simply listing them may be an adequate reminder that leads to action. All homeowners know how to turn down the thermostat; however, many do not know how to install storm sashes or ceiling insulation.

Depending on the speaker's purpose, then, he may need to follow certain references with an explanation or demonstration that more fully develops the specific instance.

The Analogy Like an example, the *analogy* is a useful device for *clarifying* a speaker's message. It is particularly useful for introducing *relatively new* and *unfamiliar* ideas. Through the comparative process of the analogy, we can show the relationship of something new and strange to something old and familiar, and in showing this relationship, we can help the audience discover the nature of the new and strange.

Consider the speaker who is trying to distinguish between "abstract" and "concrete" language styles. He might start with a general statement such as "Abstract language provides perspective, whereas concrete language provides details." He could then *clarify* that narrative statement through use of the following analogy:

> Picture a helicopter sitting on the ground with a camera attached to its bottom and pointing straight down. Now, imagine the pilot taking a picture of the earth. Most likely the picture would reveal small rocks, a weed or two, and a few blades of grass. Now imagine the pilot flying to five hundred feet and taking a second picture. That picture will no longer reveal the small objects, but it will include a larger picture of the airport. Now imagine the pilot taking a picture at ten thousand feet. This picture is likely to provide a general perspective of things. That is, it is likely to reveal large objects like clouds, land masses, and large bodies of water; it also provides a general perspective of the geographic relationships among these objects.
>
> It is safe to say that language operates much like the camera on the bottom of the helicopter. That is, concrete language gives us the specific details like small rocks, weeds, and blades of grass. Abstract language gives us perspective; it provides the bigger picture of things; it shows the clouds, the landmasses, and the lakes; and it shows the way these things are related to each other. Depending on one's purpose, a speaker will want to use both concrete and abstract language. He will use concrete language when specific details are needed, and he will use abstract language when an overall perspective is needed.

The above analogy was used as a device for clarifying the nature of concrete and abstract language. Clarification was achieved by comparing concrete language with low-level pictures and abstract language with high-level pictures.

Analogies fall into two main categories: *figurative* and *literal*. *Figurative analogies* point to a *similar quality* in two different situations. In the above analogy, for example, the common quality in high-altitude pictures and abstract language is the level of abstraction. *Literal analogies* point to a *quantitative relationship* between two different situations. To illustrate this quantitative relationship consider the following:

> Many individuals consider the small crack around the front door of their house to be a minor source of heat loss. Yet a recent study revealed that the open space provided by that small crack is often the equivalent of a hole in the wall ten inches in diameter!

This analogy is literal in the sense that it points to a measurable equivalent for the amount of space provided by the crack around the front door—namely, the amount of space provided by a ten-inch hole in the wall.

Figurative and literal analogies are two of the most useful tools in speech construction. They can provide *clarity* and *vividness* and their process of comparison can contribute a novel *stylistic effect*. At the same time, the speaker should be aware of the limitations of these tools. For example, the figurative analogy can only point to general qualitative similarities; if misused, it can grossly exaggerate the similarity of two different situations. The literal analogy frequently requires the quantitative assessment of a qualified mathematician or engineer. In any case, the ability of the speaker to formulate ideas in communicative language is directly related to the ability to employ useful language tools such as the figurative and literal analogies.

Restatement The listener's task is somewhat different from the reader's task. A reader can read and reread a given section of an article before moving on to the next section. The listener does not have this advantage. The speaker therefore must clarify messages through adequate explanation and use supplementary techniques to bring clarity and vividness to his central ideas. The *restatement* of central ideas at key points throughout the speech is a simple and commonly used technique for achieving this goal.

Internal Summary The summary technique is an obvious means for concluding a speech. There are other uses of the summary, however, that are frequently overlooked. The internal summary can be an extremely useful technique for amplifying crucial points throughout a speech and for recapping essential points in one part of the speech while providing a transition to the next. In general, internal summaries are more useful as the speech becomes longer. In speeches that approach five minutes or more, members of the audience can experience difficulty in sorting out the speaker's major ideas. By including a brief summary of major points after each key division of the speech, the speaker can increase the audience's focus on central ideas.

Statistics Statistics provide a convenient language for summarizing quantitative relationships. The appropriate statistic will typically allow the speaker to assign a simple numerical value to an overall characteristic of a body of data. For example, statistics can provide measures of central tendency (average scores) or measures of dispersion (spread of scores).

When the speaker wishes to communicate quantitative summaries of data, the appropriate statistic can be the most useful of all available tools; in some cases, it is the only available tool. As with other forms of support, however, the speaker's ability to employ statistics successfully will depend on a knowledge of statistics, including their advantages and limitations. Because of the frequent use of statistics in speeches and because of the contribution they can bring to a speech, the speaker is well advised to gain a reasonable familiarity with this tool.

In general, the speaker should employ statistics in cases where they will provide clear and accurate summaries of important data. At the same time, a speaker should avoid unnecessary statistics that simply cloud the issues at hand and serve to confuse the audience. In the Carter-Ford debates, for example, criticism was directed at both contenders because of what appeared to be an unnecessary and confusing use of complex statistics.

ADD THE INTRODUCTION AND CONCLUSION

A speaker's primary efforts will be directed toward a clear statement of his purpose, and the development and organization of main ideas and supporting materials. After achieving these central tasks, the speaker will turn to the preparation of an introduction and a conclusion appropriate for his particular speech, the occasion, and the audience. At the very least, he should develop a few written statements that can serve as introductory and concluding remarks.

Although a well-developed speech should be the speaker's central concern, getting off to a poor start can diminish the overall effectiveness of a good speech. In addition, the speaker who does not have a clear stopping point might end the speech abruptly and awkwardly. Worse yet, for lack of a convenient stopping point, a speaker may find himself

"I see our main speaker needs no introduction."

wandering into new territories that prolong his speech and deviate from the central purpose. Many well-planned ten-minute speeches are excellent for ten minutes but become poor at the end of fifteen and unbearable at the end of twenty.

The Introduction In general, the introduction is designed to achieve one or more of the following purposes:

1. It can serve to recognize the significance of the occasion and the presence of distinguished guests.
2. It can provide the speaker with an opportunity to express appreciation for the opportunity to appear before that particular group.
3. It can make reference to preceding events and connect them to the current speech, thereby providing a transition between those events.
4. It can be used to gain attention; however, a speaker usually has the audience's attention for the first minute, and there usually is little need for attention-getting devices in the introduction.
5. In almost all cases, it should include statements that prepare the audience for the forthcoming speech. For example, the speaker might use a rhetorical question such as: "Do you know the three

most important ways of saving energy in your home?" Or he might use a simple declarative statement that focuses audience attention on the central issue of the speech: "If you are an average homeowner, your monthly utility bill is twice as high as it needs to be!"

Frequently, the introduction is a kind of audience briefing in which the speaker provides a survey of the territory he or she intends to cover. In this case, the speaker may simply indicate the nature of the speech and the major topics to be considered.

The lay speaker often seems to feel that a speech should start with a joke, probably in the belief that a good joke will establish a friendly and more relaxed relationship between himself and the audience. But what happens if the joke "bombs"? If you feel that a joke can contribute to your presentation, there is an excellent strategy for preventing its backfire: Always select a joke that *ties directly* to the ideas in your speech. If a joke ties directly to a point that you are about to develop, it will seldom backfire. If the audience responds, so much the better; if it doesn't, the joke still serves a useful purpose by introducing your next point.

In some cases, it may be desirable to make last-minute changes in the introduction to a speech. At public gatherings, a number of events occur just prior to a speaker's presentation. A prior speaker may have stressed a major point; the person introducing the speaker may have included a comment that deserves a response; or a sudden noise may have startled the audience. An imaginative speaker might use one of these events as a springboard to his own speech. The effect can be a creative and original transition from prior events to the speaker's presentation. Nevertheless, a speaker should not assume that she or he will be blessed with a last-minute stroke of genius. A preconsidered and planned introduction should be available and utilized except when last-minute changes suggest a novel approach.

The Conclusion The conclusion of a speech is usually influenced by the purpose of the speech. If the purpose was to inform, the speaker is likely to provide a summary of the main ideas. If the purpose was to persuade, he might summarize the main arguments in support of his point of view. Typically, the concluding remarks serve to restate or emphasize ideas already developed in the main body of a speech.

The speaker occasionally can achieve a more stylized or dramatic effect by employing a piece of prose or poetry that captures the essential meaning of his messages. Or he might conclude with an enthusiastic call for action on the main proposal of the speech. In any case, if the speaker is able to achieve his major purpose he is likely to do so in the body of his speech. Usually, the conclusion can do little more than provide a sense of completion and closure and summarize or emphasize points the speaker has already developed.

In all aspects of speech preparation, speaker originality can provide a refreshing departure from the more standard and predictable patterns of speech development. At the same time, originality includes a greater element of risk. The speaker must always consider his motives and determine whether he prefers the safety and predictability of an established path or whether he prefers to take on the adventures as well as the risks that go with cutting a new path.

Finally, then, after the basic speech is developed, the speaker will usually spend some time reviewing his product. The energy devoted to this task will depend on the available time and the importance of the speech event. During this final critical review, the speaker will typically ask such questions as:

1. Do all included materials contribute to my central purpose?
2. Are all materials sufficiently clear and organized for my intended audience?
3. In the case of persuasive speeches, are all arguments sound and adequately supported?
4. Are planned introductions and conclusions appropriate for the purposes of the speech?

THE PRESENTATIONAL FORM

To this point we have discussed the basic elements that contribute to a coherent, organized, and well-developed set of ideas and supporting materials. We have also suggested that these ideas and supporting materials can be recorded on separate index cards and then arranged and rearranged until the speaker is able to achieve the desired sequence. If this procedure is followed the speaker may find that his or her set of index cards provides an adequate if not preferred basis for presentation of the speech to an audience.

The organization of speech materials onto index cards offers the speaker a number of advantages:

1. Index cards make a neat and convenient package. They can be carried in a coat pocket or a purse.
2. Index cards are unobtrusive. They are less of a visual distraction than large sheets of paper. When handled, they do not make "crumpling" or "rattling" sounds that can be picked up by a microphone.
3. By writing on only *one side* of the index cards the speaker can move smoothly through the cards without "flipping" them from front to back.
4. Sooner or later the speaker's neatly prepared materials are either dropped on the floor, blown by the wind, or slide from the speaker's stand. By *numbering* each card in a consistent and visible way the speaker can easily and quickly reorganize the set of cards and proceed with a minimum of disruption.
5. The speaker may present the same speech to a variety of audiences that provide different time limits. By organizing separate speech units on separate cards it is possible to delete certain cards for a shorter speech or add cards for a longer speech. To achieve a shorter speech the speaker may use fewer illustrations or examples or even eliminate a particular section of the speech. If added time is available the speaker may wish to include more materials that serve to elaborate main ideas or "localize" the speech by relating ideas to the local community. A variety of suggestions for organizing your note cards is summarized on the following pages.

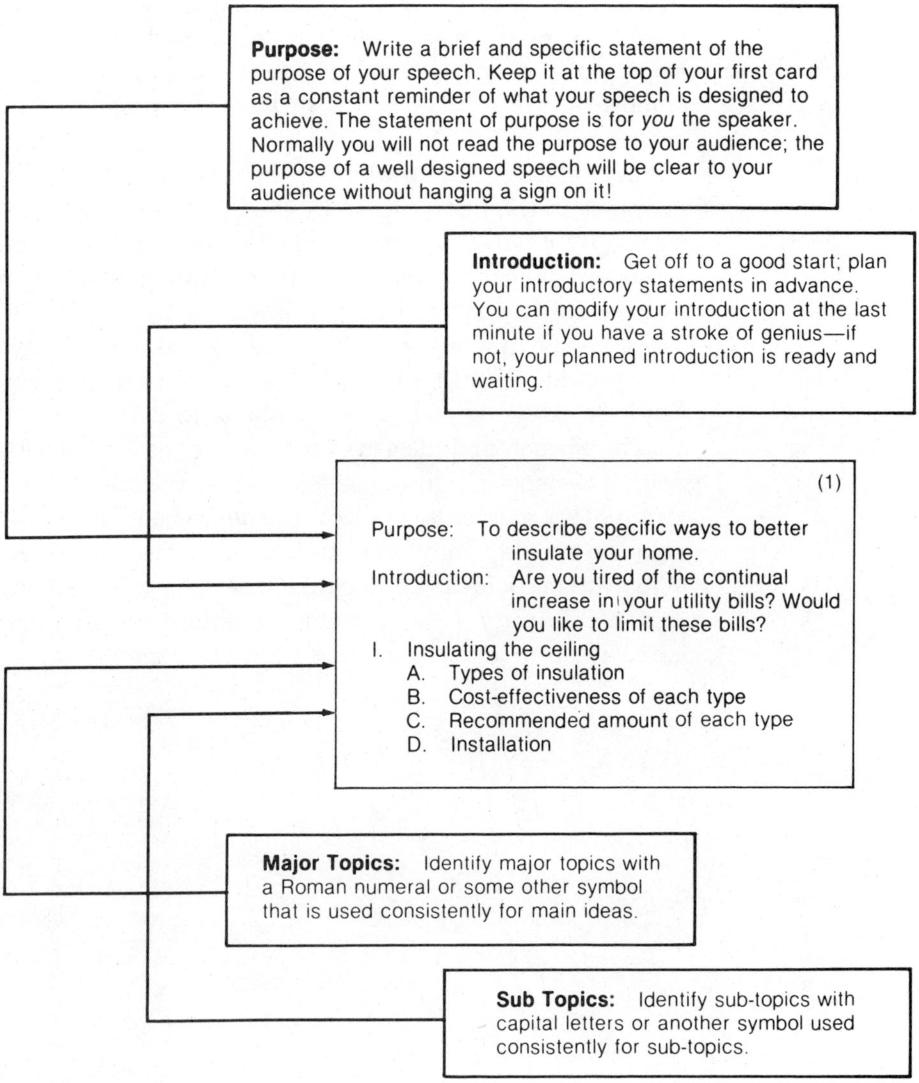
Purpose: Write a brief and specific statement of the purpose of your speech. Keep it at the top of your first card as a constant reminder of what your speech is designed to achieve. The statement of purpose is for *you* the speaker. Normally you will not read the purpose to your audience; the purpose of a well designed speech will be clear to your audience without hanging a sign on it!
Introduction: Get off to a good start; plan your introductory statements in advance. You can modify your introduction at the last minute if you have a stroke of genius—if not, your planned introduction is ready and waiting.
(1)
Purpose: To describe specific ways to better insulate your home.
Introduction: Are you tired of the continual increase in your utility bills? Would you like to limit these bills?
I. Insulating the ceiling
A. Types of insulation
B. Cost-effectiveness of each type
C. Recommended amount of each type
D. Installation
Major Topics: Identify major topics with a Roman numeral or some other symbol that is used consistently for main ideas.
Sub Topics: Identify sub-topics with capital letters or another symbol used consistently for sub-topics.

FIGURE 7-1a

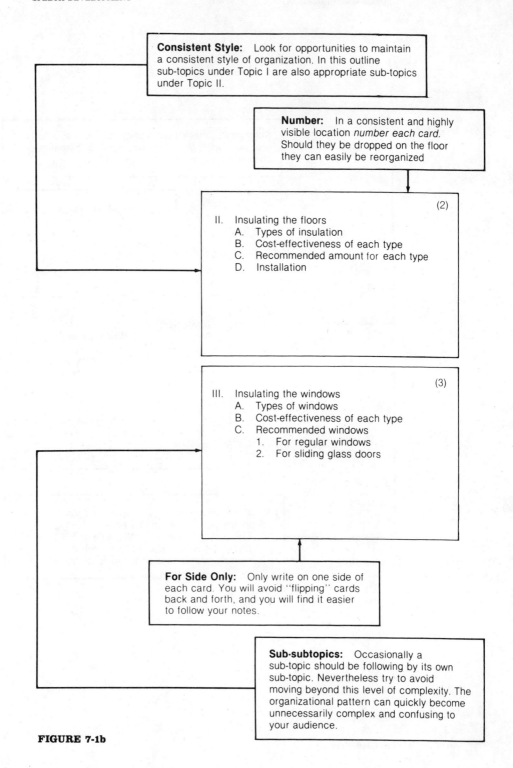

Consistent Style: Look for opportunities to maintain a consistent style of organization. In this outline sub-topics under Topic I are also appropriate sub-topics under Topic II.

Number: In a consistent and highly visible location *number each card.* Should they be dropped on the floor they can easily be reorganized

(2)

II. Insulating the floors
   A. Types of insulation
   B. Cost-effectiveness of each type
   C. Recommended amount for each type
   D. Installation

(3)

III. Insulating the windows
   A. Types of windows
   B. Cost-effectiveness of each type
   C. Recommended windows
      1. For regular windows
      2. For sliding glass doors

For Side Only: Only write on one side of each card. You will avoid "flipping" cards back and forth, and you will find it easier to follow your notes.

Sub-subtopics: Occasionally a sub-topic should be following by its own sub-topic. Nevertheless try to avoid moving beyond this level of complexity. The organizational pattern can quickly become unnecessarily complex and confusing to your audience.

FIGURE 7-1b

Summary: Internal summaries capture the essence of your messages. (A closing summary can also provide a convenient way to end your speech.)

Limit Number of Cards: A minimum number of cards usually results in better eye contact and a more spontaneous and interesting style. Only use cards when they are really needed.

(4)

SUMMARY: In Brief:
A. Where to insulate
B. What insulation to be used
C. What you can save

Conclusion:
— It is frustrating to keep getting higher and higher utility bills
— And, you don't have total control over those bills
— But you can save a great deal through proper insulation of your home

Conclusion: Carefully plan your conclusion in advance. Have a prepared way to bring closure to your speech. Without a specific planned way to stop, a good speech can begin to wander and become a poor speech.

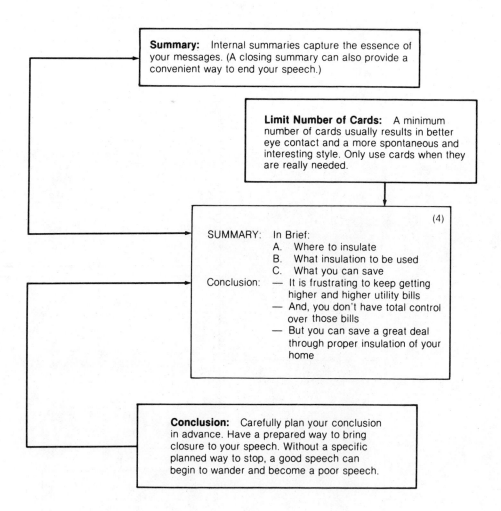

FIGURE 7-1c

ALTERNATIVE PRESENTATIONAL FORMS

Use of the index cards and the organizational techniques just discussed prepare a speaker for the *extemporaneous* form of presentation. With sufficient preparation and rehearsal, the speaker need only glance at each item on the card to deliver a relatively smooth presentation. Also, this minimum involvement with notes usually results in a natural tendency toward better eye contact and a more dynamic and spontaneous style.

Nevertheless, the trained public speaker will want to be aware of alternative presentational forms as well as their relative advantages and limitations. Accordingly, the four basic presentational forms, the *manuscript* speech, the *memorized* speech, the *impromptu* speech, and the *extemporaneous* speech are now considered in some detail.

THE MANUSCRIPT SPEECH

Manuscript speaking involves word-for-word reading of a prepared text. The speech is a carefully written essay, and the speaker reads it to the audience with little or no deviation from the precise wording.

Manuscript speaking is tempting to use for several reasons. First, the speaker is reasonably confident that what he had planned to say will be transmitted accurately so long as he adheres to the manuscript. For example, important officials, such as the President and the Secretary of State, who are speaking not just for themselves but for large institutions or entire nations, must be assured that their words are delivered as planned without deviation. During delicate international negotiations, officials spend hours and even days preparing carefully worded documents for public dissemination.

Political campaigners have also come to rely on the manuscript. With increasingly heavy news media coverage of important elections, politicians frequently are unwilling to chance a slip of the tongue that could damage their campaign. For example, during the 1968 presidential campaign, candidate George Romney returned from a tour of Vietnam and spontaneously announced in a news conference that he had been "brainwashed" by the American military command, that it had given him loaded or one-sided information. The single word *brainwashed* became Romney's biggest liability as his opponents and the press continually challenged his judgment and credibility. Politicians today are rarely "off the record," and from bitter experience many have learned to read from a manuscript whenever their remarks might be quoted.

Like politicians, business and professional people realize that their remarks often become part of a permanent record and should not be modified on the spur of the moment. Not only does a manuscript assure conformity of their remarks with organizational policy, but it also lends itself to prior review and modification by colleagues. In most courtrooms, judges may not deviate from a previously approved set of jury instructions; even a slight variation in wording may bring complaints from the attorneys or a reversal of verdict by an appeals court. In short, subtleties in the wording of a speech sometimes have important implications, and a manuscript helps protect the speaker and the people represented.

Another reason some speakers use a manuscript is to allay fears about making mistakes in front of an audience. The manuscript becomes a kind of security blanket, which assures that the speaker will not forget or seriously misstate the prepared comments. In a basic speech communication class, the student who reads from a manuscript is often one who is especially bothered by stage fright.

A third rationale for using a manuscript involves timing. Radio and TV broadcasters measure air time in seconds and must know precisely how long certain kinds of messages will last. Speakers at some formal occasions are given a time limit for their remarks and are asked not to deviate from that allotted time. A speaker at a noon meeting of a service club knows that the membership must return to their jobs before 1:00 P.M. A classroom lecturer knows that when the bell rings, the students will get up and leave. The speaker who has practiced the manuscript speech will know fairly accurately its reading time.

While manuscript delivery may be appropriate for some of the specialized speaking situations noted above, the method should be used with caution. First, preparing the manuscript is often an enormously time-consuming task. For a relatively short speech of, say, fifteen minutes, the speaker needs about seven or eight pages of typed, double-spaced manuscript. When we think of ministers giving weekly half-hour sermons or professors giving daily hour-long lectures, the sheer volume of writing may be prohibitive. Because preparation of a manuscript speech is laborious, people who regularly use this delivery strategy are usually those who have a staff of speech writers. While corporate executives or U.S. senators may be able to afford this luxury, most of us cannot.

A second reason for avoiding the manuscript strategy is the difficulty of maintaining a natural speaking style. In everyday conversation, we use emphasis and pauses without conscious thought in a spontaneous expression of complete thought units. When reading from a manuscript, however, we are tempted to "read words accurately" rather than "express ideas meaningfully." Too many readers pause at awkward places —for example, the end of a printed line rather than the end of a thought unit. A monotone delivery often develops. Eye contact with the audience is infrequent because the speaker is "buried" in the manuscript. The style becomes too formal, and the speaker appears rigid and aloof. If the written manuscript has long complex sentences and unfamiliar words, the speaker is likely to sound even more awkward and unnatural. In general, a natural manuscript reading style comes only after long experience (as with newscasters or actors) and usually cannot be accomplished by the beginning speaker.

The most important indictment of the manuscript strategy is that it is not conducive to spontaneous audience adaptation. The authors believe that speech communication should be audience-centered, and later in this book we shall discuss strategies for adapting to unexpected audience behavior. Here we note that some adaptation is usually warranted in *any* public speaking situation. For example, this adaptation might involve a reference to the remarks of a previous speaker, adding more detailed explanation when the audience appears not to understand, cutting material to conform to new time limits, pausing to respond to a comment or question from the audience, or changing speech content to be consistent with events of the last few days or hours. Whatever the reason, when a speaker wants to modify the presentation on the spur of the moment, he is severely hampered by a prepared text. He may simply ignore the needed change because he is too "locked into" a precise manuscript.

If a speaker is convinced that, despite the problems, a manuscript delivery is justified, he or she should practice reading the speech in advance, striving to deliver complete thought units through careful expression. The following points might be useful:

1. Write the speech with simple sentence structure and wording. Remember that the audience will hear it only once and cannot reread it.
2. Practice reading the speech aloud. Frequently, sentence wording will not sound natural and can be modified before the speech is

delivered. Practice reading in complete thought units as they might be uttered in conversation.

3. Work on eye contact with the audience. Try "gulping in" a whole line of print and speaking that line while looking up at the audience.
4. Make reminder notes in the margins like "slow down," "louder," or "eye contact." Underline key passages that need vocal emphasis and use parentheses to assure good phrasing.
5. Be willing to deviate from prepared comments if the audience clearly needs more elaboration.
6. Use a typed, double- or triple-spaced manuscript with clear divisions or notations at main points.
7. Number the manuscript pages, but do not staple.
8. Always end the typewritten page with a complete sentence. Never divide a word or sentence to put on the next page.

THE MEMORIZED SPEECH

One of the ancient canons or fundamental norms of good speechmaking was *memoria*, or memory. Greek and Roman schoolboys, in developing their rhetorical skills, would memorize the speeches and writings of orators and statesmen. A good public speaker in those days did not rely on notes but formally recited his prepared remarks from memory. Not surprisingly, these speeches when read today appear flowery and poetic, as much a literary as a rhetorical effort.

The use of memory as a delivery strategy continued throughout the development of speechmaking in America. Even in the early 1900s, the ability to recall extended passages of great literature or famous speeches was admired. It was encouraged by schools, which asked students to "declaim" great speeches in classrooms and in speaking contests.

Only during the last two or three decades has verbal memory training decreased in the schools. Whether the de-emphasis is beneficial or harmful is not important here. What is important is that the memorized speech strategy is no longer viewed as viable for most public communication events. The same disadvantages noted above for manuscript speaking apply here—only more so. Preparation time is enormous, the speaking style is usually unnatural, and adaptation to the unique situation is nearly impossible. Most important, should the speaker forget his intended words, he is in deep trouble. Almost everyone can remember with horror a time when he "blew his lines" in a play, ceremony, or contest. Those experiences alone should deter a speaker from using memorization as a delivery strategy.

THE IMPROMPTU SPEECH

A popular event in student speech contests is the impromptu speech. The contestant is given a general topic. He or she considers it for a few moments, usually no more than a minute or two, and then gives a five- to seven-minute speech on that topic. While the exercise may be good practice for developing spontaneous communication skills, the speeches themselves tend to be shallow in content, confusing in organization, uninteresting, and not very fluently delivered.

In the real world, speakers with significant background and expertise in a particular topic area are sometimes tempted to forego extensive preparation for a public speaking engagement. From past experience they know that they can expound on that topic intelligently and fluently regardless of the time limits or audience. Such speakers are very rare, however, and most of us, regardless of how well we know a topic, cannot employ this strategy effectively.

One problem we face in spontaneous delivery is organization. Though we may have a general plan in our heads for structuring three or four key points, substructure is often confusing and digressions are common. Recall, for example, someone telling a story or describing an event, continually expanding on irrelevant information while the listener is thinking, "Get to the point!"

Another problem with impromptu speaking might be called the paradox of information. The more knowledgeable a speaker is in a particular field, the more difficult it is for him to sift through a huge body of data and ideas to come up with a meaningful message for a specific time limit and a nonexpert audience. In general, the more information a speaker has, the more care should be taken in sorting, condensing, and arranging it.

A final argument against the impromptu strategy resides with the audience. Most listeners can quickly tell when a speaker has not prepared his remarks. He has no notes, his comments lack fluency and organization, he is repetitious, and he often appears to be confused, as if he were groping for ideas. What that speaker may be saying indirectly or at least what the audience might *think* he is saying is "I did not consider you, the audience, or this occasion to be important enough to waste my time in extensive preparation."

While the impromptu strategy should be avoided, sometimes spontaneous public communication is necessary. Public officials may be called on to answer detailed questions at a press conference or public meeting. A professor may need to respond at length to a student's question. (Most professors do respond *at length!*) An executive at a business conference may be asked to discuss policy alternatives. A job applicant may have to outline career objectives for an interview committee. A law school student may be asked to analyze an assigned case for the class. A legislator may need to answer arguments against his proposed bill. The possibilities seem endless and suggest that almost everyone who becomes involved in public situations will eventually have to use the impromptu delivery strategy.

People who are regularly in the public eye should try to predict the kinds of information others might request. The President and other public officials often have briefing sessions with advisors to go over potential questions and answers. Leaders of corporations or labor unions try to bone up on statistics and examples that can be used as support for their arguments when they are asked to defend their organization's position. We believe that to some extent a person can *prepare and plan* for impromptu speaking situations, even though the specific situational variables cannot be known.

When a speaker finds himself in a situation that obviously calls for extensive impromptu comments, he should first be certain that he understands what is expected. Is the question clear? Does he grasp the argument that the previous speaker has made? (We have all experienced the frustration of having a speaker answer a question in lengthy detail, only to finish and have the inquirer say, "That wasn't my question.") This clarification process may also "buy time," giving a few extra moments for the speaker to consider a reply, permitting him to develop a general organizational plan. Depending on the speaker's natural abilities, the message might still lack fluency and continuity, but at least it can be a thoughtful, relevant response. The impromptu speaker should recognize, too, that an audience does not expect these spontaneous replies to be polished prose and will excuse minor deficiencies in presentation.

THE EXTEMPORANEOUS SPEECH

To many people, the word *extemporaneous* denotes "off the cuff," "impromptu," "ad lib," or "off the top of the head." Even dictionary definitions suggest that the word means "makeshift" or "spur of the moment." These are not the meanings that we shall use in discussing the extemporaneous delivery strategy. Rather, we shall define the term as it has come to be used by most speech communication instructors.

With an extemporaneous strategy, the speaker assembles information and materials, carefully structures an outline, and even rehearses the delivery. However, the speech is not written verbatim; it is not a manuscript. Rather, the speaker lets the *specific language* of the speech develop naturally as he delivers the speech from the outline. That is the key: careful preparation and practice and spontaneous language development.

One disadvantage of the extemporaneous strategy is that the exact length of the speech is difficult to predict. Hence, the strategy is more difficult to adapt to speech situations that require precise timing like radio or TV presentations. Another disadvantage is its lack of formality (most people do not naturally speak in flowery or highly styled prose), rendering the extemporaneous mode an unlikely strategy for such events as inauguration addresses or formal ceremonies. Perhaps the biggest problem with this strategy is that it may intimidate the beginning speaker. In preparing for a speaking situation, the novice may fear that the right words won't come to him when he needs them, that he may stammer and grope for the proper phrasing, that he may be unable to expand on a point in the outline. Hence, he succumbs to temptation. He writes out more and more of the speech until soon he is using the manuscript strategy with its attendant shortcomings.

Nevertheless, speakers should utilize the extemporaneous mode as much as possible; it is the optimal strategy for most speaking situations, even for the beginning speaker. The main advantage is that it combines the best elements of the manuscript speech (careful preparation of ideas and organizational plan for a particular speaking situation) with the best elements of natural delivery (simple and spontaneous word choices and normal, unaffected vocal inflection).

Another advantage of the extemporaneous mode is that the speaker makes the best use of preparation time. Since an extensive manuscript and tedious memorization are unnecessary, the speaker can spend more time collecting and arranging materials and practicing the delivery.

A third advantage is ease of adaptation. With little trouble, the extemporaneous speaker can make last-minute changes, inserting new information, deleting sections to shorten the speech, or altering the wording of key points. After the speaker has begun, he can spontaneously elaborate on an idea if the audience does not appear to understand, or eliminate planned explanation if he notices that time is running short. The speaker can even stop in the middle of the speech and ask for questions from the audience.

Again, the extemporaneous strategy demands that the speaker not become preoccupied with precise language or perfect fluency. But if key ideas demand precise phrasing, a sentence outline will assure that such careful wording can be used for main points. Portions of the introduction or conclusion might also be written out, and, of course, all quotations of outside sources must be delivered verbatim.

After developing the speech and organizing the material into a desirable presentational form, the public speaker will want to turn his or her attention to the second major concern — delivery — which is the subject of the next chapter.

SUMMARY

Public speaking continues to be one of the most important means of human communication. In general, the main purposes of speeches are (1) to inform, (2) to persuade, and (3) to provide ceremony. The basic purpose of an informative speech is to communicate information to an audience. The basic purpose of a persuasive speech is to influence the attitudes, feelings, or behaviors of the members of an audience. The usual purpose of a ceremonial speech is to provide a meaningful experience in keeping with audience expectations and past traditions.

The materials for a speech may come from a speaker's own experiences, or they may be available from "authorities" who have special training and experience. As speech topics become more specialized, the speaker will increasingly need to rely on such outside sources for at least part of the materials needed for speech development.

Speech preparation can be more effective if the speaker approaches the speech in a sequence of five steps: (1) development of a clear statement of purpose, (2) identification of topics or arguments that relate to the purpose, (3) determination of an overall plan of organization, (4) development of appropriate supporting materials for each main point in the speech, and (5) development of an appropriate introduction and conclusion.

Several patterns of speech organization were discussed. These are: (1) the time pattern, (2) the topical pattern, (3) the logical pattern, and (4) the problem-solution pattern. Several techniques were described for the development of materials supporting the speaker's main ideas: (1) explanation, (2) example, (3) specific instance, (4) analogy, (5) restatement, (6) internal summary, and (7) statistics.

Finally, basic presentational formats were discussed. These included the manuscript speech, the memorized speech, the impromptu speech, and the extemporaneous speech. For most occasions the speaker was encouraged to use the extemporaneous approach.

QUESTIONS

1. When does a public speech serve useful purposes? When would it be appropriate to employ an alternative form of communication?
2. What are the inherent advantages and disadvantages of the one-to-many public speaking settings?
3. Are the various forms of support interchangeable or does each form serve a unique function?
4. What purposes are served by developing a speech outline?
5. Under what circumstances does a speaker constitute his or her own best source for speech materials?
6. Under what circumstances should a speaker provide documentation for statements included in the speech?

SUGGESTED READINGS

Andrews, James R. *A choice of worlds: the practice and criticism of public discourse*. New York: Harper & Row, 1973.

Monroe, Alan H., and Douglas Ehninger. *Principles and types of speech communication,* 7th ed. Glenview, Ill.: Scott, Foresman, 1974.

Scheidel, Thomas M. *Speech communication and human interaction,* 2d ed. Glenview, Ill.: Scott, Foresman, 1976.

Vohs, John L., and G. P. Mohrmann. *Audiences messages speakers.* New York: Harcourt Brace Jovanovich, 1975.

8

DELIVERY STRATEGIES AND PROBLEMS

PREVIEW

Public speaking is an artistic enterprise, not only in the preparation of a speech but also in its actual presentation. Listeners may not be preoccupied with how a speaker looks and sounds, but they will certainly notice delivery, especially if the speaker has bothersome, distracting mannerisms. Speakers themselves, though they should be primarily concerned with speech content, develop anxiety about their delivery. As a society, we tend to appreciate people who are fluent and attractive in a one-to-many communication setting. Public advertising, news broadcasting, and political speaking are examples of communication events in which we expect articulate, fluent delivery.

It would be nice to believe that delivery doesn't matter—that the important thing is what people have to say. But realistically it *does* matter. It matters to the listeners. If two speakers have essentially the same message, the one with better oral and visual style will usually be more successful in eliciting the desired audience response. It also matters to the speaker who wants to be thought of as an effective communicator. So we offer this chapter to try to help speakers develop their delivery skills, noting that without those skills even the most important messages may go unheard and unappreciated.

OBJECTIVES

To discuss audible and visual aspects of speech delivery

To provide specific suggestions for improved audible and visual styles of delivery

To consider the problem of excessive "speech fright"

To provide specific suggestions for developing a more relaxed and more comfortable style of delivery

EIGHT We have discussed some of the factors involved in the development of a well-organized and effective speech. Although speech preparation is crucial to good public communication, it is by no means the most difficult or intimidating element of speechmaking for most people. A much more threatening prospect is the actual delivery of this message to a particular audience.

Nagging questions continually arise. What if I forget what I want to say? Will the right words come to me when I need them? Will the audience like me? How should I dress? What should I do with my hands? What if I say the wrong thing? Can everybody hear me? What if people get bored, fall asleep, or walk out while I'm talking?

Our concern for *delivery*—the actual presentation of the message—is not unjustified. We know it will affect the speech outcome. No matter how good the speech content, the speaker's oral effectiveness is crucial to audience understanding and approval. Because we recognize that many things can go wrong during a speech presentation, we want to be assured that we have made the best choices among the many strategies for presentation available to us. In this chapter we explore some of these strategies for optimizing a public communication event. Specifically, we focus on audible and visual aspects of speech delivery. We also consider the common problem of "speech fright" or "excessive anxiety" in the speech setting.

AUDIBLE FACTORS

In addition to deciding on the form of presentation of a speech, the speaker has to decide what vocal style to use. How loudly should he speak? How rapidly? How precisely should sounds be enunciated? How varied should the inflection be? How planned or calculated? Are there oral mannerisms or problems that should be avoided? These questions are among those that need to be asked when considering audible style —vocal characteristics that the audience hears.

The speaker has two major options—the *formal* style and the *casual* style. The formal style has a long history. Many famous public speakers have used a stately, oratorical style with carefully planned inflection, dramatic pauses, increased volume, overly precise enunciation, and other vocal traits that give the speech a formal ceremonial tone. We can all remember speakers who, when they got behind the podium and began to speak, seemed almost to become different people because their oral style changed so radically. Many people have come to expect this formal style simply because it has been used so often. When we get up to speak, we may find ourselves changing our delivery style to fit what we assume to be audience expectations.

But the point of any speech should presumably be the content, the *message* the speaker wants the audience to receive. Our goal should not be to impress an audience with a beautifully modulated voice; rather, it should be to maximize the chances that the audience will attend to and understand our message. We therefore suggest for most public communication the second option—a natural, casual style. Our term for this style is *conversationality.* With this strategy, a speaker uses language and vocal inflection much as in normal, face-to-face conversation. The emphasis given to words and phrases, the speed and loudness of the delivery, the word choices—indeed, all audible characteristics of the presentation—are similar to the speaker's oral style in everyday interaction.

Of course, some changes from a purely conversational delivery may be necessary. A speaker may have to talk more loudly or articulate more carefully because of poor acoustics. More precise language usage may be required to assure message accuracy as, for example, with a technical engineering report. In addition key points sometimes need special vocal emphasis, which might not be characteristic of a natural delivery. In general, however, we recommend that a public communicator strive for a conversational, spontaneous oral style.

The conversational strategy fits nicely with the extemporaneous delivery mode. The speaker appears more relaxed and warmer; he may be more relaxed simply because he is exerting much less effort in presenting the message. Still, a speaker's habits and stereotypes may make it difficult to escape from a more formal style, and he may want to remind himself not to lapse into an unnatural delivery by inserting reminders in the outline notes to "relax!" or "be conversational."

For most people, a conversational style is easy to develop and causes few problems. As in normal conversation, the speaker can expect some imperfections in fluency—an audible pause like "uh," a minor pronunciation error, a grammatical slip, or a slurred phrase. Fortunately, while the speaker may notice these minor errors, the people in the audience rarely do. As in more casual interaction, the listeners filter out these flaws and focus on content. For a very few speakers, however, the vocal characteristics and gaps in fluency may be serious enough to call attention to themselves. In a study of over 1,600 college freshmen, for example, 133 (about 8 percent) had discernible speech disorders (Fair-

he
has
ha

cloth, 1966). Probably a larger percentage have occasional problems that are noticeable and distracting, although not technically "disorders." The remainder of this section explains some of the problems that, if uncorrected, may impede a conversational delivery. Voice scientists often refer to four categories of communication disorders: articulation, language, voice, and rhythm.

ARTICULATION

Articulation problems are essentially the improper formation of speech sounds by the articulatory mechanism—the teeth, tongue, lips, and hard and soft palates. Sometimes the problem is substitution of sounds. The cartoon character Elmer Fudd's error was to substitute *w* for *r*—"I'll twap that awnwy wabbit!" Another example is Tweety Bird's classic line, "I tawt I taw a puddy tat!" Some substitution is due to different cultural backgrounds. People of German background may substitute *v* for *w* ("I vant it"). A native-born Japanese may insert *r* for *l* ("flied lice" for "fried rice"). People on the East Coast may substitute *er* for the final *uh*, as in "Ameriker" or "Afriker." And, of course, we are aware of substitutions in a southern accent, as in "oil" pronounced like "all." But audiences are not necessarily distracted by articulation errors that stem from cultural differences. The problem instead is in improper articulation that is not tied to regional language or culture, errors that stand out from the rest of a speaker's generally correct speech.

A common substitution is the lisp, using *th* for *s*. American culture has regrettably come to associate a male lisp with effeminacy and homosexuality and a female lisp with childishness. It is almost always distracting.

Another articulation problem is distortion. Some speakers simply do not enunciate carefully enough, and sounds become slurred and partially omitted. Others are hampered by organic problems, as in the case of a person with a cleft palate. Still others have dental devices like bridges or orthodontic retainers that impede clear articulation. Whatever the cause, distorted or mumbled speech may call attention to itself, thus distracting the audience away from the speaker's message.

LANGUAGE

Language is a symbol system used for communication. *Language disorders* is a broad term that refers to a person's limited ability to use this symbol system in oral communication. Common language problems

"Well, to make a long story short. . . ."

faced by public communicators are errors in *pronunciation* and *grammar*. A speaker may distract or confuse an audience if his natural speaking style includes, *from the audience's point of view*, improper use of language. The key factor is the audience perspective. Some usage is not improper though the listeners may think it is. For example, for many years speakers who used the so-called black English were considered "substandard" in their use of language. They pronounced words differently, appeared to err in grammar and syntax, and used a vocabulary that was unfamiliar or confusing to non-black audiences. Black English is a legitimate and systematic variation from general American dialect, yet even today, some black speakers have difficulty gaining acceptance from audiences due to their language usage.

Many language problems are linked not to culture but to individual characteristics. A person's educational background may have limited his language development. The home, school, and community environments of children sometimes preclude varied and accurate language learning. Problems may be caused by emotional or neurological deficits during childhood. Sensory deprivation like a hearing loss also causes language deficiencies. Anyone who has observed language training for deaf children knows what an enormously handicapping problem deafness can be.

Fortunately, most public speakers are not bothered by serious language handicaps, but people who make errors in normal conversation are likely to transfer those flaws to the public arena. For example, a speaker may show a limited *vocabulary* by continually using the same descriptive terms throughout the speech. We recall a student speaker who was describing her trip to Europe and using color slides. For nearly every slide, she noted that the experience it depicted was "really interesting" or "a lot of fun." After more than thirty slides, this vocabulary flaw became tedious for the audience. Younger speakers today use "like" and "ya know" repetitiously and usually as substitutes for more varied descriptive language.

Pronunciation errors are deviations from a culturally accepted or dictionary prescription of the sounds of words. Standards of pronunciation are based on conversational utterances of educated or literate speakers. Standards vary, with region, of course, and are subject to gradual change. Most audiences have a general awareness and expectation of "good" pronunciation. Glaring errors distract us from a speaker's generally fluent delivery, especially when committed by experienced communicators like newscasters, politicians, the clergy, or teachers.

In general, pronunciation errors include, first, the use of the *wrong sound* (*February*, "FEB ru ary," not "FEB you ary"). A second type of error is an *omitted sound* (*police*, "po LEECE," not "PLEECE"). Third, an error can include an *extra sound* (*drowned*, "DROWND," not "DROWN ded"). Fourth, a speaker may use a *misplaced accent* (*cement*, "suh MENT," not "SEE ment"). Whenever a public communicator reads or quotes from manuscript, she or he should try to anticipate pronunciation errors and even write phonetically the difficult words so that they will not cause a glaring distraction.

Grammar can be broadly defined as the choice, forms, and placement of words in a sentence. Fortunately, most speakers exhibit reasonably correct grammar in normal speech. But occasionally speech habits or colloquialisms divert audience attention from the message. The double negative is common, as in "I won't never do it." "This here" and "them there" are substandard. So are improper verb forms ("I've been woken up" or "I drunk it all down"). Hundreds of examples of such grammatical errors can be found in any basic composition text. In general, when we consider a sentence like "My daddy he done it real good (rather than "My daddy did it well"), we can understand why some ungrammatical speakers have difficulty communicating with an audience. People sometimes equate poor grammar with low intelligence or bad ideas or other negative qualities. The irrepressible Dizzy Dean never suffered because of poor grammar ("He slud into second base but got throwed out anyways"), and some speakers purposely use an uneducated language style as a ploy to win favor of an audience they believe to be uncultured. But for most of us, a failure to detect and remedy common grammatical errors will usually be a serious handicap in many different communication situations.

VOICE

The human voice consists of three primary variables: *pitch*, or the vibration frequencies that determine the highs and lows; *loudness*, the force or volume of the sound; and *quality*, or overall characteristics of the vibration and resonance of the sound waves. For most speakers, the conversational style naturally integrates these three variables with little conscious effort, but voice problems can become public speaking problems for a few people.

In terms of pitch, some male speakers' voices are too high and some females' too low for audience expectations, suggesting effeminacy in men and masculinity in women. People of both sexes can develop a *monotone* delivery, an absence of regular pitch variation or inflection. The monotone is especially common among speakers who choose the manuscript delivery strategy. Embarrassing breaks in pitch may affect boys in adolescence whose voices are changing. Older speakers suffering a gradual hearing loss may have trouble monitoring and controlling the pitch levels.

Loudness can be a problem for the public speaker, especially some women who must strain or shout to be heard in a large room. While such speakers may be advised, "Project your voice," the fact is that for many low-volume voices an attempt to increase loudness could seriously strain or damage the vocal mechanism. We notice, for example, how a person who must speak loudly for extended periods (like a cheerleader) often experiences hoarseness or loss of voice. What has happened is that the vocal chords have become aggravated and swollen from the continued high volume and will not vibrate normally. A person with a low-volume voice should use an efficient loudspeaker system for any speech to a large audience. Some speakers try to speak too loudly, perhaps due to habit or to personality factors, sometimes because of a hearing loss, and sometimes because our culture has perpetuated the notion that vocal intensity indicates a dynamic, fluent, forceful speaker. Also, many speakers develop the same monotone in the area of loudness that is so common with pitch—no variation between loud and soft.

Vocal quality is much more difficult to define and identify than pitch or loudness. We often use vague adjectives like *gravelly*, *strident*, *hoarse*, *piercing*, *mellow*, or *harsh* to describe vocal quality. *Hypernasality*, a more precise term, refers to the occasional problem in which too many of the resonating sound waves pass through the nasal cavities instead of through the oral passages. In the English language only the *m*, *n*, and *ng* sounds are formed with air passing through the nose. When other sounds, especially vowels, are uttered with most of the air going through the nasal passages, a speaker is hypernasal, and the vocal quality is unpleasant. In contrast, *hyponasality* (also called *denasality*) results when the air that should be resonating in the nasal passage passes through and resonates in the mouth instead. We experience this problem when we have a severe cold, as do a few people who have permanent sinus or bone structure problems that can only be corrected by surgery. The reader can experience denasality simply by holding the nose and saying "Spending money is nice." The *m*, *n*, and *ng* sounds become more like *b*, *d*, and *k*, and the sentence becomes "Spedink buddy is dice."

A *hoarse*, *gravelly*, or *raspy* voice may be caused by swollen vocal chords or mucus on the vibrating mechanism. We notice how distracting a speaker can be when he sounds as if he needs to clear his throat. Audiences may squirm helplessly, totally unaware of the message and preoccupied with the unpleasant vocal quality. Still another problem is *breathiness* in which too much air escapes through the vocal chords giving the voice a whispery quality. Although the Hollywood starlet may consider breathiness sexy, for the public speaker, especially one using a loudspeaker or recording equipment, this vocal flaw is highly detrimental.

Many voice problems can be corrected. But since they may be the result of physiological and psychological problems, the speech pathologist—not the public speaking instructor—is probably the best source for advice and therapy. Speakers should become aware of their vocal characteristics, and one way is to listen to a tape recording of one's delivery. At first it may be an unpleasant experience. "That doesn't sound like me" or "I sound terrible" are common responses. (Actually, the way we hear our own voice is determined not only by sound waves through the air but also by bone conduction, the sound vibration through the skull. The tape recorder "hears" our voice the way other people do, through air conduction only. Thus, the playback is a fairly accurate indicator of the way other people hear us.) Listening to the tape and getting feedback from others can be useful in either confirming effective vocal traits or identifying particular problems that may be distracting to the audience.

RHYTHM

Every language has an oral dimension called *rhythm*, the speed of utterance and recurring patterns and intervals between speech sounds. In learning a second language, we usually develop vocabulary and grammatical competence before we gain rhythmic competence. Hence, it is usually easy to tell that a person is just learning our language simply by noting the different rhythm patterns.

Delivery speed and intervals between sounds develop naturally in most children, and these patterns continue through adulthood. As noted in Chapter Three, our culture ascribes meaning to rhythmic variation, and it becomes an important component in the total process of oral communication. Because rhythm is both natural and communicatively meaningful, we have earlier advocated a conversational public speaking style. The problem is that too many speakers become inhibited, overly formal, or frightened in front of an audience and have trouble maintaining the conversational style. Rhythmic patterns become awkward and hard to listen to, and the natural process of vocal inflection is altered. Since the new, unnatural delivery does not necessarily convey the same messages as a more natural mode, the speaker loses a valuable communication tool.

One rhythm problem is a delivery that is *too rapid.* Though some people speak rapidly in normal conversation, the speed may increase in the public situation. The cause may simply be anxiety, a desire to make the unpleasant speech situation as brief as possible. Another cause is the tendency to try to cover more information than can be presented in a limited time. We have all heard the rapid-fire disc jockey reading a commercial; presumably the sponsors want to say as much as they possibly can in a thirty- to sixty-second time slot. We have heard professors who, anticipating the bell, rush through the last portions of a lecture. There is evidence that increasing words per minute cuts down the time available to comprehend each verbal symbol and, beyond a certain speed, leads to a decrease in understanding (Foulke, 1968; Sticht and Glasnapp, 1972).

The obvious corollary of a rapid delivery is one that is *too slow*—that is, the regular intervals between words and phrases is too long. Even at the normal English speech speed of about 100 to 125 words per minute, the audience can think much more quickly, somewhere between 400 and 500 words per minute (thought speed). This means that listeners can anticipate what might come next and even think about other unrelated ideas. When the speaker's delivery sinks below normal rates, the audience may become nervous and impatient, anticipating words that are too slow in coming. Or the audience will discover that it can attend to other things and still listen enough to understand the message. The most important flaw of a too-slow rhythm is that it more closely resembles a monotone style as the longer pauses between each sound make the pattern of naturally varied inflection more difficult to hear.

A third rhythm problem is the *unnatural pause.* Speakers who rely on a manuscript or quote from printed material too often pause at the ends of printed lines, after all punctuation marks, or after a predictable grouping of five or six words. An example of unnatural pauses is the novice actor trying to read Shakespeare. Although the great playwright utilized a poetic form called *iambic pentameter* (ten-syllable lines with a two-syllable rhythm pattern), he did not intend the lines to be read in predictable one-line patterns like those of a children's poem. If our novice actor pauses at the end of each line rather than at the end of a complete thought unit, the meaning may be lost. Another example might be an inexperienced broadcaster who has not yet learned to read conversationally; his awkward rhythm patterns are distracting. In sum, the pause is a meaningful rhythm characteristic that we use every day without thinking. But when poorly timed or omitted, it can retard an otherwise effective delivery.

A final rhythm problem is especially serious—*stuttering*. Though stuttering is a complicated disorder and difficult to define, for our purposes we can simply think of it as an obvious and distracting interruption in the flow of speech, one that is likely to recur. It can include repetitions of single sounds or "blocking" on particular syllables or words (inability to utter the sound at all). Severe stuttering may be accompanied by facial distortions or other unnatural bodily movement. Most stutterers are well aware of their speech problem, and many tend to avoid public communication situations. Those who do speak publicly have learned to manage their stuttering. While severe stuttering is rare, *all normal speakers have some occasion to repeat or hesitate on speech sounds*. When these situations arise, the speaker should not be preoccupied with the problem. Since it occurs in normal conversation, there is no reason to try to eliminate it from public speaking. As a speaker gains experience, he or she will learn to disregard occasional stutters and focus instead on the message.

In this section, we have examined vocal factors in speech delivery. We urge speakers to utilize a conversational vocal style. The only exception is if, in using that natural delivery, specific vocal characteristics become counterproductive. Only then, through self-awareness, reminders, and practice should the speaker try to modify his or her normal style.

VISUAL FACTORS

In Chapter Three we suggested that the nonverbal dimension of oral communication has a significant impact on the meanings that are given to verbal messages, and we discussed several of the factors that affect nonverbal meanings. Here we shall apply those factors—everything about the speaker that the audience sees—to the public communication event.

People in an audience notice two things about the speaker's visual presentation. They notice the way he or she looks—the physical features and clothing. They also observe physical behavior. Both elements combine to affect the speaker's impact on the audience.

Speech teachers once referred to a speaker's dress and grooming as "stage presence." That term is probably inappropriate because it implies that the speaker should be performance-oriented with both costume and role for playing a part in a theatrical production. Today we tend to think of physical appearance more as an *identifying* link between speaker and listener. Instead of emphasizing speaker-audience differences and separation with special dress and grooming, a speaker needs to narrow the sender-receiver gap by assuring that these nonverbal factors are not a distraction while at the same time enhancing audience receptivity.

A primary requirement of a speaker's clothing is that it be comfortable. Some high-heeled shoes, tight-fitting pants or dresses, and heavy, hot fabrics may distract the speaker with physical discomfort. Dress and grooming habits can also affect a speaker *psychologically*. A new hairstyle, new glasses, or avant-garde clothing might be a source of apprehension if the speaker fears audience disapproval.

Even more important than speaker comfort is message effectiveness. Obviously, if listeners become distracted by a speaker's physical characteristics, attention to and comprehension of the message may be lost. What is appropriate physical appearance? It can be argued that suitable dress and grooming criteria can only be determined by the individual, in this case the speaker. Some people use a self-reference criterion, applying purely personal needs and tastes as to what is acceptable appearance with little regard for audience expectations. A speaker who adopts the "do your own thing" standard has every right to do so, but he should not be surprised at negative responses from some audiences.

We suggest that a more meaningful point of view is *accommodation*: a move away from a speaker-centered orientation ("I'll do what makes me happy") toward a more audience-centered basis for communication behavior. If the message the speaker wishes to communicate is truly important, if receiver understanding and acceptance are sincerely sought, the speaker must be willing to adjust to audience standards of acceptable physical appearance. Accommodation means neither deception nor abandonment of personal convictions. Rather, it is simply the willingness to make minor adjustments in normal preferences so as to increase the chances of communicative effectiveness. By considering the relative formality of the speaking occasion and dressing appropriately or by avoiding clothing or accessories that are distracting, the speaker can enhance speech effectiveness with attention to appearance.

MEN ON THE MOON
YESTERDAY-
WOMEN WILL
LIBERATE
THE

An audience is also acutely aware of the way a speaker moves. We often hear students criticizing a professor's lecture style in terms of bothersome physical mannerisms. "He's always pacing back and forth; it drives me crazy!" "She keeps tapping her pencil on the podium." "He buries his head in his notes and never comes up for air." "Those glasses —on and off, on and off!" Certainly professors are not unique. Many public communicators have physical behaviors that may become distracting. While listeners do not necessarily focus on these behaviors, and may receive the message accurately regardless of the speaker's physical action, one should never assume that such movement can be irrelevant to the communication process. As we learned in Chapter Three, listeners *always* develop meanings—sometimes unconsciously—from nonverbal action. Eye contact, facial expression, gestures, and postural changes are all important visual factors.

EYE CONTACT

What strategies should the public communicator use? In terms of eye contact, we suggest that the speaker gain as much freedom from notes as possible and try to vary direct person-to-person eye contact with many people in the audience. One outmoded suggestion for eye contact is: "Look just above the last row in the audience, perhaps at the back wall." We categorically reject this suggestion. To utilize the conversational delivery style discussed earlier, a speaker needs to establish the kind of eye contact that is appropriate for face-to-face dialog.

The importance of eye contact can be demonstrated with a simple experiment. In a casual conversation with a friend, try closing your eyes while that person is talking. Your friend will probably stop abruptly and ask what's wrong. You then reply, with eyes still closed, "Nothing is wrong. I'm hearing you. Go right ahead with what you were saying." Your friend will probably be unwilling to continue the conversation until you respond to his message with "normal" eye contact. This little test suggests the effect of eye contact on our willingness to communicate. Like the students who become frustrated with the teacher who buries his head in his notes, we in the audience want the public speaker to acknowledge our presence and importance with direct eye contact.

A by-product of good eye contact is an increased ability to hold attention. If a speaker looks directly at a person in the audience, his eye contact has a "grabbing" effect. (Most teachers know that the easiest way to get a daydreaming student to listen to the lecture is to look directly at him.) Conversely, looking away from a person is a kind of psychological "release" that permits the listener to attend to other things. While eye contact cannot guarantee complete audience attention, especially if the message is inherently uninteresting, it is an important factor in audience receptivity.

For several reasons, speakers may avoid regular eye contact with the audience. One common explanation is that they simply have not practiced it in a public communication context. Often, eye contact is not used because the speaker has relied too heavily on a manuscript. Or a speaker may have psychological blocks. He may simply be frightened. The audience may seem threatening, and the speaker learns that if he never looks up at them he will never receive negative nonverbal feedback. Sometimes a speaker will maintain eye contact with only those people who appear to be giving positive responses to his message, avoiding those who appear passive or hostile. Sometimes the speaker becomes so engrossed in his speech content that he simply forgets that the audience is out there. Whatever the reason, eye contact in general American culture is among the most significant visual factors affecting communication.

FACIAL EXPRESSION

Another visual factor is *facial expression.* The facial muscles are capable of enormous variation in movement and positioning. As we know from actors and pantomimists, facial communication can not only be highly meaningful (certainly the focal point of bodily posture) but can also be developed through practice. In other words, facial expression can be a *conscious* strategy for the communication of feelings and ideas.

The problem with *planned* facial expression is that it too often appears contrived and insincere. The painted smiles in automobile showrooms, beauty contests, and political campaigns are good examples. But the opposite extreme—passive, expressionless facial features—is equally unacceptable. When the speaker is discussing happy themes, he or she should look happy. Grave or unhappy messages should be accompanied by more serious looks of concern and even sadness.

How can the speaker make facial expression congruent with the mood of the message without appearing artificial? If the speaker uses the conversational speaking style, facial expression is likely to develop naturally. If the speaker selects topics of real personal concern, enthusiasm, or commitment, natural expression will be more likely than if the speaker selects a topic of only casual interest. Viewing one's speech on videotape is a good way of becoming aware of one's nonverbal facial behavior in a public situation. A speaker may discover, "I'm really coming across too seriously; I'm too grim. Next time I'll try to smile more." Or, "I really do look bored. No wonder the audience seemed restless. I'll try to show my enthusiasm." In general, however, we caution against becoming too concerned with a facial strategy. The normal expressions that people exhibit in everyday conversation will develop, in most cases, as a speaker grows increasingly familiar with the public speaking situation.

GESTURES

A third factor in the speaker's movement is *gesture* or *bodily action.* Though facial expression can be included in this category, for the moment we shall consider primarily hand and arm movements, bodily stances or postures (including postural changes), and "footwork" or shifting of positions in front of the audience. Obviously, the number of different kinds of gestures and combinations of movement are practically infinite; the speaker has an enormous range of options. And almost any movement, positioning, or posturing carries symbolic content or meaning. Hence, the speaker's animation serves as a potentially flexible and varied tool for enhancing audience comprehension and increasing message impact. The speaker obviously cannot ignore the action dimension of his presentation.

To what extent should gestures be *strategic*—that is, carefully planned to help achieve specific objectives? The answer of speech theorists over several centuries has been that bodily action should be as carefully prepared as verbal content. Students who were a part of this tradition often planned animation for a public speech as carefully as they would have rehearsed for a starring role in a dramatic production. Some teachers developed elaborate notational systems and training devices so that students could gesture fluently with specific movements in appropriate places. The practice of cultivating stagelike gestural emphasis continues to some extent, and students preparing for speech contests or formal occasions may spend hours developing subtle, finely tuned physical actions to complement an equally precise manuscript and oral style.

For several reasons, a formal gesture strategy is usually inappropriate. First, as with other nonverbal factors, a planned movement or gesture may appear unnatural and thus distract or confuse the audience. A planned gesture may be mistimed, appearing out of proper sequence with the idea being expressed. It may be overdone or appear stiff or awkward. Like facial expression, the planned gesture also may lack congruence with the spoken idea. Natural gestures accompanying normal conversation, in contrast, are nearly always properly timed and appropriate to the ideas being expressed. The reader may recall a heated argument, a conversation at a party, a child describing a new toy, or a salesperson closing a deal—all illustrations that bodily action need not be planned to be meaningful. We all gesture fluently every day and usually without conscious thought.

A careful gesture strategy is appropriate for a manuscript or memorized delivery mode, the speaking style we discourage as impractical for most speaking situations. In the extemporaneous mode, on the other hand, a speaker lets the specific wording develop naturally as he moves through his outline. Planning gestures to enhance particular phrasing is thus futile.

Some speakers discover that, despite their interest in a natural, spontaneous bodily action, their movement in public communication is infrequent, inhibited, and awkward. They make comments like, "I don't know what to do with my hands," or "I can't find a comfortable posture," or "I just freeze up and no movement seems appropriate." These comments are typical of beginning speakers. We have found that with increased exposure to the speaking situation, a person tends to become more involved in the message and less preoccupied with physical behavior. The result is usually the gradual development of natural gestures.

Bodily action may require serious attention, however, if particular mannerisms become distracting. A common problem is random pacing. The speaker wanders back and forth at regular intervals, often as a subconscious release of tension. Another problem is repetitious hand and arm gestures. A typical movement is the "apple-picker gesture" in which the speaker moves his hand out and back, out and back (like a person picking apples) almost as if he were reaching out to grab the words that come next in the speech. Another overused gesture is a perpetual chopping motion with one hand. A postural distraction is the constant shifting of weight from one foot to the other with possible shuffling of whichever foot is not supporting body weight. And, of course, facial mannerisms like a nervous tic can also bother the listeners.

Inappropriate movement not only hampers message effectiveness, it also neutralizes the potentially potent tool provided by the visual dimension of the speaker's presentation. The inventory of potentially distracting gestures is large. The important thing is to get adequate feedback from students or instructors so that a speaker will recognize his or her unique mannerisms in a simulated situation rather than an actual one. It has been found that bodily action can be improved through regular feedback in a basic public speaking class (Brooks and Strong, 1969).

SPEECH FRIGHT

Perhaps no problem is more overwhelming for the beginning speaker than *speech fright*—the anxiety and sometimes panic that so often accompanies the actual speech presentation. A common reason that some students avoid a basic speech communication class is not necessarily that they feel communication to be unimportant, but rather that they are thinking ahead to the inevitable public speaking projects in which they will have to stand alone before the class and present their ideas for the scrutiny of critical listeners. Because this problem is so compelling to so many people, we shall spend some time in this section developing an understanding of this age-old bugaboo and suggesting some strategies for managing it.

The term *stage fright* is often used instead of *speech fright* to characterize anxiety and nervousness in public speaking. It is probably an intimidating term because of its suggestion of a theatrical format for public communication. In any case, if the speaker thinks of the speech as a *staged* presentation, his communication task may seem much more awesome and threatening due to the implied emphasis on pleasing or entertaining an audience with a polished, flawless "performance." Although speech instructors sometimes use the term *stage fright* because of its popularity and common meaning, the reader should not necessarily associate the public speaking event with a *stage* presentation. We prefer the term *speech fright.*

In this section, we begin with some observations about the public speaking setting and general characteristics of speaker anxieties. From this perspective, we then explore symptoms and causes of speech fright and suggest ways of managing it. The reader will not find a handy-dandy set of rules for *curing* the problem. It *is* possible, however, to learn better ways of assuring that speech fright will not impede speech delivery or effectiveness.

PUBLIC SPEAKING IN PERSPECTIVE

A public communication event should not be a totally relaxed, casual experience for the speaker. A speech should be a challenge for which we should prepare psychologically. Just as an athletic coach worries when the team appears to be too blasé about the approaching game, so the speaker should be concerned if he or she does not feel at least a twinge of apprehension. If worry and nervousness do not play a part in speech delivery, the actual presentation will probably be bland and the speaker unenthusiastic. While this premise may be of little consolation for the beginning speaker, we are convinced that experienced communicators come to view speech fright as a potential ally in making the best possible presentation.

Second, we should realize that speech fright is common for *most* speakers in *most* public situations. The overwhelming conclusion of empirical research into speech fright is that, regardless of experience, speakers regularly face the problem of coping with their anxieties before an audience (Lomas, 1937; Clevenger, 1959; Baker, 1964; Klee, 1964; Mowrer, 1965; Friedrich, 1970). When the beginning speaker assumes that he faces special or unique problems of nervousness, he impedes his speech progress, and he is grossly inaccurate. Speech fright is a *life fact* of public communication, not an accidental psychological quirk for a few novices.

Third, anxiety is common to nearly any situation in which a person's behavior is open to immediate scrutiny by others. Athletes, actors, ministers, politicians, musicians, singers, teachers, dancers, attorneys, broadcasters, and many others regularly report anxiety before and during their audience-centered activities, even after years of experience.

Fourth, speech fright usually dissipates and sometimes disappears after we begin the public presentation. For the football player who quietly loses his dinner just before the big game, the first physical contact with an opponent usually begins the process of fear abatement, and after a few moments nervousness is no longer a conscious factor. A stage actor, after a few lines, quickly gets "into the role" and becomes absorbed in her performance. Similarly, we have heard many beginning speech students report that they can actually feel the nervousness leaving them after they get into their speech. In a short speech of, say, five to seven minutes, speech fright may not diminish completely, but it is important for the beginning speaker to recognize that for nearly everyone the process does in fact occur in varying degrees. One reason the experienced speaker is not preoccupied with speech fright is that he knows from past experience that the symptoms gradually vanish as the speech progresses.

Fifth, speech fright will not necessarily affect the communication event. Some symptoms of speech fright are more distracting or disruptive than others. Some do not affect the speaker's presentation in any discernible way but merely cause internal discomfort for the speaker. While speech fright may affect the smoothness or fluency of presentation, however, and while a speaker with manifest nervousness may not fulfill completely his speech objectives, it is extremely rare that speech fright totally negates the desired effects of a public presentation. However, when speech fright is a potential impediment to our fulfillment of public communication goals, we are justified in learning how it affects us and how it can be managed.

SPEECH FRIGHT SYMPTOMS

Symptoms are perceivable indicators of deeper psychological or physiological conditions that cannot be observed. Speech fright has many symptoms. One indicator of speech fright is avoidance of the public communication situation. Some people regularly turn down opportunities to speak publicly. Others construct their lifestyle and environment so that the chance of facing an audience will rarely arise. Others back down from previous commitments to speak, as in the case of the speech class student who is regularly and conveniently absent on the day he or she is scheduled to make a presentation.

Another set of symptoms involves withdrawal behavior. Withdrawal behavior is demonstrated verbally with self-belittling comments like "I'm really no good at this," "I haven't had much time to prepare," or "I'm probably not saying this right, but. . . ." Nonverbally, the speaker may withdraw through a lack of eye contact, unenthusiastic tone of voice, facial expression showing resignation, confusion, or frustration, and a slouched posture.

We can describe and clarify stage fright symptoms by identifying behaviors in the speaker that appear to deviate from normal communicator characteristics. One study grouped these observables into three categories (Clevenger and King, 1961). *Fidgetiness* includes such nervous, nonpurposeful movements as shuffling feet, swaying body, swinging arms, stiffness of arms and legs, a lack of direct eye contact with the audience, and pacing back and forth. *Inhibition* involves a deadpan facial expression, trembling knees, hands in pockets, a pale face, nervous hands, and returning to one's seat while speaking.

Finally, *autonomia* is the excessive reaction of the autonomic nervous system — the unconscious and relatively automatic body regulator of muscles and glands — producing such symptoms as moistening lips (perhaps indicating inadequate salivation), blushing, heavy breathing, and repeated swallowing or throat-clearing.

We must make an important distinction between *observed* symptoms and *experienced* symptoms. What the listeners may actually notice is not necessarily what the speaker is feeling emotionally or physically, and an audience assessment of speech fright will probably differ from that of the speaker. Our experience has been that speakers *overestimate* the degree to which they are affected by speech fright and the extent to which audiences perceive those symptoms. There is some evidence that audiences tend more often to *underestimate* student fears (Robinson, 1959). Obviously, some of the symptoms are simply not observable to an audience. Listeners cannot see apprehension, anxiety, embarrassment, or self-consciousness; they can only infer them from what they hear and see. They often do not even notice things that may antagonize the speaker and magnify his problems — the slightly quavering voice, unnatural inflection, trembling hands or knees, flushed or pale face, rigid posture, dry mouth, heavy breathing, difficulty in finding the right words. If these characteristics are noticed at all, the degree of nervousness and inner fear they represent usually are underestimated by the observers.

It may be of little consolation to the public speaker to know that the audience does not fully notice the extent of his nervousness. "So what if the audience doesn't *see* it? I still *feel* it, and that's the important thing!" Although the speaker's "comfort level" is an important consideration, we also believe that it is especially important for the speaker to recognize speech fright symptoms, and to learn to understand and control the ways in which those symptoms might affect the presentation. An analogy might be common physical illnesses, aches, and pains. We learn that these problems are inevitable, that they are uncomfortable, but that there are ways of managing them. Being able to identify and understand the symptoms does not always eliminate our physical discomfort, but such knowledge can soothe our anxiety when we recognize the symptoms as common and predictable. In contrast, we react strongly to symptoms we do not understand or cannot correctly identify. We wonder what is happening to us and worry that it might be serious. The beginning speaker may be confused and startled by the radical changes in physical and mental functioning; a growing awareness of these changes is an important factor in our ability to accept and cope with our public speaking fears.

One common explanation of stage fright is that it is *learned behavior*. From early development, we've been reminded that any "performing" situation is something to be feared. For example, a third-grade girl, before playing a solo in a piano recital, is told, "Now, don't be nervous, dear. You'll do a good job." A Little League ball player is counseled by his father before the big game, "I know you will do well. You won't let the team down; you'll come through."

Our society is performance- and success-oriented. We emphasize winning. We stress perfection. In so doing, perhaps we also *teach* a fear of failure. A child soon *learns* that to do well in a performance is to receive positive payoffs and to do less well is to have those rewards withheld or to be punished. The child also learns that people admire those who succeed and ridicule those who err. Since we view ridicule as a kind of punishment, and since public speaking exposes us to many people who may mock our mistakes, we learn that the public communication situation is highly threatening.

We also learn, incidentally, that when the speech has ended and we return to our seats, the speech fright vanishes. But why? People still see us and hear us as we speak in more casual interaction. If we say something foolish they may still laugh at us. Our self-esteem is just as vulnerable — we are still risking just as much — as when we were standing before the audience. What is involved in the simple act of moving from a standing position behind a lectern to a seated position? Could it be that we not only teach fear of a speech presentation, but we also define the limits or boundaries of that performance? That is, perhaps we learn that informal situations are not threatening (at least they are not *defined* as threatening), so that in moving from perceived formality to perceived informality our speech fright vanishes.

Other possible sources of speech fright have been outlined by Buehler and Linkugel (1962, 36–38). We list them below with our own brief explanations:

Fear of Physical Unattractiveness The speaker believes that he or she is not handsome or pretty or is improperly dressed.

Fear of Social Inadequacy The speaker fears exhibiting behavior that the audience will perceive as inappropriate or crude. This fear implies social inferiority.

Fear of Criticism The speaker may be overly sensitive to, and unable to cope with, negative feedback from the audience.

Fear of Failure We discussed earlier this cultural trait; although we know that success is sweet, we preoccupy ourselves with the possibility of a blunder.

Fear of the Unknown We cannot predict precisely the spontaneous developments of a speech situation. Although beginners may be especially prone to this fear, even experienced communicators may succumb to the uncertainty of public speaking, especially if they have been unexpectedly embarrassed in a previous speech.

Fear of Speech Fright The mere thought of being afraid, of having to cope with the burdensome speech fright symptoms, may itself prompt us to fear upcoming speeches.

Conflicting Emotions When we must face simultaneously a strong desire to succeed in a task and an equally potent fear of failure, the emotional turmoil may add to our distress; we know that either we speak and face failure or we don't speak and deprive ourselves of rewards.

Excitement from Anticipation The anticipation of a big event, of an intoxicating, ego-enhancing experience, of the opportunity to have many people sit captivated while we present our ideas, may prompt the same physical reactions as when we experience extreme fear.

MANAGING SPEECH FRIGHT

We have argued that speech fright is inevitable for most people, that it need not detract from speech effectiveness, and that some nervousness may be an aid to the speaker in spurring him to a better presentation. Therefore, we do not urge an attempt to *eliminate* speech fright (assuming that were possible). Instead, we suggest that the speaker learn to *control or manage* speech fright so that its physical and psychological symptoms do not impede the effectiveness of a presentation. (We recall one student who thought he had developed a surefire scheme for eliminating speech fright. About thirty minutes before his speech, he would down three shots of bourbon. His speeches were free from nervousness.

They were also inarticulate, comical, pathetic, and a total waste of the audience's time!)

Nearly all speech instructors have pet suggestions for managing speech fright, and we are no different. We offer the following list somewhat reluctantly, however, because the reader may be tempted to view it as a prescription — a set of rules that can lead to predictable results. These suggestions are only strategies that may help some people and not others.

Self-Analysis Through self-analysis a person can develop a greater understanding of his own behavior. It is likely, however, that this analysis can be most useful when its focus is *objective facts* as opposed to *critical judgments.* We encourage an individual to consider his or her own learning history, and the ways in which that history may be linked to current tendencies toward speech fright.

Plan for Self-Improvement To some extent speech fright is a form of learned behavior. Accordingly, under new learning circumstances, an individual can "unlearn" speech fright behaviors and develop a higher level of self-composure. Developing and implementing a plan for self-improvement can accelerate the learning of desired behaviors.

Become Familiar with Public Communication Theories and Principles Twenty years ago, space flight was a frightening prospect. We were facing the unknown. Yet for several years astronauts traveled into space with little observable apprehension. As Neil Armstrong landed the first U.S. spacecraft on the moon, for example, his heartbeat was within the normal range for everyday activities. One factor in his or any other astronaut's coolness must have been a detailed understanding of space science — orbital mechanics, propulsion theory, communication and navigation equipment, and the like — and confidence in its ability to perform. Similarly, the public speaker can learn much about the variables of a one-to-many communication situation from ancient theories to the findings of modern behavioral research. This knowledge means the speaker is not confronting the unknown but has an accurate comprehension of a reasonably familiar environment. One means of developing this awareness is a basic speech course, which can render speech fright much less intimidating (Brandes, 1967).

Develop a Message-Centered and Audience-Centered Point of View A well-researched and well-developed message, designed to meet the needs of a particular audience, virtually guarantees a degree of audience appreciation. As a speaker becomes more involved in his message and ways to get that message to his audience, he also becomes less self-conscious and anxious. Carefully select, prepare, and organize your presentation! Though preparation is good advice for other reasons as well, it may be the *single best way* to enhance self-confidence. We are rarely anxious over things we are well prepared to do. At the same time a poorly prepared speaker has good reason to be anxious.

Welcome Repeated Exposure to Public Communication To this suggestion we have heard some students reply, "Get serious. When I finish this basic course I'll never speak before an audience again as long as I live!" That is their option, though not a very realistic one. Many people willingly impede their personal and professional growth by being reluctant communicators, avoiding public speaking at all costs. We urge students to accept and even seek out speaking opportunities because repeated exposure to the public communication setting tends to reduce the fears associated with it and, at the same time, enhance self-confidence. As their public speaking experience increases, students will learn to expect certain symptoms and accurately predict their disappearance after the speech begins.

Evaluate Feedback The responses of an audience should be viewed as *new information.* Feedback provides an evaluation. Your successes and failures can serve as an important basis for redirection and improvement. We don't have to *agree* with all aspects of the feedback but we need to *listen to* and *evaluate* that feedback. Feedback provides facts about the ways in which we *affect* members of our audience.

Project a Positive Image The way we look, move, and speak obviously affects the audience's impression of us. When our positive behavior suggests we expect to do well, the audience is unconsciously led to expect a good performance, which in turn leads us to expect even more from ourselves (Bormann and Shapiro, 1962). If we continually apologize, offer excuses, admit our nervousness, or claim inadequacy, our psychological state — and our performance — will reflect our uncertainty. For many speakers, each apology further damages an already fragile self-concept.

Recognize the Importance of Introductory Remarks Getting off to a good start can be an important boost; a confused or muddled beginning can be excruciating. Don't rush into it. Pause to arrange the notes and get oriented. Smile! Start slowly and methodically. Seek an early favorable response from the audience — perhaps with a humorous anecdote, a reference to someone in the audience, an acknowledgment of common interests, a rhetorical question. Resist the temptation to begin quickly or to speak rapidly. Positive audience feedback can boost confidence quickly.

Utilize a Casual, Conversational Delivery Style The more formal we become, the more precise we must be. We become physically tense and notice even the slightest errors. For many people, a more relaxed delivery style can induce relaxation of mind and body as well.

Use Visual Aids Visual aids (Chapter Nine) not only improve audience understanding but also give us a friendly partner during the speech, a visual support to a verbal effort. They share the communication burden.

Use Physical Techniques to Ease Tension Deep breathing, smiling, stretching, exercising, muscle relaxing, and even meditating are potentially beneficial prespeech strategies. A deep breath as we begin speaking can also help. Comfortable posture and clothing can enhance our physical and psychological comfort.

Share Speech Anxiety with Friends While we do not recommend admitting our fears to an audience, frank discussions with others before the speech can be a therapeutic release, a kind of self-disclosure that enhances mutual empathy and the realization that we all share the common human characteristic of speech fright.

SUMMARY

Regardless of how carefully the speech content has been prepared, it is meaningless until delivered to an audience. In this chapter we discussed both audible and visual factors of speech delivery.

In terms of audible factors, we recommend that the natural conversational style should be used for most speeches. However, a speaker may have distracting mannerisms of articulation, language, voice, or rhythm that may require some conscious attempts at improvement. Visually, speakers should be willing to accommodate audience expectations concerning physical appearance and natural movement. Comfortable and appropriate clothing, eye contact, facial expression, bodily action, and posture are all factors that affect audience receptivity. While the speaker should try to avoid distracting mannerisms, the main goal should be to adapt natural physical characteristics to the public communication event.

Speech fright, a common concern for most communicators, cannot and probably should not be totally eliminated. Understanding its symptoms and causes is a first step to dealing with the problem. Speech fright can be managed in several ways; helpful instruction, adequate preparation and continued exposure to public communication appear especially helpful.

QUESTIONS

1. For the following public communication situations, what might be effective delivery strategies? Why?
   religious service
   political campaign
   classroom presentation
   business conference
   orientation session
   televised speech
2. In what ways are the following terms relevant to good or bad aspects of the speech presentation?
   conversationality
   articulation
   pronunciation
   grammar
   accommodation
   pitch
   formal style
3. What are some of the implications of an audience-centered approach to speech delivery?
4. What are some common problems in a speaker's visible mannerisms? What are potential solutions?

SUGGESTED READINGS

Bronstein, Arthur, and Beatrice Jacoby. *Your speech and voice.* New York: Random House, 1967.

Eisenson, Jon. *The improvement of voice and diction*, 2d ed. New York: Macmillan, 1965.

Fairbanks, Grant. *Voice and articulation drillbook,* 2d ed. New York: Harper & Row, 1960.

Hanley, Theodore, and Wayne Thurman. *Developing vocal skills,* 2d ed. New York: Holt, 1970.

Rahskopf, Horace. *Basic speech improvement.* New York: Harper & Row, 1965.

9 INFORMATIVE PUBLIC COMMUNICATION

PREVIEW

Perhaps an unfortunate stereotype of public communication is that of the dynamic orator using all his rhetorical skills to persuade an audience to his point of view on a great issue or cause. Actually, a more realistic generalization about public communication is that more often it is an attempt to explain, to teach—to exchange information in everyday, nonthreatening, practical circumstances. The problem, however, is that because the informative speech situation is not a momentous public event, because it is a frequent and not too exciting activity, the speaker may not give it the attention it deserves. Further, informative speakers may assume that their listeners are so information-oriented, so concerned with actual content, that speech structure, supporting materials, and presentational techniques are relatively unimportant.

In this chapter, we urge informative speakers not to treat their presentations lightly, noting that audiences—students and parishioners and employees and service club members —have too often had to suffer through tedious, unimaginative, and even confusing speeches because the messages had accurate content but nothing else. We hope this chapter will provide useful guidelines for making public information exchange more effective.

OBJECTIVES

To enhance awareness of the characteristics of the informative communication process

To explore typical problems in informative speaking

To help improve skills through several suggestions, with special focus on visual aids

NINE Hundreds of times every day, human beings send and receive information. An alarm clock reminds us — none too gently — that it is time to get up. A TV announcer reveals that skies are cloudy and rain is expected. Family members discuss their plans for the day. Friends share the latest gossip. Teachers instruct students, supervisors direct employees, professionals advise clients, and associates share information to make decisions. At the end of the day, family members return to describe their activities, while the six o'clock news brings them up to date on world events. Although information exchange occurs frequently and in a variety of forms, we rarely stop to reflect on it.

Informative communication is probably the most common type of audience-centered speaking. Also called *expository* speaking, informative communication can be defined as describing facts, ideas, feelings, experiences, and perceptions with the general objective of being understood. The informative speaker wants to establish shared meaning with the audience. He seeks audience *cognition* (the process of gaining knowledge, of comprehending, or learning), regardless of the listeners' attitudes or feelings toward the information.

INFORMATIVE VERSUS PERSUASIVE COMMUNICATION

Before we proceed to the characteristics of effective informative speeches, it is useful to distinguish between *informative* and *persuasive* communication. In persuasion, the speaker seeks to influence the listeners' attitudes, values, and behavior. Persuasive objectives have not been achieved if the listeners merely understand ideas or facts. They must instead respond to the persuader's message with belief, conviction, and sometimes with a particular behavior or action before the persuasive communication can be termed successful. While information is still a crucial part of the persuader's message, the goal goes beyond simple information exchange and shared meaning.

The distinction between informative and persuasive communication is useful for the public speaker because it helps to isolate the communicative goals and assess the best methods of achieving those goals. However, a good case can be made for the notion that the distinction between informative and persuasive communication is not clear-cut. Winterowd (1968, 1–2) suggests that *there is no such thing as "neutral" language*. He means that the speaker cannot construct a message so precisely worded that it will be understood in exactly the same way by everyone. Meanings are in people, not in words; each listener will decode and respond to the language symbols in a unique, personal, subjective way. Suppose a teacher in a classroom utters the declarative sentence, "The weather report said the temperature outside is 76 degrees with clear skies." One student might think, "Yeah, and I wish I were out there instead of in here." Another might respond, "Gee, it sure seemed hotter than that during lunch hour." A third might argue, "No it isn't; I can see some dark clouds forming." A fourth might complain, "Couldn't we discuss the weather some other time and get back on the subject?" Even this simple informative message affected each listener in a different way. It changed the students ever so slightly in ways that would not have occurred had the teacher *not* commented on the weather.

Another example might be the speaker who is describing the internal combustion engine. His objective is to assure that the audience will understand how the engine works. However, he is also suggesting, at least indirectly, "Please be interested in my speech. Like me as a person and appreciate my efforts to inform you. And when I've finished my message, use the information I've given you in constructive ways." Hence, all speakers attempt, to a greater or lesser extent, to *influence* listeners' emotional or psychological states whether the main objective is to achieve understanding, modify beliefs, or change behavior.

It can be argued, then, that all communication is persuasive; all communication attempts to influence and achieves different results with each listener. From a philosophical or theoretical perspective, we agree that the informative-persuasive dichotomy may be somewhat misleading. We therefore hope that the public speaker will recognize the inherent persuasive content in any informative message.

From a practical standpoint, however, we still believe that the major functions and outcomes of informative speaking are unique and distinct from the persuasive. It is possible to inform without persuading (as with the politician who describes his program but cannot convince us to vote for him) and to persuade without informing (as with some emotionally loaded advertising). When the primary communication goal is instructional or expository, the speaker faces special problems and concerns. The remainder of this chapter examines these concerns and some approaches to informative communication. Chapters Ten and Eleven cover the logical and motivational aspects of persuasive communication.

CHARACTERISTICS OF THE INFORMATIVE PROCESS

Despite the fact that we exchange information every day with seemingly little effort, expository speaking is a challenging and difficult process.

Several characteristics of the informative process contribute to the speaker's challenge: the complexity of the process, competing information, limits of time for presentation, and the variety of available presentational options.

The process is complex. Speaker-audience interactions are made up of several identifiable stages, all critical to the effectiveness of the speaker's presentation. First, the speaker must gain the audience's *attention.* The listeners must be focused on the message, and attracting their interest can require significant effort, as noted in Chapter Twelve.

The second stage is *reception.* Transmission of the message must be effective. The audible symbols (spoken words) must be articulated clearly and with sufficient volume to permit accurate reception of their intended content. Audience *comprehension* is the third stage. The listeners must understand the received message in about the same ways as the speaker intended. *Retention and recall* are the listener's ability to store and remember the speaker's message. Computer specialists use the terms *information storage* and *retrieval*, and note that recorded information is useless unless it can be located and recalled quickly and accurately.

Finally, *application* is the use of recalled information for constructive purposes. The ultimate objective of any informative speech—from a professor's lecture to a cooking demonstration—is to impart facts and ideas that can somehow be applied in our everyday activities. Whether the information is used for solving a puzzle, answering exam questions, operating a machine, or creating new ways of seeing the world, the inherent value of information is that we can *do something with it.* It is a tool by which we can achieve our goals.

Audience feedback intervenes throughout the informative process. Feedback is especially crucial during the first three stages—attention, reception, and comprehension—but at the same time difficult to read clearly. For example, if a member of the audience is looking the speaker squarely in the eye, does that mean that he is paying attention? Not necessarily. We all know that his thoughts could be a thousand miles away. If the listener is not cupping a hand to his ear or straining forward in his seat but sitting back passively, does that mean that he is receiving the audible signal clearly? If he nods pleasantly, does that mean that he understands the message and appreciates the speaker? The instructors in our society—teachers, parents, and supervisors—are regularly surprised when feedback in these first three stages appears positive but a failure in recall, the fourth stage, proves that at least one of the first three was defective. The listener wasn't paying attention, couldn't hear, or didn't understand, because his recollection of the message proved incomplete and inaccurate. Even if feedback shows that the listener *can recall* information, we still have no assurance that he can *apply* it until we get more feedback. A business manager, unimpressed by a new employee's recitation of the courses he had taken in college, remarked, "I don't care what you know; I want to know what you can do with it."

The speaker's message must compete with hundreds of other bits of information. As a speaker presents information, the listeners hear the language of the speaker's message. But they may also receive whispers from a side conversation in the audience, an announcer's voice from a radio in the next room, or even written messages from a book or newspaper. The supposedly primary language events — those making up the informative speech — are in competition with language events from other sources.

The listeners also may respond to other competing events: audience noises or movements, bothersome physical mannerisms in the speaker, pain from an uncomfortable chair, awareness of room temperature, sights and sounds from outside the room, or any of hundreds of perceivable conditions or behaviors. Also, the listeners may think of a variety of things — ideas, people, events, dreams, the past, the future, literally anything — and our thoughts often compete with the speaker's message.

How do we manage this large and varied input? Listeners have a *channel capacity*, a limit to the number of events they can process simultaneously. The audience manages channel capacity through *selectivity*, a kind of filtering process for focusing on the events that either stand out from the larger field or appear important to personal needs and goals. For an informative speaker to achieve his objectives, he must compete successfully with the other events so that the audience responds selectively to his message.

The speaker has extensive information but limited time. The good expository speaker usually confronts a dilemma; we think it is an inevitable one. He knows the topic in depth (some speakers can legitimately be called experts or authorities) and therefore knows how broad and complex the subject really is. He feels that limited information on a broad topic can be deceptive. Furthermore, the speaker usually likes the topic. He enjoys talking about it as much as he can. However, the informative speaker rarely has enough time to discuss the topic for more than a few minutes; the constraints of the speaking situation force him to limit content significantly. Thus the dilemma: (1) Do I try to tell as much as

possible, even if I have to speak rapidly and go overtime, so that I can give the topic the credit it deserves; or (2) do I establish limited informative objectives, assuring that the audience will understand the few points I present but possibly distorting the overall picture I'd hoped to provide?

While we cannot prescribe a comfortable way out of this dilemma, we tend to favor the second alternative. The speaker with limited goals may caution members of the audience that they are not getting all of the available information and therefore should not make certain conclusions about that information. At the same time, this speaker may be appreciated by the audience because he or she has made a few manageable points meaningful and interesting.

Some instructional speakers have the advantage of several days and even weeks to present information. The college classroom, military training, and management development programs are examples. For most of us, however, the information/time dilemma remains a common problem.

The informative speaker has infinite presentational choices. Chapter Seven included several alternatives for organizing and writing the speech. Chapter Eight explored delivery strategies, and Chapter Twelve includes options for maintaining interest and attention and managing the speech environment. All three chapters imply that the speaker has wide latitude for developing unique presentations. Here we add that since any idea may be expressed in a variety of meaningful ways, the informative speaker will regularly face the problem of choosing the best strategy for any given audience. We, the authors, in writing this text experimented with several different writing styles and organizations. Competent teachers experiment with various instructional strategies. Many informative speeches fail because their writers gave too little attention to establishing the most effective combination of words, structure, delivery, style, and supporting materials.

VERBAL CONTENT

There are a number of techniques for improving the verbal content of an expository speech. Consideration of scope, topic, language, rhythm, and audience participation are all important to the speech writer. Suggestions in these areas are given below. The use of visual aids in support of verbal content is addressed in the next section.

LIMITED OBJECTIVES

As noted above, the informative speaker is tempted to try to present too much material in the allotted time. Listeners simply cannot digest large doses of unfamiliar information. Yet speakers who should know better repeatedly forget that simple fact. You are probably familiar with the professor who glances at her watch, notices that the bell will ring in five minutes, and speeds up her delivery to cover the last fifteen minutes of prepared material. A student in a speech class, planning an eight- to ten-minute speech on his favorite subject, "Baseball," starts with Abner Doubleday, proceeds through a narrative of the game's development, and concludes with a skills course in running, throwing, hitting, and sliding. The harried executive allocates fifteen minutes of a busy day's schedule for an orientation session for new employees, a time to tell them everything they need to know to work for the company.

Simply providing more information in less time does not improve informative efficiency. Instead, it probably detracts from overall effectiveness. The speaker-centered or message-centered communicator will attempt to *utter words*; the audience-centered communicator will try to assure that the five-stage informative process is productive, that the audience will benefit from the message. As one teacher wisely noted, "If at the end of my class a student knows just one important idea that he didn't know before, I think I have succeeded in my instructional objectives." This is good advice for any speaker.

SIMPLIFICATION AND CONCRETENESS

Almost any human activity or area of knowledge has a *jargon*, a set of technical or special words or idioms that insiders know and use. Sometimes these terms are useful in that they can clarify complicated concepts among those who have arbitrarily agreed on their meaning. Sometimes the words merely show pretentiousness, a phony air of expertise. And sometimes jargon is used to exclude others from the conversations of the in-group. Insiders say, "If they can't understand us, they can't interfere!" Whatever its function, jargon should be avoided in informative communication. All technical terms should be defined in simple, direct language, *even if that simplification slightly distorts the special meaning of the term*. Further, the speaker should use specific examples that illustrate such terms.

REPETITION

We have all used repetition as a means of remembering important information. Memorizing lines in a play, cramming before an exam, or learning a foreign language are examples. Reiteration of ideas (using different language each time) can enhance the *retention* capability of the audience. It can also *clarify* a complicated explanation. Each time the idea is repeated, the odds improve that a listener who didn't get the message before will now receive and comprehend it.

Of course, repetition has some risks. It can quickly become tedious or boring. The speaker may offend some listeners if he repeats points that are actually fairly simple. Redundancy also uses precious time that could be used to present more important information. Yet the payoffs, we believe, outweigh the risks, especially if the content is truly important. It is bad enough that written messages like memos, letters, instruction sheets, and even textbooks so frequently fail to give the reader the benefits of reiteration. It is even worse with oral messages, because the audience cannot go back over what they may have lost or misunderstood. Regrettably, a model for informative communication still popular is, "Listen carefully; I'll go over it just once and then I expect you to remember my instructions and do the job right." That intolerant, message-centered attitude is precisely what we are attempting to change in this chapter. Repetition is a way of saying, "I am willing to accommodate you in any way I can so you can grasp this information."

AUDIENCE PARTICIPATION

Most expository speeches involve the passive learning format. The speaker explains; the audience listens. But participative learning can enhance the speaker's effort because it asks the audience to help in the "creation" of information. One method is to let the audience come to the desired conclusion without the speaker telling them. For example, suppose a speaker wants to describe a problem and then explain a solution, a common informative speech theme. He might build interest and suspense in his description and then ask the audience to come up with a solution. He could then interact with them informally on their suggestions. Or the speaker might let the audience develop examples that illustrate his key points. He might ask, "Can anyone think of an actual communication event in which a person's role affected the outcome?" In suggesting an example, the listener would probably understand and remember the principle that "roles affect communication behavior."

The speaker faces certain risks in using participative devices. Some audiences have gotten used to a passive role and feel comfortable with not having to exert the effort to respond. They may resent the speaker's requests. Other audiences are unable to respond because they cannot think creatively about the speaker's ideas. (Most teachers have had this experience. Because of the mood of their students on a particular day, they simply cannot generate any voluntary reactions from the class.) Finally, the participative framework is difficult to plan. If the audience takes off on a subject, the speaker may not have time to do some of the other things he had planned. Hence, the speaker must either be tactful in getting back on the topic or have the ability to adapt the ideas generated through audience participation to the planned content. Whatever the possible drawbacks, however, audience involvement in developing information is a creative and increasingly popular approach.

FEEDBACK

Throughtout this text we emphasize the importance of feedback in the communication process. The informative speaker will continually receive and interpret feedback. As noted, it is difficult to interpret accurately listener feedback indicating whether we have accomplished the five stages of informative communication — audience attention, reception, understanding, retention/recall, and application. Hence, we believe that the speaker should *actively seek* specific kinds of feedback to improve his understanding of audience responses.

One method is to write into the speech outline specific stopping points at which to seek response. The speaker might ask, "Is there anyone who would volunteer to tell us what he understands about this first point?" Or, "Is there anything you'd like me to go back over in this first section?" The common phrase, "Are there any questions" may achieve results, though some people are reluctant to ask because they do not want to appear stupid or they fear an angry, defensive response from the speaker. Another technique is to identify particularly difficult terms and concepts, and spend some time interacting with the audience, as by asking someone to paraphrase the speaker's definition.

Like other techniques, seeking feedback can cause problems. The speaker may learn that he has been an ineffective communicator. Some people would really rather not know if their effort was successful; to seek responses, especially during the speech, is just asking for trouble. Arrogant speakers take a different view: "If they don't understand, it's their own fault; I'm not going to clutter my carefully prepared message with a lot of irrelevant audience comments." But if the message and the consequent audience behavior is important, and if the speaker has a sincere concern for the audience, clear feedback is essential.

THE USE OF VISUAL AIDS

Public speaking situations have a visual dimension. The audience sees the speaker, his posture, dress, and movement. The visual dimension can be exploited best if the speaker supplies other observable devices to enhance or clarify the message. In this section, we examine some of those devices and suggest some ways to use them most effectively. Visual aids are used most frequently in the informative speaking environment. However, they are also productive in other types of public and small-group communication.

We need not dwell on the ability of visual aids to improve the audible message. At all five stages of the informative process discussed earlier, the visual dimension provides a perceptual cross check and amplifier of the verbal. However, if poorly selected or displayed, visual aids may also distract or confuse the audience. A speaker should not assume therefore that, once conceived, the visual aspect of the informative speech will take care of itself; careful planning is necessary.

TYPES OF VISUAL AIDS

The Human Body When a speaker personally demonstrates a particular behavior (like swinging a tennis racquet, doing yoga exercises, or operating a machine), his body becomes a visual aid that provides information above and beyond his normal animation. In addition to personal demonstration, the speaker may select another person to help him, as with a speech on self-defense maneuvers, lifesaving or first-aid techniques, or modeling clothing. The main advantages of the body as a visual aid are animation, adaptability, and realism. We can move around to appropriate positions and postures, change behavior to meet unexpected situations, and actually show how a particular activity is performed.

One problem with the speaker's use of his own body for demonstration is that he may have difficulty continuing an effective speech delivery. We once saw a speaker demonstrate modern dance steps. She became so winded that her speech was uttered in strained, awkward gasps. Another problem is greater difficulty in using notes during the physical demonstration. If another person participates, he or she may behave with awkwardness or embarrassment and become distracting.

Physical Objects Audiences appreciate seeing appropriate physical objects. If the object being discussed is physically present, we have the advantages of exactness and realism. Sports equipment, products of arts and crafts, and various mechanical devices are common visual aids in this category.

Objects are sometimes too big or too small to be practical for a particular speech environment (New Trends in Single-Engine Aircraft, Techniques of Diamond Cutting). With some objects we are unable to show the inner workings (The Catalytic Converter in U.S. Automobiles). Some objects are unavailable for display (Primitive Artifacts), and others may have to be shown out of proper perspective or context because the larger objects of which they are a part cannot be exhibited (Radar Devices in U.S. Missiles). Nevertheless, the informative speaker will discover that objects, when appropriate, can attract attention and enhance a complicated verbal explanation.

Models Models are replicas of the real thing. Their size can be varied to be practical (Aerodynamic Features of the SST, The DNA Molecule), and cutaway views in some models permit us to concentrate on the important aspects. For example, medical instruction often utilizes plastic models of body parts that can be further disassembled to show inner workings. Models also can prevent embarrassment, as with the life-size dummy used for demonstrating mouth-to-mouth resuscitation.

Unfortunately, appropriate models are often expensive and difficult to obtain. They are less than realistic, and precise model dimensions and features are difficult to achieve. But for some types of instructional messages designed to train people for specific tasks, either real objects or their replicas are crucial.

Electronic Media Included in the electronic media category are projections of slides, filmstrips, movies, and transparency materials. The category also includes videotaped replays on television monitors. Such visual aids can supply movement, variety, color, rapid changes of image. They can also provide large amounts of information in a brief time. Most instructional programs developed in the last few years utilize electronic media to some extent.

Though the advantages are significant, visual aids that depend on electronic media can pose significant problems for the one-time-only informative speech. Equipment and facilities are usually costly. Setup of devices requires technical expertise and adds significantly to speech preparation time. Many more things can go wrong during the speech than with other types of visual aids — power failures and faulty equipment, for example, can cause havoc. Most important, the personal audiovisual appeal of the speaker is minimized, especially when lights are dimmed, sound is loud, and most of the audience attention is directed to the visual media rather than to the speaker's commentary. Use of electronic aids requires practice, but these aids are clearly becoming more popular than any other form of visual support, and most public speakers will have to learn to use them.

Pictures and Diagrams Almost any audience likes to look at pictures, photographs, paintings, and drawings; they can enhance the interest and clarity of a presentation. They are usually easy to obtain, and we can develop them especially for a particular speech. Obviously, topics involving particular places, people, or artistic themes must rely heavily on pictorial content (Western American Artists, My Vacation in Scandinavia, Famous Actors I Have Known). Diagrams or drawings of actual objects can depict three-dimensional views and concentrate on important features.

Certain kinds of pictures, like large color photographs or original paintings, are sometimes too expensive or inaccessible for a one-time-only presentation. Some speakers make drawings and diagrams too complicated with irrelevant information or too small to be seen by a large audience. And some speakers may be unable to prepare these visual aids themselves because of the artistry or time necessary for effective results.

Graphs and Charts Charts and graphs illustrate statistical and conceptual relationships. The pie, line, and bar graphs can summarize bulky statistical information in relatively simple form, and the statistical chart can show interrelationships (for example, the amount of rainfall according to year and location). Organization charts demonstrate very well the links between various subgroups.

The problem with a graph or chart is that the viewer must spend time getting oriented to what it is designed to show and how it should be read. For example, if a speaker were discussing economic trends over the past few years, he would first have to explain carefully the terms, symbols, and lines on the graph. From reading some textbooks, we know how long a process that can be. Furthermore, since the speaker usually utilizes only a portion of the data, the excess information in the chart or graph may become distracting.

Maps Because they show dimensions, shapes, contrasts, and geographic relationships very well, maps are often indispensable. Speeches on the weather, international politics, travel, transportation, military activities, historical topics, and various business and government issues all demand the effective display of maps.

Appropriate maps often are hard to obtain without considerable expense. Printed maps are usually too small and almost always show unnecessary details that either confuse or distract, as with a common automobile road map. Hand-drawn maps are rarely precise or neat, though they can be constructed to the appropriate size and without irrelevant data.

Chalkboards By far the most popular visual aid, the chalkboard is readily accessible in almost any public speaking environment, often in the form of a movable panel. The speaker can adapt his writing or drawing for the size of the audience, and ease of erasure permits spontaneous modifications.

This aid sounds ideal, doesn't it? We take quite the opposite, and probably controversial, point of view that *except for everyday classroom situations, the chalkboard as a visual aid should be avoided.* We believe that speakers commonly use the chalkboard as a substitute for better visual alternatives because they lack energy and creativity. They lose audience contact while they are writing or drawing. The materials are rarely neat, precise, or artistic. Previous erasures show as messy smudges, and the new writing is sometimes not dark enough to be seen clearly. Glare from lights or a window may restrict the view of part of the audience.

The availability of a chalkboard also tempts unplanned use on the spur of the moment. Suppose the speaker senses some confusion in the audience. Instead of simply elaborating verbally, he says, "Well, uh, perhaps I can show you what I mean here on the board." He searches for chalk, draws an image that is inaccurate and too small, hunts up an eraser, tries again, and perhaps eventually writes or sketches something that may or may not clarify his point. The audience watches him struggle and may lose interest. The haphazard attempt to use a quick visual medium has actually detracted from the speech. Again, we urge that the chalkboard be used sparingly; there are better ways. A possible improvement over the chalkboard for spontaneous sketching or writing is the large tablet on an easel, with colored felt-tip markers. This aid is portable and less messy. And, if the speaker prefers to prepare information beforehand, the tablet is also superior to the messy and erasable chalkboard.

VISUAL AIDS PREPARATION

The effective use of visual aids requires careful planning and preparation of the materials, always with an eye to the purpose and main ideas of the speech and the audience for whom it is intended. The following suggestions will help the speaker achieve maximum effectiveness of the visual dimension of his or her speech.

Advance Planning and Preparation Prepare visual aids well in advance of the speaking situation. Last-minute attempts to find appropriate pictures, draw charts, or arrange for demonstration equipment is not only a hectic process but also reflects negatively on the speech. The audience can usually sense the lack of careful preparation. If the visual aid is another person, it is crucial to discuss his role with him beforehand so that he will know *precisely* what is expected of him. Spontaneous volunteers rarely do an optimal job in a demonstration and may even sabotage (usually unintentionally) the speaker's objectives.

Relevance Make the visual aid and all its components relevant to the speech topic. Too often, informative speakers toss in extra materials as an afterthought simply because the aid is available, looks good, and "might as well be shown." We once heard a slide-illustrated lecture about a trip through Aztec ruins in Mexico. The speaker could not resist spending about five minutes showing slides of his wife and children on a side trip through Disneyland!

Sometimes speakers use visual aids simply to impress an audience with their advance preparation, even though the materials are not needed; perhaps they want to prove to their auditors (or to a speech instructor) how hard they've worked on the project. The speaker should screen visual materials carefully. Are these devices really necessary? What do I hope to achieve that cannot be gained without them? Will I insult my audience's intelligence by using an aid for so simple an idea?

Simplicity and Clarity Make certain the visual aids are simple and clear. If a speaker must make a lengthy explanation about what the visual materials are supposed to illustrate, the materials become less "aid" and more new speech topic. Visual aids must be large enough to be seen, and dark or contrasting colors can help. A series of simple charts, graphs, or pictures may be more comprehensible than one large complicated one.

Rendering Style If the visual aids involve writing or drawing, be neat and artistic. Speakers in business or professional settings often have artists or printers prepare their visual aids because they know that sloppiness causes a *transfer* of negative attitudes about the visual aids to the speaker's own speech objectives and ideas. Frequently in this text we have argued that the verbal and nonverbal processes are intertwined and inseparate. Thus the speaker with verbal fluency can be betrayed by the nonverbal impact of a pencil-drawn chart on a torn piece of notebook paper, a graph on smudged posterboard, messy writing on a blackboard, and even an object or model in disrepair.

Practice Practice using the visual aids beforehand. This step in speech preparation is frequently overlooked. The speaker practices the verbal message orally and occasionally *thinks* to himself, "At this point I will pick up the object and show how it is used." But he doesn't actually *do* the demonstration ahead of time; he just imagines himself doing it. As a result, many speakers have been surprised by unexpected problems. Perhaps the color slides were not in order, or a device would not work properly, or an important detail had been omitted from a diagram, or the aids were bulky to hold, clumsy to manipulate, and difficult to set up. Practicing will not guarantee that unexpected problems will be avoided, but it can significantly reduce their likelihood and improve speaker confidence. We especially encourage the speaker to rehearse *in the presence of a listener*, asking that person to interrupt whenever he cannot see or understand.

THE PRESENTATION

No matter how well prepared, visual aids that are ineptly presented can be at best useless and at worst a distraction. The following suggestions will help optimize a speaker's use of visual aids during the presentation.

Audience Viewing Make certain that visual aids, during use, remain in clear and constant view of the entire audience. Do not let the hands, body, podium, or other visual aids obstruct the vision of particular audience groups. Everyone should be able to see without effort or strain. If some cannot, they will either lose interest or become resentful that the speaker does not appear concerned with their well-being. Except for a few well-planned lecture or conference rooms, most speaking environments are *not* ideally suited for visual presentations. Hence, the speaker may have to spend some time moving around with the visual aid so everyone has an opportunity to benefit from it. Some speakers nervously play with demonstrated objects, bouncing them around as the audience struggles to focus on them. As a rule, speakers should touch the visual aids only when absolutely necessary for displaying them.

Eye Contact The speaker should maintain *eye contact* with the audience. Visual aids may become security blankets. We find it more comforting to look at them because, unlike the audience, these *things* we have prepared do not glare back at us, do not threaten us. Hence, we may look at the visual aids throughout the entire speech. As with touching the materials, we should look at them only when absolutely necessary — when we must see where to point or when we must manipulate them in some way. The listeners may decide whether they want to look at us or at the materials. Since eye contact has such potency for maintaining audience attention, the informative speaker cannot abandon this crucial tool.

Timing Use or display visual aids at the *proper psychological point* in the speech. The use of visual materials usually has only two possible outcomes: (1) improved audience understanding and interest, or (2) distraction of the audience from the speaker's message. If visual aids are in view before or after the speaker actually applies them, the audience will notice. The speaker cannot simply say, "Don't pay any attention to that; I'll get to it in a minute." The audience *does* notice and is thus prepared psychologically to think about it. We recall the speaker who was discussing poisonous snakes. He had a cage with a live rattler moving around inside. The cage appeared to be open at the top so the snake could crawl out. As the audience squirmed nervously, the speaker tried to present five minutes of background information about snakes in general before he described the live one in the cage. He remained naively unaware that the audience didn't hear a word he said!

Though sometimes it is impossible to hide the visual aids (like an intricate blackboard drawing that must be done beforehand, a large object like a motorcycle or a large animal), we should make every attempt to assure that materials are *visual* only when we want them to be.

Handouts *Avoid* handouts during the speech. Handouts are such things as pictures, objects, and printed materials that one or more audience members can look at while the speech is in progress. Most of the time these devices only distract the audience. If passed around, a single handout inevitably means that three or four people are not listening to the speaker at any particular moment; they are looking at the handout or are involved in passing or receiving it. Meanwhile, a person in another part of the room notices the handout's progress and thinks, "I'll bet the speaker is finished before I get to see it." Some people see the handout at the wrong time, after the speaker has already moved on to another point.

Sometimes we are tempted to hand out duplicated materials so that everyone can read along while we elaborate the listed material. While this procedure is productive in certain classroom, small-group, or conference settings, it has a problem: once the listeners have printed materials, the speaker cannot prevent them from reading during other parts of the speech. Many teachers have learned this lesson when they handed back a graded exam at the beginning of the period and then tried to give a forty-five-minute lecture.

It is much better to find ways to let everyone see a visual aid at the same time, perhaps by using larger materials or an overhead projector or by asking people to come up after the speech has ended to see tiny objects or pictures. Presentation of a single document or picture to the entire audience at once is not only cheaper and quicker, but it also directs attention to material at the times and in the manner the speaker prefers.

THE DEMONSTRATION

Perhaps the most challenging type of informative speech using visual media is the *demonstration.* A demonstration is not simply the *display* of visual aids but rather the *use* of those aids in showing the audience, through the speaker's behavior, a process or procedure. Table 9-1 indicates the difference between normal informative speaking and demonstration.

Demonstrations have strong audience appeal because they leave little to imagine. As an instructional device, demonstrations are crucial on topics like arts and crafts, athletics, and equipment operation. However, in any physical process many things can go wrong. What if the speaker must thread a needle? Carefully slice a vegetable with a razor-sharp knife? Bring water to boil quickly? Comb the hair of a frisky dog? We

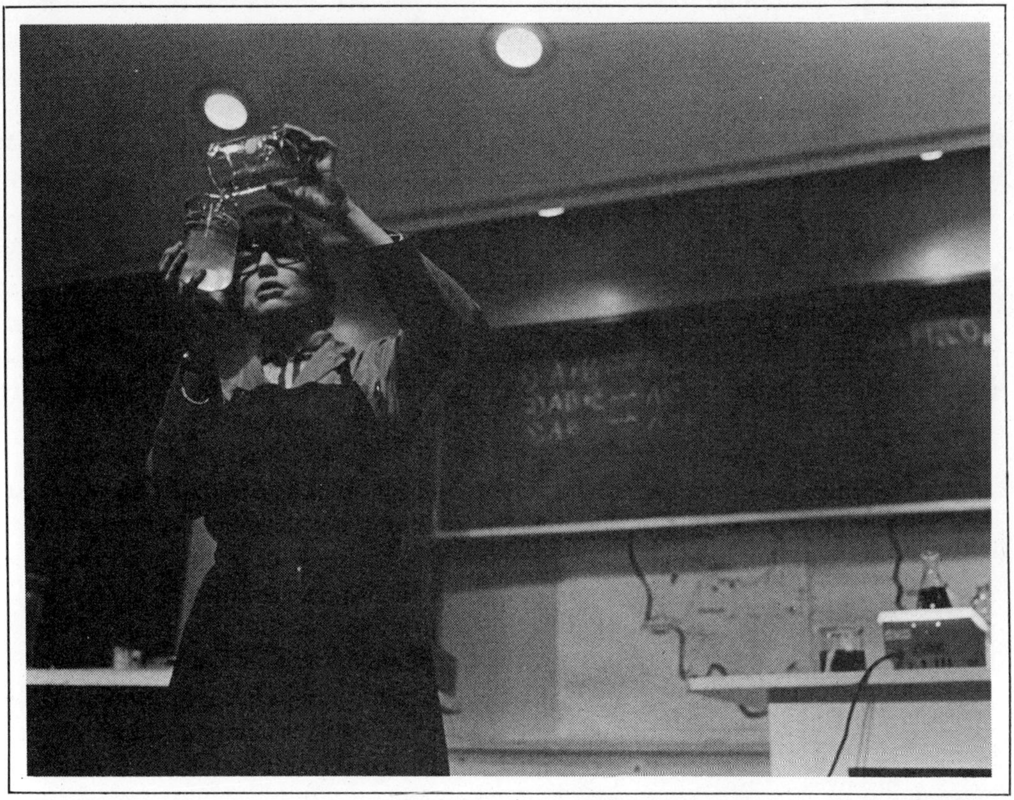

have seen many well-prepared informative speakers fail because of unexpected events in the "doing" phase. One student demonstrated karate. Because of nervousness, he could not concentrate fully and broke his hand instead of the brick! A woman explaining wine tasting accidentally sent a fifth of cabernet sauvignon crashing to the floor. An ardent golfer swung his three wood and demolished a light fixture. A guitarist broke a metal string and spent several minutes replacing it before he could continue. Most speech instructors can describe numerous horror stories of the demonstration-gone-awry.

TABLE 9-1 DEMONSTRATIONS AND VISUAL EXHIBITS

Visual Exhibits	Demonstrations
a chart showing proper tennis court positions and strategy	using a tennis racquet to show proper serving techniques
color photographs of imaginative food servings	preparing and mixing ingredients for a new recipe
slides or films that illustrate techniques of firearm maintenance and safety	dismantling and cleaning a firearm
charts and graphs that show the effects of exercise on cardiovascular functioning	doing pushups, running in place, and then taking blood pressure, pulse, and respiratory readings
showing human models with new hairstyles	styling a person's hair

In preparing speeches that involve demonstrations, we should remember an important axiom: whatever *can* go wrong *will*. We must be able to predict potential trouble spots. Ask these questions beforehand: What events have to happen as planned for my speech to succeed? If one of these events does not go smoothly, what are my options? What visual materials can become defective? After considering potential trouble spots, try to eliminate them ahead of time. For example, if a speaker anticipates that nervousness will lead to trembling hands, he may want to do some of the intricate manipulation ahead of time (threading a needle, pin-striping with paints, assembling tiny machine parts, and the like).

Be especially conscious of *time*. Rarely does a demonstration run shorter than expected; it almost always takes longer. Run through the speech ahead of time, precisely as it will be done during the actual presentation. If it is too lengthy, ask again the crucial question: Which portions of the demonstration are really necessary and which are not? Any demonstration should have carefully limited objectives. The speakers who encounter problems are frequently those who tried to do too much in a short time.

Avoid extended *silent demonstration*. Though there are exceptions to this rule, most audiences expect continuous commentary from the speaker. Experienced demonstrational speakers actually plan for filling periods of physical activity with anecdotes or additional information. They know that some people become uncomfortable during these silent phases, and continuity in speaking eases the problem. If the speaker has practiced using the visual aids, he knows when these moments of silence are likely to occur and can plan accordingly. Anyone who has ever watched helplessly as a speaker quietly struggled with a troublesome visual aid knows how useful supplementary verbal materials can be for this type of situation. While the speaker need not apologize for circumstances beyond his control, he should frankly explain the problem and trust the audience to be reasonable. Audiences are usually not malicious or sadistic people who enjoy seeing a speaker flounder in unexpected problems. Most of us feel real empathy for the speaker in difficulty. Some people will even try to help with the demonstration.

SUMMARY

Informative speaking is the description or exposition of facts, ideas, feelings, experiences, and perceptions so as to be understood. Persuasive speaking, on the other hand, seeks changes in audience attitudes and behavior.

Problems with informative communication include the complexity of the information-exchange process, competition with other types of information, the dilemma of having significant information and limited time, and a large number of presentational choices. We have suggested that the informative speaker should limit his objectives, simplify his speech with concrete language and repetition, and encourage audience participation.

The speaker has many options for visual aids: the human body, objects, models, electronic media, pictures and diagrams, graphs and charts, and the chalkboard. These aids must be used carefully, however. Clear, neat, and artistic results are crucial. The speaker should practice using the aids, with special concern for assuring an unobstructed audience view, maintaining eye contact, and using at the proper psychological point in the speech. In general, handouts should be avoided as visual aids.

Demonstrations involve not simply the display of visual aids but also their actual use as the speaker explains a process or activity. Demonstrations have strong audience appeal but are prone to unexpected problems; therefore, the speaker needs to plan and practice the speech even more carefully than he prepares for the use of visual exhibits.

QUESTIONS

1. Elaborate on the concept of audience participation or feedback in expository speaking. Can you think of typical informative speech situations in which the potential of audience involvement is ignored and the listeners are left in a somewhat passive role? Are there situations in which audience participation would be inappropriate in an informative speech event?
2. Why can it be said that all language is persuasive—that even an expository speech includes attempts to influence an audience? In a typical informative speech, what are some of the persuasive messages that the speaker would be sending?
3. What are some of the common problems in the informative communication process? What are possible suggestions for resolving each problem?

SUGGESTED READINGS

Bormann, Ernest, and William Howell. *Presentational speaking in business and the professions.* New York: Harper and Row, 1971.

Dale, Edgar. *Audio-visual methods in teaching,* 3rd ed. New York: Holt, 1969.

Olbricht, Thomas. *Informative speaking*. Glenview, Ill.: Scott, Foresman, 1968.

Wilcox, Roger P. *Oral reporting in business and industry*. Englewood Cliffs, N.J.: Prentice-Hall, 1967.

10

PERSUASION THROUGH ARGUMENT

PREVIEW

Most of us like to think of ourselves as rational individuals. We place a high value on the sending and receiving of messages that seem reasonable. Argumentation is a form of communication that is reasonable. In this chapter, we examine some basic concepts in argumentation—logic and reasoning, propositions, issues, and evidence—and how these elements fit together in the production of rational communication about what is true, what is good, and what we should do to improve our circumstances.

The study of rational, persuasive communication is important because rational arguments play an important role in many contexts—the courts, legislative bodies, and public forums. It is important to recognize that rational argument plays an equally important role in less formal settings, too. It is basic to science, the classroom, and any other context where rational decision making is in order—dyads, small groups, or formal public speaking settings.

OBJECTIVES

To develop some basic concepts in argumentation

To improve understanding of the nature of logic and reasoning and their role in communication

To help develop practical skills in arguing a reasonable point of view

To sharpen critical skills in interpreting argumentative communication

TEN This chapter and the following one address a form of communication called *persuasion*. In Chapter Nine, we discussed informative communication in which the communicator's purpose is to share information about matters of fact. In persuasion, the communicator's purpose goes beyond sharing beliefs about matters of fact. The communicator seeks to influence the listener's values, attitudes, and behavior. Attempts to get the listener to vote for a political candidate or course of action, to buy a particular product, or to change judgments are examples of persuasive communication. Persuasion is still concerned with matters of fact; what distinguishes it from purely informative communication is the added emphasis on influencing values, attitudes and behavior.

We have elected to devote two chapters to persuasion, one on argumentation and one on motivation. Argumentation has to do with the logical, rational, intellectual aspects of persuasive communication—reasoning, logic, truth, issues, propositions, and evidence. The chapter on motivation deals with extralogical, extrarational appeals whose persuasive effects depend more on psychological or emotional processes than on logic and reasoning. Like the distinction between informative and persuasive communication noted in Chapter Nine, the distinction between persuasion through argument and persuasion through motivation is an arbitrary one. Appeals to reason are effective because we are motivated to evaluate communication on rational grounds. But reason is by no means the only motivating factor in persuasion, as we'll see in the following chapter.

ARGUMENTATION

An argument is a line of reasoning—a set of logically related statements designed to induce belief in the truth of a specific conclusion. *To argue* does not mean "to fight." It is unfortunate that the term is often used that way. *To argue* is to *engage in persuasive communication that appeals primarily to the rational faculties of the listener.*

No single assertion, proposition, conclusion, or statement constitutes an argument. Remember that an argument is a *line of reasoning* involving more than one statement. If we merely say "There is life on Mars," we have not made an argument. We have an argument when we offer at least one more statement showing our reason for believing the truth of the other statement, such as "We believe this because Mars changes color on parts of its surface as the Martian seasons change." We're not saying that this is a particularly good argument, but it does consist of two distinct statements, one lending logical support to the other.

An argument is said to be *valid* if its conclusion follows logically from its premises. When we communicate a set of statements that together seem reasonable, we have made a line of reasoning. The reasonableness of a set of statements depends on two factors—the *truth of the individual statements* and the *logical connections among them.* When an argument fails to persuade, it fails either because the truth of one or more statements has not been established or because the logical relationships among the statements are not valid.

LOGICAL REASONING

There are two basic types of logical reasoning: *deductive* and *inductive.* Deductive reasoning is based on the rules of formal logic. In a deductive line of reasoning, the *conclusion follows logically from its premises,* because it merely restates information that is already implied in the premises. For example, consider a simple deductive line of reasoning consisting of two premises and a conclusion, called a *syllogism*:

	All metals conduct heat.	*Major premise*
	Tin is a metal.	*Minor premise*
Therefore:	Tin conducts heat.	*Conclusion*

Notice that the conclusion of this syllogism really doesn't say anything new. What it says is already implied by the premises; it clarifies information that is already there.

When we reason deductively, we are simply arranging a series of statements so that the listener can understand how the information contained in the premises leads inevitably to the conclusion. If the premises are true, and the rules of deductive logic are followed, then the conclusion will be true. Most people know the rules of deductive logic intuitively and are able to detect faulty reasoning, especially when fairly familiar concepts are involved.

The problem in getting a listener to accept a valid deductive conclusion seldom involves his inability to understand the rules of formal logic. Rather, the problem usually has to do with gaining his acceptance of the truth of the premises, and this is usually a problem in *inductive* reasoning.

In inductive reasoning, the *conclusion derived from a set of premises always contains new information* that is not already contained in the premises. The plausibility of an inductive conclusion depends upon the number and quality of specific premises on which the general conclusion is based. We are reasoning inductively when we generalize on the bases of specific observations:

	Tin conducts heat.	
	Lead conducts heat.	
	Copper conducts heat.	*Premises based on observations*
	Iron conducts heat.	
	Silver conducts heat.	
Therefore:	All metals conduct heat.	

Notice that the conclusion, a generalization, is by no means an inevitable logical consequence of its premises. It would be if every possible metal were included in the premises; because some are missing, however, the conclusion says more than the premises do. In inductive reasoning, we can never be absolutely certain that the conclusion follows logically from the premises. The best we can expect is a fairly high level of expectation that the conclusion is a valid logical *inference*.

EVALUATING THE VALIDITY OF A LINE OF REASONING

We said earlier that a line of reasoning is valid if its conclusion follows logically from its premises. It is relatively easy to ascertain the validity of deductive reasoning, since all that is required is that the conclusion restate something implied by its premises. Inductive validity, on the other hand, is not so readily determined, since the conclusion of an inductive line of reasoning is a generalization inferred from an incomplete set of premises.

DEDUCTIVE REASONING

In the case of deductive reasoning, it is possible to judge the validity of the reasoning apart from the truth of the individual statements. Considered by itself, validity in deduction has nothing to do with the truth of the premises or conclusion.

Table 10-1 illustrates the way logical validity and truth operate independently in deductive reasoning. The quadrants of a 2 × 2 table are called cells. Cell *A* is a valid syllogism with true premises and a true conclusion. In cell *B*, both premises and the conclusion are true, but the reasoning is invalid because the conclusion is not a logical consequence of the premises. As it is written, the syllogism fails to identify the logical relationships among the terms and does not measure up as a line of reasoning even though all three statements are true.

TABLE 10-1 LOGICAL VALIDITY AND TRUTH

Truth of Conclusions	Validity of Arguments: *Valid*	Validity of Arguments: *Invalid*
True	*A* All men are mammals. Leonard Bernstein is a man. Therefore, Leonard Bernstein is a mammal.	*B* Some students are athletes. Some athletes wear glasses. Therefore, some students wear glasses.
Untrue	*C* All beagles have feathers. Charlie Brown is a beagle. Therefore, Charlie Brown has feathers.	*D* Many tennis players are men. Chris Evert Lloyd is a tennis player. Therefore, Chris Evert Lloyd is a man.

Cell *C* is a syllogism with three untrue statements, but the reasoning is valid because the conclusion follows logically from its premises. In cell *D*, both premises are true, but the conclusion is false. The syllogism itself is invalid, and in spite of the true premises, there's no guarantee of a true conclusion unless the reasoning is valid.

When confronted with a problem in determining the validity of a deductive argument, it may help to draw a *Venn diagram* — a set of overlapping circles, each of which represents all the members of a particular categorical set of objects. Figure 10-1 shows some Venn diagrams indicating the relationships implied by the premises of the syllogisms in Table 10-1.

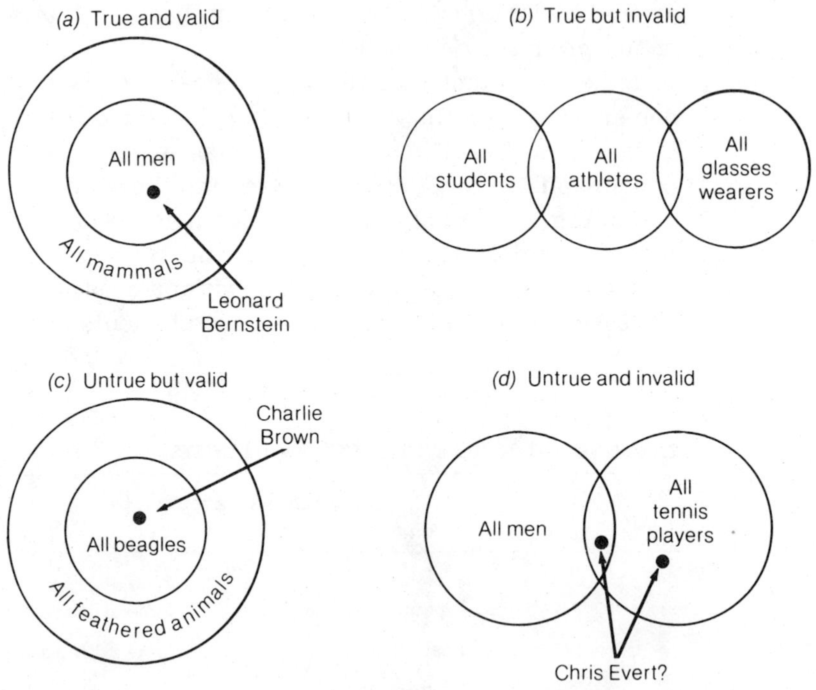

FIGURE 10-1

INDUCTIVE REASONING

Unfortunately, no one has ever been able to discover an adequate set of rules for determining with certainty when an inductive conclusion follows from its premises. There are no handy devices such as the Venn diagram to help us judge the validity of inductive reasoning, so we use informal, somewhat intuitive rules in checking inductive validity.

In general, however, the logic of induction is the logic of *probability*. When we infer something on the basis of past experience and state our inference in terms of probability, we are reasoning inductively. The validity of an inductive argument is intimately related to what we believe to be the truth of our conclusion – the degree of confidence we have that the conclusion is accurate. Suppose you find that it rains every time you invite friends over for a barbecue. You are planning a barbecue for next weekend, and you say "Chances are it will rain next weekend, since I'm giving a barbecue." This is a probability statement. If you tune in to a radio weather forecast and hear "There will be a 10 percent chance of rain over the weekend," you are hearing another probability estimate. The weather bureau's estimate is presumably more valid than yours because it is based on more careful and systematic observations, but both are inductive conclusions.

In practical argumentation, most of the difficulties a persuader encounters have to do with disagreements over probability estimates. Some probabilities can be stated in numbers. For example, the probability of drawing the ace of spades at random from a deck of cards is 1/52. The probability of drawing any ace is 4/52 or 1/13. The probability of drawing any spade is 13/52 or 1/4. Reasonable people will probably not dispute these odds.

Subjective estimates of probability are a different matter, however. If you ask ten different people what the chances are that China will attack the United States with nuclear missiles within fifteen years, you'll find a wide range of estimates. Most of the issues we argue about—in law, politics, religion, science, morality, or whatever—involve important estimates of subjective probabilities. None of us can escape the obligation to make such estimates and to base our actions on them. For example, if you are driving a car and see a child by the roadside, you must make a subjective probability estimate of the likelihood that the child will dart into your path. If you estimate wrong and hit the child, you may be accountable. If you estimate wrong about the likelihood of another car entering your path, you may not live long enough to be bothered with accountability.

When an individual is called to account for some action in a court of law, the concept of the "reasonably prudent person" is frequently used to decide whether or not the action in question is justifiable or defensible. It is assumed that there are community standards for estimating subjective probabilities, and that a defendant should be held legally accountable for failure to act in accordance with those standards. How many times have you heard statements like these offered in defense after a catastrophe:

> I didn't know the gun was loaded.
> I never expected the kid to dart out in front of my car.
> I was only kidding about hijacking. Can't you take a joke?
> I never expected that when I told them to get the information "by any means necessary" they would actually break into the office.
> I had the right-of-way after all.

Each of these statements illustrates someone's failure to make a reasonable subjective probability estimate of the consequences of some act.

Arguments over issues of public policy require many different kinds of probability estimates. Should marijuana be legalized? What are the chances that doing so would increase the abuse of more dangerous drugs? Should the United States unilaterally limit development of strategic arms? What are the chances that this would precipitate aggression by the communist superpowers? Should we permit abortion on demand? What are the chances that this would result in the abuse of abortion as a risky means of birth control? Since we have no way to assign objective probability estimates to these potential outcomes, we must base our decisions on some sort of consensus about subjective probabilities. Thus, you can see that the validity of an inductive line of reasoning depends on our confidence about the probable truth of its conclusion.

Let's consider an example. The artificial sweeteners known as cyclamates were banned in 1969 by the Food and Drug Administration because researchers found that high dosages of cyclamates can produce cancers in rats. Some opponents of the ban argue that the dosages used to induce the rat cancers were the equivalent of between one hundred and five hundred bottles of soda pop per day for humans and that therefore the probability of human cancers owing to cyclamates must be assumed to be minutely small or totally nonexistent. The FDA and certain consumer health advocates argue that the evidence shows a risk, however small, and that the ban should stand. Ask yourself these questions: Even if we knew the exact probability of contracting cancer from cyclamates in normal doses, what would you consider to be an acceptable level of risk? Since we have no such objective probability, what is your subjective estimate of the risk based on the evidence we have? To decide the validity of the FDA's argument, you must make intelligent guesses on both questions.

The persuasive force of an argument involving probability estimates depends on the quality and quantity of evidence on which the estimates are based. In a later section we discuss the nature of evidence and its role in the estimate of probabilities.

DEDUCTIVE AND INDUCTIVE ARGUMENTS

Rational argumentation would be child's play if we were equipped with an exhaustive list of major and minor premises that are true. All we would have to do is apply the rules of formal logic to tease out valid and

TOTE TICKETS PAY
ODDS
TIMER
TIME OF DAY
TOTAL
WIN
PLACE
SHOW
POST TIME
4 RACE

true conclusions. We have no such list, however, so we must base our deductive reasoning on premises inferred from inductive reasoning. In other words, it isn't possible to rely exclusively on deductive reasoning because the premises used in deduction are themselves *conclusions* based on inductive reasoning.

When you use deduction in arguing a case, just be sure that your premises are *acceptable to your listener as true* and that your logic conforms to *accepted rules of deduction*. Your conclusions should be accepted by a reasonable listener so long as you express your argument clearly. What may seem reasonable to you may not seem reasonable to someone else, however. No message is inherently true and reasonable because its meaning is *assigned* by the interpreter. Personal standards of truth and reasonableness vary, and productive argument requires that you and your listener come to a shared understanding of each other's standards for judging truth and reason.

When resorting to inductive arguments, an unavoidable strategy, you have two major tasks to accomplish. First, you must convince the listener that your probability estimates are reasonably accurate. You need not bother with numerical estimates unless you have a good basis for calculation. Just give the listener an indication of how sure you are of your points. "I believe it is highly likely that . . ." is preferable to "The probability is .84 . . ." in most situations because such precise objective probabilities cannot be ascertained. Second, you must convince the listener that your estimates constitute either a high and dangerous level of risk or a desirable level of gain with respect to whatever you are talking about. Suppose you knew that even one bottle of soda pop sweetened with cyclamates produces a 10 percent increase in the chance of contracting cancer. By itself, this information may not convince your listener to avoid cyclamates. Only if he personally considers this figure to represent an unacceptable risk will he avoid the offending agent. Or suppose you could convince the listener that a 10 percent increase in defense spending could reduce the risk of war by 20 percent. Only if your listener finds this cost/benefit ratio acceptable will he join you in advocating the increase.

This is why it is important, when you reason inductively, to know what a listener already believes about the probabilities involved. There's not much point in trying to convince people of something they already believe. Spend your time speaking to the probability estimates on which you disagree.

In practice, most arguments take the forms of *categorical*, *causal*, or *analogical* reasoning. Almost all categorical reasoning is deductive. Its purpose is to identify the membership of events or ideas in various categories. All the syllogisms discussed earlier include examples of categorical reasoning. Causal reasoning is inductive and consists in describing and explaining events and phenomena in terms of cause-effect relationships. There are some serious philosophical and methodological problems involved in causal reasoning, but constructing an argument without it is almost impossible.

An analogy is a figurative illustration in which the properties of a familiar object or event are used to describe or explain the properties of a less familiar object or event. We are using analogical reasoning, for example, if we describe the flow of electricity through a wire as being similar to the flow of water through a pipe. Analogical reasoning is an exceptionally powerful rhetorical technique because it takes advantage of the familiar in explaining the unfamiliar. It is also highly susceptible to abuse, however, because it is easy to find common analogies for almost any situation, but difficult to find analogies that do not fall apart under careful scrutiny. Analogical reasoning is purely inductive.

An analogy is a reasonable argumentative device if and only if two conditions are met: (1) the analog (familiar object) corresponds on all important features with the object, event, or phenomenon of interest, and (2) the analog introduces no irrelevant but potentially misleading features for which there are no meaningful correspondences in the object of interest.

Try these two tests on the following analogies:

A woman without a man is like a fish without a bicycle.

Breakfast without orange juice is like a day without sunshine.

Permitting students to participate in university governance is like letting the inmates run the asylum.

The energy crisis constitutes the moral equivalent of war.

Capital punishment is tantamount to institutionalized murder.

Laws making marijuana possession a crime are as foolish as the Eighteenth Amendment to the U.S. Constitution (prohibition).

Of these three types of arguments, the categorical variety is probably the most rational, and analogical arguments are the least rational. The more rational forms are not necessarily more persuasive. The persuasiveness of an argument does not simply result from logical rigor.

To illustrate these three types of arguments, let's turn to a topic that produces vigorous argumentation in contemporary society—abortion.

Below are some arguments frequently advanced on this topic. We offer them as examples only, and not because we necessarily agree with any of them.

Categorical Argument Abortion is murder, since murder is defined in the law as the willful and premeditated taking of a human life, and a human embryo is certainly both living and human.

Causal Argument The availability of abortion-on-demand fosters irresponsible behavior in the form of failure to take adequate precautions to avoid unwanted pregnancies.

Analogical Argument A human embryo is not a person just as a kernel of corn is not a plant. An embryo, like a seed, is a set of plans for a person. To abort an embryo is no different in principle from preventing any given sperm cell and ovum from getting together in the first place.

Whatever your views may be on the reasonableness of these arguments, it may be helpful for you at this point to analyze the reasoning in them. Before you read on, take a few minutes to dissect each argument, and try to create rebuttal arguments for each one.

An argument is not the same as a fully developed persuasive speech or essay. A fully developed speech consists of many arguments, not just one. An argument is a logically coherent subunit of a speech—like a single girder or span in a bridge—leading to the persuader's major conclusion. The persuader who expects to lead listeners to the conclusion must be sure that the bridge is complete. A missing argument may weaken the bridge or make the crossing impossible.

PROPOSITIONS

Persuasive communication is motivated by the persuader's perception of some basis of disagreement with the listener. The persuader must discover that basis if the disagreement is to be resolved through argument. A proposition is the most important conclusion in a line of reasoning, the argument. There are three basic types of proposition: propositions of *fact*, propositions of *value*, and propositions of *policy*. When you wish to persuade someone, then, you must find out whether your disagreement is over facts, values, or policies. If you disagree over facts, then your arguments should be based on observable evidence. If you disagree over values, then your arguments should speak to likes and dislikes that you share with your listener. If your disagreement is over policies, then your arguments should address the rationality of your prescription in light of the listener's knowledge of the facts and his or her value judgments.

PROPOSITIONS OF FACT

A proposition of fact is a statement about reality – about some observable feature of the world around us. When used in this context, the word *fact* does not necessarily impart truth or accuracy to a statement. Rather, it indicates only that the statement can be verified by observation. "There is a unicorn in the garden" is a proposition of fact even though it is untrue. It is a proposition of fact because we would check its accuracy by looking in the garden. Scientific theories are arguments involving statements of fact, since the truth of a theoretical statement is verified through observation.

PROPOSITIONS OF VALUE

Propositions of value are statements about what is good or bad, right or wrong, just or unjust, beautiful or ugly. They signify someone's feelings about something – someone's likes and dislikes. To say that cigaret smoking causes cancer is to state a proposition of fact. A statement that cigaret smoking is *bad* because it causes cancer is a proposition of value.

Sometimes it is difficult to distinguish between propositions of fact and value. For example, you might assert that Bob Dylan is a better singer than John Denver or the other way around. To support your view, you might point to some observable evidence such as record sales or the critical judgments of respected music critics. You should be aware, though, that your evidence in this case would consist of indicators of the likes and dislikes of selected individuals. There is a subtle but important difference between statements of *fact about likes and dislikes* and the judgmental statements themselves. The latter are propositions of value.

PROPOSITIONS OF POLICY

Propositions of policy call for action. Statements of fact *describe what is*, statements of value *appraise what is good or bad*, and statements of policy *prescribe what should be*. Our propositions of policy are based on what we say about what is true and what is good. "Cigaret smoking should be outlawed" is an example of a proposition of policy. *Any* statement that prescribes is a proposition of policy.

ISSUES

It is impossible to conduct a rational inquiry or to advocate a rational point of view without identifying an intelligent question about the topic under consideration. Such a question is called an *issue*. An issue is not the same thing as a topic or subject. An issue is a question about the topic that must be answered satisfactorily before a decision about the topic can be reached. The three types of issues correspond to the three types of propositions: issues of fact, value, and policy. When you argue an issue, you must be prepared to provide reasonable answers to these three types of questions: What are the facts? What is good or bad about these facts? And what should we *do* about the situation?

Whenever you enter into persuasive argument, whatever your purpose, you must speak to the issues of concern to your listeners. Make it your first order of business to clearly identify the issues that need to be addressed – the questions your message must answer to gain listeners' acceptance. Never lose sight of the fact that it is the listeners who ultimately decide what issues need to be resolved and what constitutes a satisfactory answer to questions of fact, value, and policy. One of the worst obstacles to rational persuasive communication is the failure to identify the issues over which the participants disagree.

EVIDENCE

Evidence is anything offered to prove, support, or gain a listener's belief in a conclusion or claim. It is information calculated to influence beliefs. In the legal context, a clear distinction is drawn between the evidence presented in a trial, and the attorneys' arguments, which are interpre-

tations of the evidence and appear at the end of the trial after the evidence has been presented. Jurors are instructed that their decisions must be based on the evidence, and the evidence alone, and that attorneys' arguments are not evidence, but interpretations of the evidence with which the jurors may choose to agree or not.

Evidence used in any argumentative context may take many forms — statements made orally or in writing by authoritative sources, statements made by persons who made first-hand observations of events in question, graphs, charts, and other visual aids, and even actual objects such as documents, artifacts, or even persons. The persuasive impact of evidence depends primarily on three factors: (1) the evidence itself, (2) where it comes from, and (3) the receiver's willingness to believe the claim for which the evidence provides logical support. The evidence itself must have a clear bearing on the claim; it must be relevant. It must be self-consistent and uncontradictory. It must be understandable to the listener, and it must provide him with material reasons for believing in the claim.

The source of the evidence must be reliable. For example, where the evidence consists of someone's testimony about personal observations, the testifying person must be a competent, trustworthy person who is not motivated to distort or misrepresent the facts he has observed or the meanings he has assigned to his observations. Frequently, where technical inferences are involved, the source's credibility requires a high level of special training or expertise.

Finally, and perhaps most important, the evidence must meet the listeners' needs. To be convinced, different listeners will require different kinds of evidence, in terms of both quality and quantity. If the listener is initially disposed to accept the claim, it may take very little evidence to cause him to believe it. If he is initially disposed to deny the claim, no amount of evidence may change his mind. This makes it imperative that the persuader know as much as possible about his audience so that he can tailor his message to their requirements for proof.

Below are some tests of evidence summarized from Freeley (1971, 97–110). We have found them useful in preparing persuasive arguments and evaluating the arguments of other speakers.

1. Does *enough* evidence exist to support the conclusion?
2. Is the evidence *clear* to the audience? Are most receivers likely to understand it quickly and easily, especially in terms of what conclusions the evidence is intended to support?
3. Is the evidence *consistent*? Is it *externally* consistent with other information that exists? (Does other evidence tend to corroborate

or refute the evidence in question?) Is it *internally* consistent? (For example, does the first part of an eyewitness' account jibe with later parts of his same story?)

4. Is the evidence *verifiable*? Can a speaker go back to original sources to check on the accuracy of statistics, examples, or testimony? Can someone other than the speaker, like a political opponent or a member of the audience, gain access to the same information?
5. Is the source of the evidence *competent*? Has printed material from which examples or statistics are taken come from someone qualified? Is testimony given by someone who observed and was mentally and physically able to report that observation accurately, or whose background equips him or her to provide competent opinions?
6. Is the source of the evidence *reliable*? Is someone who testified trustworthy, truthful, and unbiased? Do printed materials have a good reputation for fairness and thoroughness?
7. Is the evidence *relevant*? Does it support the conclusions that the speaker claims it supports? Does it lead logically and directly to the conclusion?
8. Is the evidence *statistically sound*? Are statistical criteria followed rigorously—such as accuracy, appropriate classification, valid sampling procedures, statistically significant results, reporting in context, and fair visual representations?
9. Is the evidence *recent* or current? This judgment is obviously relative; it depends on the topic. A business executive, attempting to persuade colleagues to adopt a particular investment program, needs up-to-the-minute statistics. In contrast, an advocate for prison reform might need not only reasonably recent evidence about current conditions, but may also use historical materials about past failures in the system.
10. Is the evidence *adaptive* to the information and interest levels of the receivers? Sometimes a speaker with the same topic and purpose must use significantly different supporting materials when speaking to different audiences, like the anti-smoking advocate who used primarily statistical evidence with a group of older smokers, and used extended illustrations with a teen-age group.

The selection and use of convincing evidence requires exceptional analytical skill and judgment. We frequently hear people remark, "Let the facts speak for themselves." The assumption here is that some facts, in and of themselves, lead to self-evident truths about a situation. It is important to distinguish between statements of fact and *inferences* based on statements of fact. An inference is a conclusion based on observation; it is not the observation itself or a purely descriptive report of the observation.

Consider the following hypothetical case: John Jones is found dead with a gunshot wound to the head. Jones' next-door neighbor discovers Bill Smith standing over the corpse holding a smoking revolver with one bullet expended. The discovery is made thirty seconds after the neighbor hears the shot. Had anyone else fled the scene between the time of the shot and the discovery of Smith over the body, the neighbor would have crossed paths with the fleeing party. Here we have strong evidence that Smith shot Jones.

Do the facts speak for themselves? They do not. Facts never speak for themselves in the sense that they point conclusively to the truth of a single inference. If you examine the above circumstances carefully, you will find that no one fact in the case leads conclusively to the inference that Smith killed Jones. Not until all the facts are interpreted collectively to provide a reasonable reconstruction of the event could we make a plausible case against Smith. Even then, the plausible reconstruction is by no means self-evident.

Any case against Smith would be based on circumstantial evidence and would require inductive reasoning. Are you willing to accept the truth of a major premise that says "A person found with a gun over a recently shot corpse is the person who pulled the trigger?" Of course not.

In fact, it was later determined that Smith had not fired the gun that killed Jones. It turned out that Smith was Jones' minister. Jones had telephoned Smith announcing his intention to commit suicide, and Smith had rushed to Jones' apartment to prevent the deed. How do we know this to be the case? Smith so testified to the police and later at the coroner's inquest. Jones had been a member of Smith's parish for many years. According to other parishioners, the two men had been close friends. Furthermore, police investigators found no motive on Smith's part for killing Jones. At the coroner's inquest, Smith proved a highly credible and competent witness, and his version of the shooting was accepted. Thus, the final verdict on the circumstances of Jones' death was based on Smith's testimonial evidence about what he directly observed.

To help back up Smith's story, another neighbor testified that he had seen Smith running to the scene of the killing moments before the shot was fired. Usually, wrongdoers are seen running *from* the scene of their crime. Here, inductive reasoning by analogy helped support Smith's story.

We use rational argument when we need to reconstruct something that happened in the past that can no longer be observed, when we are trying to interpret the meaning of our present observations, or when we are predicting what will happen in the future. We base our judgments on available evidence gained through observation. We are faced with a question for which there is no simple answer: How much and what kind of evidence is required to prove a statement of fact that is inferential* —that is, not verifiable through immediate and direct observation? There is no simple formula that provides an answer to this question.

Bear in mind that inferences based on inductive reasoning are not absolute truths. They are *decisions*. The best we can expect is that decisions based on good evidence and reasoning will be true. What we call truth is nothing more than what we *decide to believe*.

THE STRUCTURE OF ARGUMENT

When you have some occasion to put together a rational persuasive message, you must accomplish each of the following objectives:

1. Clearly and concisely identify the crucial issues to be addressed.
2. Show how each issue is related to the major issue at hand.
3. Establish a definite claim about every issue.
4. Support each claim with convincing evidence—evidence that is relevant, substantive, self-consistent, credible, and sufficient to the requirements of the audience. *Document your sources!*
5. Demonstrate the logical connections between each piece of evidence and the claim it supports.
6. Organize your message so that the arguments presented build on one another to form a logically coherent whole.

Failure to accomplish any one of these objectives is likely to result in a failure to persuade. If your message reflects careful attention to each objective, it is likely that you will be judged a competent and rational communicator. You may not achieve your persuasive purpose, but you will win respect for your position and your rationality.

*Speaking of requirements for proof, you might be interested to learn that, two weeks after the coroner's inquest ruled the death of John Jones a suicide, the Reverend Mr. Smith ran off to South America with Jones' widow.

Toulmin (1958) has developed a structural model of argumentation that is useful in preparing and evaluating rational persuasion. By now, you should be familiar with most of its components. It has six major ones and is applicable to both inductive and deductive lines of reasoning. The components are as follows:

Data Data are statements about evidence and serve as premises. *Data* and *evidence* are synonymous terms. In an argument, data are statements that are generally acceptable to the interpreter without additional proof, offered to provide logical support for a conclusion or claim that does require additional proof.

Warrant A warrant is a connecting premise, such as the minor premise in a syllogism, showing the logical connection between a piece of data and its corresponding claim. The warrant justifies, or shows the reasonableness, of inferring the claim from the data.

Claim A claim is simply a conclusion — a statement requiring proof.

Backing Backing consists of statements providing support for the warrant in a line of reasoning, where the warrant itself requires additional explanation or proof.

Rebuttal or Reservation A rebuttal is a reservation about the warrant, showing how the data and the warrant could conceivably lead to an alternative claim other than the one being advanced. Usually, the rebuttal is a statement anticipating conditions under which, given the data and the warrant, the claim would not logically follow.

Qualifier A qualifier is a word or phrase in the argument indicating the degree of certainty of the persuader's belief in the claim. The qualifier discloses the persuader's probability estimate that the claim is true.

Let's look at some different kinds of arguments analyzed with Toulmin's model.

You can see from the illustrations in Figure 10-2 how the Toulmin model can be used to diagram the logical flow of an argument from premises to conclusions. The model is not a formula for structuring a fully elaborated argumentative speech, but it should help you to organize your thinking about a topic and developing lines of reasoning from available evidence. It can assist you in discovering issues needing consideration and help you anticipate potential rebuttals to your claims.

The most important component in the Toulmin model is the warrant. It is the warrant that provides the logical connection between data

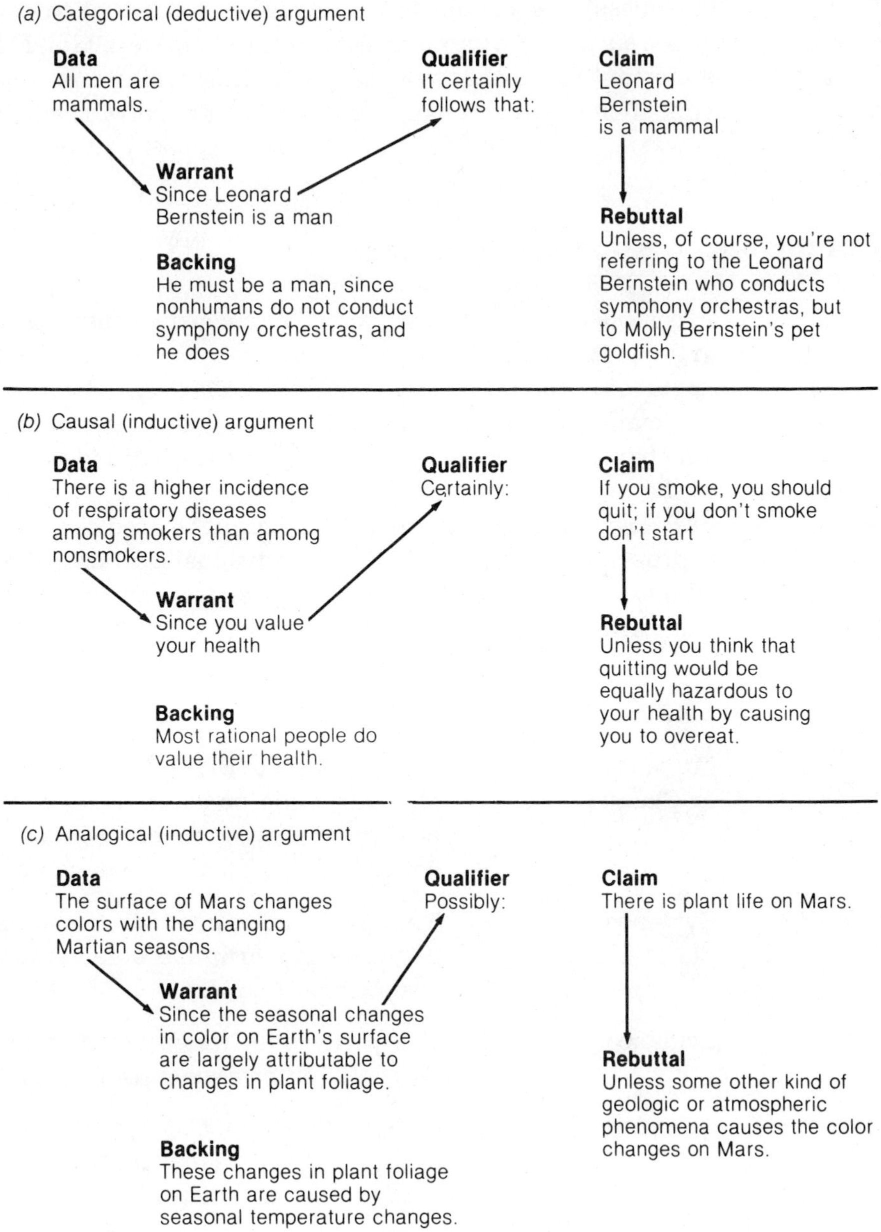
(a) Categorical (deductive) argument
Data
All men are mammals.
Qualifier
It certainly follows that:
Claim
Leonard Bernstein is a mammal
Warrant
Since Leonard Bernstein is a man
Backing
He must be a man, since nonhumans do not conduct symphony orchestras, and he does
Rebuttal
Unless, of course, you're not referring to the Leonard Bernstein who conducts symphony orchestras, but to Molly Bernstein's pet goldfish.
(b) Causal (inductive) argument
Data
There is a higher incidence of respiratory diseases among smokers than among nonsmokers.
Qualifier
Certainly:
Claim
If you smoke, you should quit; if you don't smoke don't start
Warrant
Since you value your health
Rebuttal
Unless you think that quitting would be equally hazardous to your health by causing you to overeat.
Backing
Most rational people do value their health.
(c) Analogical (inductive) argument
Data
The surface of Mars changes colors with the changing Martian seasons.
Qualifier
Possibly:
Claim
There is plant life on Mars.
Warrant
Since the seasonal changes in color on Earth's surface are largely attributable to changes in plant foliage.
Rebuttal
Unless some other kind of geologic or atmospheric phenomena causes the color changes on Mars.
Backing
These changes in plant foliage on Earth are caused by seasonal temperature changes.

FIGURE 10-2

(premises) and conclusions. Arguments that fail to convince usually lack a sufficient warrant linking the data to the claim. Moving from one statement to another through reasoning is like crossing a logical canyon. If the listeners can't find the bridge, show them the way!

THE RATIONAL PERSUASIVE SPEECH

A complete persuasive speech may consist of many arguments. Each argument must stand as a logically coherent subunit of the speech. No arguments should be included unless they contribute to the support of the main idea being advanced in the speech; similarly, no argument may be omitted that is required to prove the main idea to the satisfaction of the target listeners.

Below are some arguments that might be used in a speech advocating a proposition of policy—"that additional standards be imposed for admission to practice of trial law, above and beyond the successful completion of state bar examinations."

ARGUMENT

Contention or Claim:	Every citizen of the United States who enters into civil litigation or is brought to trial on criminal charges is entitled to representation by competent counsel.
Evidence:	The Sixth Amendment to the Constitution guarantees a criminal defendant the right to assistance of counsel.
Evidence:	The Fourteenth Amendment guarantees the citizen "due process of law."
Evidence:	Citation of several Supreme Court decisions based on the Sixth and Fourteenth Amendments which apply to concrete situations.

The issue addressed here is "What are the rights of U.S. citizens respecting representation by an attorney in courts of law?" The claim advanced may need more or less support in the form of elaboration of the evidence, depending upon the audience. For example, a group of judges and lawyers may already be familiar enough with the Constitution and with recent applicable Supreme Court cases to warrant a cursory review of the evidence, but a lay audience may need more detailed and fully documented information about their rights.

ARGUMENT

Contention or Claim:	In recent years there have been numerous cases in which trial lawyers have performed inadequately in representing their clients in the trial courts.
Evidence:	Public comments by such authoritative sources as F. Lee Bailey and Chief Justice Warren Burger.
Evidence:	Increased incidence of appellate reversals of trial court verdicts based on grounds of incompetent or inadequate representation by counsel.

The issue addressed by this argument is absolutely essential to the purpose of the speech—"Is there a need for change?" Several subordinate issues may need to be addressed to advance an adequate answer to this question, including the specific question posed here—"Has the performance of trial court lawyers met the standards implied by the U.S. Constitution?"

Once again, depending on what the audience knows about the claim and the evidence used to support it, the evidence may need further elaboration. For most persons, F. Lee Bailey and Warren Burger are familiar names and recognized as credible authorities on jurisprudence, but for some, mere reference to their views on the subject may not be persuasive. Similarly, some listeners may require additional support for the evidence cited on the increased incidence of appellate reversals, perhaps in the form of actual cases and the citation of sources in which the listeners can find the court opinions.

ARGUMENT

Contention or Claim:	Law school training alone does not equip an individual with the skills necessary for competent trial practice.

Evidence:	Survey of law school curricula showing that law students receive minimal training in trial advocacy; law students spend most of their time reading and listening to lectures, and very little time arguing cases in moot court settings.
Evidence:	Great Britain has long recognized the different skills demanded of the trial lawyer, and provides different training for barristers (trial lawyers) and solicitors (office lawyers).

Here again, the argument speaks to the issue of the need for change. The specific question is whether or not our law schools provide adequate trial law instruction. Note that even if our evidence gains the listener's acceptance of the claim, we still haven't proved that there's anything wrong with our law schools. That's another issue entirely, and one which we may or may not choose to address, depending on our best estimate of the solution to the problem posed.

We still haven't proposed a solution to the problem, although we've implied that one way to deal with the problem is to augment law school instruction in trial advocacy. But there might be a better way to solve the problem, for example, by requiring trial lawyers to complete an internship program similar to that required of medical doctors. It might not even be necessary to advocate a plan for solution to the problem. Remember that the policy proposition advocated refers only to "additional standards . . . for admission to trial law practice," and says nothing about how these standards might be implemented. This exemplifies the importance of clearly specifying the purpose of the speech, preferably in a single proposition of fact, value, or policy that points directly to specific issues needing attention.

A persuasive speech on the above proposition would need to include arguments on additional issues. It might be useful for you to do two things after you've finished the last few pages of this chapter: (1) Make a complete list of the issues you believe are relevant to this proposition, and (2) create arguments on these issues, perhaps using the Toulmin model to diagram your reasoning.

As with any kind of speech, the persuasive speech must be organized in such a way as to help the listener understand it. A logical progression of statements helps a listener remember, and a speech that is remembered is more likely to be accepted than one that is forgotten.

Above all, remember that the meaning of a message is assigned by the listener. In persuasion, this means that the reasonableness of a persuasive speech depends on the critical criteria of those hearing the speech and is not something that is inherent in the message itself. A poorly designed and delivered message may be effective with uncritical listeners, but a critical listener may reject even a very sound conclusion if it is based on sloppy reasoning.

When you wish to communicate rationally, there is one very important principle to keep in mind. Rational communication is not just a matter of finding the right answer or reaching the correct conclusion. What matters is how you get there.

SUMMARY

Argumentation is persuasive communication that appeals to reason. An argument is a line of reasoning — a set of logically related statements. Lines of reasoning take two basic forms, called inductive and deductive. Deductive reasoning yields conclusions that merely restate information implied by a set of premises, while inductive reasoning produces conclusions containing new information.

A line of reasoning may be evaluated against two criteria: logical validity and truth. Reasoning is valid when a conclusion follows logically from its premises. Thus, validity is a criterion applicable to entire arguments. Truth, on the other hand, must be determined individually for each premise and the conclusion in an argument. Truth and validity can be evaluated independently of one another. That is, an argument may be valid, but untrue. Similarly, a set of statements may be true but not a valid argument because the statements are not logically related.

The statements that comprise an argument are called propositions, of which there are three types: propositions of fact, value, and policy. Propositions of fact can be verified by observation. Propositions of value signify likes and dislikes. Propositions of policy signify prescribed courses of action. When arguable questions are posed about facts, values, or policies, these questions are called issues.

Evidence is anything offered as a statement of fact to prove a proposition. The effectiveness of evidence as proof depends on the nature of the evidence itself, its origin, and a given interpreter's willingness to accept the evidence in the context of a particular issue.

Toulmin's model of argument is a useful tool for designing and evaluating the structure of arguments. It is applicable to both deductive and inductive lines of reasoning. The model permits a systematic analysis of the logical structure of rational speech communication.

QUESTIONS

1. What is the difference between inductive and deductive reasoning?
2. What is the difference between a topic and an issue?
3. Can you think of any evidence that would enable you to assign probability estimates about the occurrence of the following events:
   a. Worldwide zero population growth by the year 2000
   b. A nuclear war by 1990
   c. Manned exploration of Mars before 1990
   d. A cure for most forms of cancer by 1985
   e. The likelihood of a snowfall in Denver during the month of June
   f. That Lee Harvey Oswald acted alone in the assassination of John F. Kennedy
4. Name the components of Toulmin's model of argumentation and explain the function of each component.
5. Identify and describe as many different communication contexts as you can in which argumentation plays a vital role.

SUGGESTED READINGS

Beardsley, Monroe C. *Thinking straight*, 3rd ed. Englewood Cliffs, N.J.: Prentice-Hall, 1966.

Bettinghaus, Erwin P. *Message preparation: the nature of proof.* Indianapolis: Bobbs-Merrill, 1966.

Fearnside, W. Ward, and William B. Holther. *Fallacy: the counterfeit of argument.* Englewood Cliffs, N.J.: Prentice-Hall, 1959.

Freeley, Austin. *Argumentation and debate*, 3rd ed. Belmont, Calif.: Wadsworth, 1971.

Huff, Darrell, and Irving Geis. *How to lie with statistics.* New York: W. W. Norton, 1954.

Kahane, Howard. *Logic and contemporary rhetoric*. Belmont, Calif.: Wadsworth, 1971.
Sherwood, John C. *Discourse of reason*. New York: Harper & Row, 1964.

11

PERSUASION AND MOTIVATION

PREVIEW

Human beings are rational animals; we like to base our behavior on good reasons. We are also rationalizing animals; we often find good reasons *after* we've gone ahead and done what we please.

This chapter examines persuasion in terms of human motivation, which utlimately determines the success or failure of persuasive communication. First we discuss the nature of beliefs, attitudes, and values and how they influence behavior. Following that, we review the relationships between reasoning and emotion and review how our behavioral choices are influenced by both. Human tendencies that affect our reasoning, but fall outside the domain of purely rational processes, are also identified and discussed. Next we show the relationship between persuasive effectiveness and the fulfillment of needs, and finally, we try to persuade you to apply these ideas when you undertake to persuade others.

OBJECTIVES

To familiarize you with some basic concepts in the psychology of persuasion

To extend your understanding of the role of logic and reasoning in the context of other motivational factors in persuasion

To offer some practical advice on persuasive strategies and tactics

To help you understand the persuasive tactics of others who attempt to influence your behavior through persuasion

ELEVEN In the previous chapter, we defined argumentation as a form of persuasion having to do with logical, rational, intellectual aspects of communication. This chapter approaches persuasion from the broader perspective of its motivational bases.

Persuasion is more than logic and reasoning, the ingredients of argumentation, because human beings are more than calculating machines. We have desires and values. We seek gratifying forms of stimulation—intellectual, emotional, and physical. Unlike computers, we fight against being turned off, both literally and figuratively. We have needs, some biological and some created spontaneously by our own efforts.

We also have some extrarational response tendencies—patterns of thinking and feeling and acting that cannot be explained in terms of our ability to calculate logically. As creators of persuasive communication for the consumption of others, and as consumers of persuasion created by others, we must develop our understanding of these extrarational processes along with the development of our reasoning skills.

In the mid-1960's, the TV program "Star Trek" gained enormous popularity and enjoyed a long run. Today, the series still gathers a large following as it is rerun over and over again. Most of you are familiar with Mr. Spock, the logical, rational Vulcan-human, whose computer-like mind is often bewildered by the emotional side of his purely human shipmates. Spock is a character whose behavior in the series is attributable entirely to the logical stuff of our last chapter. Or is it?

Presumably, Mr. Spock is a creature without emotions—a purely rational fellow whose deductions and actions are governed entirely by logical rules. He is free of the emotional foibles of his human comrades. He regards their human emotionality as a weakness. There is irony in Spock, however. Perhaps because he is a creation of human writers unable to conceive of a purely logical creature, perhaps because he is half-earthling, or perhaps because there can be no such thing as a purely logical lifeform, Spock frequently displays subtle clues to the emotional side of his makeup. "Interesting!" and "fascinating!" may be the most emotional terms in his vocabulary, but his use of these terms tells us he is a creature of values, just as we humans are. He values logic! He likes reasoning! And so do we.

Spock displays several other characteristics that we usually attribute to basic human values and emotions. He is loyal, dedicated to his work and his friends; his shipmates are not merely co-workers, but friends. To be sure, he is quick to argue the rationality of his loyalty, his dedication, and his treatment of others, but he is not a value-free individual. Deep down he is motivated by value premises, primitive beliefs about what is good and bad.

We ordinary humans, of course, are governed by our values. We are motivated to pursue valued goals and to adhere to preferred standards of behavior in achieving those goals. Like Spock, most of us tend to place a high value on logical, rational decision making, although not all of us to the same degree. Some of us are more deliberative and analytical, while others are more intuitive and impulsive. We have different styles of meeting life, styles of thinking, feeling, and acting, and these differences reflect our basic values. Persuasive communication is effective only when it adapts to these differences and takes advantage of them. Persuasive communication tailored exclusively to persons with the inclinations of Mr. Spock will influence very few "mere humans."

THE ELEMENTS OF MOTIVATION

A persuader is rarely content to believe that his message will influence only the beliefs, attitudes, and values of his audience. Such influence is a means to an end, but not the end itself. Ultimately, the persuader is concerned with the practical consequences of his message—its effects on the *behavior* of the audience. The success of his message is measured by *feedback*, in this case, *changes* in the behavior of the audience. The politician looks at behavior in opinion polls and election results. The advertiser looks at sales.

When your goal is to persuade, state your goal explicitly in terms of the behavior you want your listener to adopt. For example, if you want to simply change the listener's mind about some issue of fact, make it your goal to get the listener to declare verbally his new belief. Seeking such a behavioral objective serves two purposes: First, it increases the chance that the persuasive effect will persist; second, it gives you some feedback on your effectiveness.

DEFINITIONS—BELIEFS, VALUES, ATTITUDES

Your listeners will decide whether or not to behave according to your prescription on the basis of their beliefs, attitudes, and values. Thus, your message must appeal to these motivating elements, as well as to the behavior changes you seek to induce. Following are some definitions of key terms.

Beliefs Beliefs are intrapersonal statements—basic units of what we commonly call "thinking." Unexpressed beliefs are private, purely intrapersonal statements about reality as each of us perceives it. When expressed publicly in speech or writing, they are called *opinions*. Just as a sentence represents a relationship between subject and object, beliefs represent *perceived relationships* between subjects or between a subject and one or more of its attributes. Each of our beliefs is characterized by a degree of confidence in its truth—the probability we assign to its accuracy. Virtually any idea that can be expressed as a declarative statement beginning with "I believe that . . ." is a belief.

As defined here, even those things that we "know for certain" are beliefs, as are all those things we accept tentatively with varying degrees of assurance. All of these statements are expressions of beliefs:

> The sun rises in the east and sets in the west.
>
> God exists.
>
> Every action is accompanied by a reaction, equal in force and opposite in direction.
>
> All behavior communicates.
>
> Murder is wrong.
>
> John will be late for our meeting.

Values Values are beliefs that are evaluative or judgmental in nature. When expressed verbally, they include value terms such as *good*, *bad*, *right*, *wrong*, *just*, *unjust*, *pleasant*, or *unpleasant*. Most individuals have a relatively small number of basic values, perhaps as few as ten or twenty, but these basic values form a core of judgmental beliefs that may be relevant to thousands of other beliefs. For example, if you have a basic value that might be called "reverence for all living creatures," this value will bear directly on many related beliefs, ranging from beliefs about weapons and war to beliefs about pesticides and pollution.

Attitudes Attitudes are clusters of fact and value beliefs relevant to some central object of judgment, called an *attitude object*. *Values* included within the cluster determine the favorability of the attitude object. These clusters of beliefs may be thought of as general likes and dislikes, and serve as predispositions to behave in somewhat consistent and predictable ways toward their objects. Virtually anything that can be named can be an attitude object—material objects, ideas, or events.

For example, consider flying (in airplanes) as an attitude object. An individual holding a favorable attitude toward flying is one whose beliefs about flying, taken together, are consistent with the individual's basic values, goals, and objectives. Such an individual might typically hold the following beliefs:

1. I believe that my life is worth preserving. *Value belief.*
2. I believe that my time is worth conserving. *Value belief.*
3. I believe that flying (as a means of transportation) can help me conserve time. *Fact belief.*
4. I believe that pleasurable activities are worth pursuing. *Value belief.*
5. I like flying. *Value belief.*
6. I believe that flying is a sufficiently safe form of transportation, among the available alternatives. *Fact belief.*
7. I believe that flying is an economically competitive mode of transportation for a person with my responsibilities and resources. *Fact belief.*

This is obviously not an exhaustive list of an individual's beliefs that are relevant to flying as an attitude object. Each one suggests the existence of other beliefs about related objects and issues, such as travel, safety, the efficient use of time, costs, and so on. Nonetheless, this small list of representative beliefs suggests a consistent attitude toward flying, one that would predispose the individual to fly in airplanes in the pursuit of his or her goals.

Now consider another individual who is deathly afraid of flying. It is likely that such an individual will seek out evidence for factual beliefs consistent with this fear, such as:

8. I believe that airline safety practices are inadequate.
9. I believe that airplane travel is excessively expensive.
10. I believe that most pilots are basically daredevils.
11. I believe that there are many flaws in the FAA's air traffic control procedures.
12. I believe that airplane manufacturers frequently make major mistakes in aircraft design.

Such a cluster of beliefs constitutes an unfavorable attitude toward flying, predisposing the individual to avoid flying.

The Venn diagram depicts the relationships among the concepts *beliefs*, *attitudes*, and *values*. As you can see, a person's beliefs, both

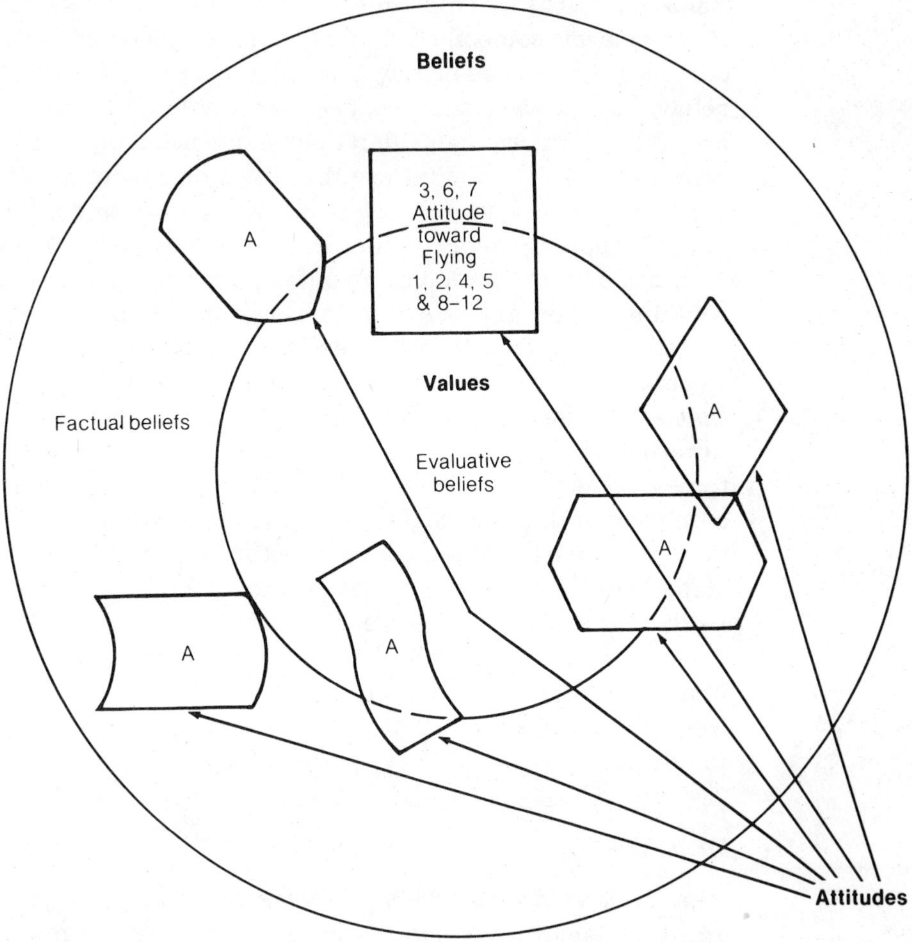

FIGURE 11-1
Numbers refer to belief statements about flying on page 302.

factual and evaluative, can cluster in limitless combinations to form attitudes, and the number of attitudes that may form is enormous. Each individual's system of attitudes is unique, since the combination of beliefs that comprises it is a product of individual experience. It is also clear that each individual's conception of what is *relevant* to a given attitude object or topic is likely to differ from anyone else's conception of relevance.

Behavior Broadly defined, behavior is anything that people do that is observable by someone else. The unit of behavior is the *act*. Beliefs, attitudes, and values held by an individual are not observable to others; behaviors are. We cannot see, hear, feel, taste, or smell beliefs, attitudes, and values, but we can infer their existence from the ways in which people behave. Do you believe that littering is wrong? If so, there's no way for anyone else to know it unless you act to disclose your belief, either by saying so or by taking pains not to litter. Whether you state your belief as an opinion or go out of your way to deposit trash in trash containers, you are behaving in a way that indicates your beliefs.

Attributing beliefs, attitudes, and values on the basis of indirect evidence often results in errors. For example, it is absurd to conclude that all military personnel like killing or have favorable attitudes toward war simply because they have chosen to serve in the armed forces. Some persons fly in airplanes in spite of enormous fear of doing so, choosing the better of two unattractive alternatives. (Perhaps they're even more fearful of seasickness, yet must travel overseas.) Too, direct statements of belief are not always reliable indicators of what people really think and feel. People lie, even to themselves. The only way to draw reliable inferences about what a person really believes is to observe him over a period of time long enough to determine whether his verbalized opinions are consistent with his behavior with respect to the beliefs in question.

ORIGINS

We are not born with beliefs, attitudes, and values. Nor are we born with all the behavioral repertory and patterns of a mature adult. These are acquired in the process of maturation, and are profoundly influenced by our interactions with other people in symbolic communication.

It seems obvious that a person's behavior is motivated by his beliefs, attitudes, and values. Less obvious but just as reasonable is the proposition that our beliefs are consequences of habitual behavior (Bem, 1970, 54). For example, consider public speaking as an attitude object about which an individual may form beliefs. Have you ever known anyone who never makes speeches but truly believes that public speaking is an enjoyable and important activity? Probably not. Many, if not most, people are initially frightened about public speaking and develop favorable beliefs about speaking only after they have given some speeches and discovered some form of personal satisfaction in doing so. The behavior occurs *prior* to the formation of favorable beliefs about the topic. A little reflection about some of your own favorite activities and how they came to be favorites will reinforce this point.

Recall the individual whose fear of flying was justified in terms of beliefs about its inherent dangers. Frequently, an individual who fears flying is obligated to fly in spite of his fears because of job requirements. It is not uncommon for him to find that, over the years, his fear of flying diminishes as a consequence of his flying experience. As the fear subsides, his beliefs about the risks of flying will also change.

RATIONALITY AND CHOICE

When we judge the behavioral choices made by others, whether they are based on self-persuasion or outside influence or both, we often confuse the *rationality* of their decisions with the extent of our agreement with their basic premises, especially their value premises. Furthermore, it is common to find people judging the reasonableness of another person's decisions by the consequences of those decisions rather than by the reasoning that led to the decisions in the first place. The following story, based on fact, is illustrative.

Back in late 1967, a young Navy pilot, whom we'll call Carl, faced a tough decision. He had been assigned to a newly formed aviation squadron scheduled for deployment to Southeast Asia in January 1968. The squadron's mission was an especially dangerous one involving reconnaissance patrols in the Annamese mountains over the infamous Ho Chi Minh trail. Carl was informed by intelligence personnel that he and his crew of about fifteen men could anticipate about a 10 percent chance of surviving the one-year tour of duty. They would be flying World War II patrol planes fitted with new electronic equipment designed to detect and locate enemy infiltrators into South Vietnam. The planes were large and slow—extremely vulnerable to antiaircraft fire during their low-level reconnaissance runs.

Carl was prohibited from disclosing many details of his mission to friends and family members, but he did prepare at least one close friend for what might happen, asking the friend to look after his wife and children in the event of Carl's death. He told his friend that he had considered and rejected courses of action that would get him out of the mission. It is a naval aviator's prerogative at any time to turn in his wings and assume the duties of a ground officer. It is also relatively easy for a Navy pilot to fail the rigorous predeployment flight physical without appearing to be a malingerer. In short, there were ways of avoiding the mission without a complete loss of honor, though perhaps at the cost of some self-respect.

In conversation with his friend, Carl stated a number of opinions bearing on his decision to carry out the mission. The conversation, as recalled by the friend, went something like this:

CARL: I've given it a lot of thought, and I can't weasel out just because I don't like the odds of survival. I'd be in good company if I did. One senior officer developed eye trouble all of a sudden. Two other guys just turned in their wings, and nobody has made much of a fuss about it.

FRIEND: Carl, I don't want to meddle in your affairs, but I've got a couple of questions. First, do you think the survival odds they gave you are accurate estimates? Second, do you think those odds are good enough to warrant the Navy's decision to proceed with the mission? Finally, do you think you're really obligated to take that kind of a risk in an undeclared war that is enjoying less support from the public every day?

CARL: Yes, I think they're leveling with me on the chances of coming through this thing. And I respect them for that. It's almost as if they're inviting me to cop out here and now if I choose to. As to whether the mission is justified — or the whole damned war for that matter — that's something I can't judge objectively at this point. A person has to trust the judgments of other people sometimes. When I bought into this man's navy I affirmed my trust in the leaders of the country. I made a commitment. I knew there was risk involved. I think we'd all be in a hell of a mess if we went around second-guessing the decisions of people we trust only when our own rear-ends are on the line.

FRIEND: Maybe so, but if a few more Germans had second-guessed Hitler, maybe . . .

CARL: Yeah, I know. But I don't think that's a fair analogy. There are bad guys on both sides in any war. Besides, we're not just talking about some simple moral judgment here, we're talking about keeping me alive, and that's a pretty selfish and narrow viewpoint.

FRIEND: And your crew.

CARL: They've got the same decision to make that I have. And they've got the same information. Everybody has heard about the risks.

FRIEND: But you're an officer and a pilot. That makes you an opinion leader. . . . Oh, hell. I said I didn't want to meddle, and listen to me. I guess it's easier for me as a civilian to have less confidence in the country's leadership, and when it gets close to home like this. . . . The whole thing begins to look like a kamikaze mission in a losing situation.

CARL: Yeah. You and I have talked about the war and we both have about the same misgivings. You got out of the Navy, and I suspect the war had a lot to do with your decision to leave. I'm a lifer. I love to fly. I love my job — most of the time, anyway. The Navy gave me a college education, and I don't feel right about letting them down now. Up to now I've had good duty. Up to now they've never asked me to do anything that didn't make sense, so maybe this mission makes sense, too. I want to stay alive as much as you do, believe me. I love my wife and kids. I owe it to them to protect myself. Hey, I'm not the kind of guy who's cut out to be some kind of hero, living or dead. I'm a big chicken down deep. But I've got to do this thing.

Carl made his decision. He based it on his beliefs about facts and values. He placed his life in danger after long and laborious deliberation, careful reasoning in which he anticipated the probable consequences of his alternatives, evaluated the factual evidence available, and examined and reexamined his basic motives and values as he understood them. A number of different attitudes affected his decision: attitudes toward the war, his family, his job, flying, and the concepts of duty, honor, loyalty, obedience, and commitment. From the standpoint of his own fact and value premises, Carl's decision was rational and logically coherent.

A few weeks after his arrival in Southeast Asia, Carl wrote his friend saying that his plane had sustained numerous hits from small-arms fire, mostly in the tail section. He joked about his gratitude that the pilots had front-row seats, and announced that he was "too stupid to be scared and too skinny to get hit." One week later, he was shot down. He is still missing and officially presumed dead. His plane, his remains, and the remains of his fellow crewmen have never been recovered.

Was Carl's decision a rational one? What does it mean to say that a decision is rational or irrational, logical or illogical? It means simply this: *within a given system of beliefs, the decision was reached on the basis of internally consistent logic, on coherent reasoning from premises to conclusions.* Logic and reasoning do not give us the means to evaluate the truth or wisdom of our starting premises. They merely give us a means of deriving conclusions that are consistent with those premises. All reasoning must proceed from some unquestioned, unchallenged starting premises. We can argue back to first premises, but once these are challenged, either new, more basic first premises are discovered or an impasse is reached. All reasoning has to start somewhere. Without unquestioned first premises, the process of reasoning becomes an infinite regression, undecidable, unending, and pointless.

We do not always agree with one another on the truth or wisdom of first premises, especially value premises. When a man says, "I would rather lose my life than my *way* of life, and that's that!" he is making a statement about first premises — fundamental beliefs that are difficult or impossible to change. We must therefore assess the rationality of a decision stemming from such premises entirely on the basis of his subsequent reasoning. It is fruitless to second-guess his starting assumptions, once they've been discovered and affirmed. Furthermore, it is pointless to judge the rationality of a decision on the basis of hindsight, with the benefit of subsequent knowledge about the consequences of his decision.

In Chapter Ten we discussed decision making in terms of subjective probability judgments. We are often required to anticipate the consequences of our decisions in terms of such probability estimates. It is patently absurd to judge the rationality of a decision in terms of its consequences; if we do, we are introducing information into our judgment that was unavailable to the decision maker at the time the decision was made. This is like adding a fool's corollary to the old poker player's rule: "Never try to fill an inside straight, *unless, of course, the next card is the one you need.*"

MOTIVES AND BEHAVIOR

If you wish to persuade someone to adopt a behavior, it is necessary for you to make use of the listener's existing beliefs, attitudes, and values. You cannot replace your listener's beliefs and habitual behaviors with new ones appropriate to your cause. You must take advantage of motivational factors that are already there. You must induce — motivate — the listener to engage in the behavior you prescribe *because it makes sense in light of his or her existing values, attitudes, and beliefs.*

To accomplish your objective, you must know as much as possible about the beliefs, attitudes, values, and habitual behaviors of your listener. Without such knowledge, you cannot adapt your message to appeal to the listener's motives. Know your listener! Discover what he already believes about your subject matter. Find out what is important to him: his fears, aspirations, sources of gratification, and basic value assumptions. Direct your message at these motivating factors. Remember: the meaning of a message is the listener's response to it, and the response to a *persuasive* message is governed by the listener's motives. Remember, too, the principle of participation; the listener must voluntarily participate in the process of his or her own persuasion.

The persuader's task is to show the listener that compliance with the persuader's message is *rationally consistent* with the listener's motives. The listener's motivation to comply is based on his perception that noncompliance means a discrepancy or inconsistency between one or more of his important beliefs and his actual behavior. Thus, the strategy of persuasive communication is to induce this perception of inconsistency and prescribe an attractive way of reducing it through a change in behavior.

We assume that human beings make behavioral choices as a result of the resolution of internal conflict among competing motives. One especially strong motive is to be rational or logically consistent, but there are additional motivating factors that may work against reason and logic. We'll turn now to a discussion of some of these additional factors.

EXTRARATIONAL MOTIVATORS

Human psychology is not yet an exact science and perhaps never will be. We simply do not understand enough about the workings of the human mind to make accurate predictions about what people will do under all circumstances. Since we do not fully understand why people think and act as they do, it isn't possible to set forth hard and fast principles of persuasion that suggest guaranteed techniques of influence. Nonetheless, careful and systematic observation of human behavior has led to some tentative conclusions about general human tendencies that can be of use to persuaders. We will briefly discuss some of these tendencies, stated as general principles of human information processing. Some of them are rooted in the logical, rational side of human nature, and some of them are extrarational and extralogical—outside the domain of purely rational processes. Keep in mind that these principles are not hard and fast laws of human nature; they are

not applicable in every persuasive situation. But they will give you guidance about what is required to win the battle of internal motives that is persuasion.

PSYCHOLOGICAL ECONOMY

We tend to form beliefs, attitudes, and values in such a way as to minimize the psychological effort involved in doing so. This means that, given the choice between laborious and difficult psychological processing of information and simpler, more efficient processes of decision making, we tend to favor the latter. This tendency means, on the one hand, that we tend at times toward intellectual and emotional laziness—toward reaching snap decisions where careful thinking is in order, toward stereotyping others when we should look further for individual differences, toward making black or white judgments where there are many shades of gray. On the other hand, this tendency implies that we have a natural tendency toward energy conservation in our thinking. For example, a good theory should include the minimum number of concepts, terms, and principles necessary to satisfactorily account for the phenomenon to which it applies. It should not include any excess baggage in terms of units of thought that don't really add anything to the explanations required. Thus, there are both beneficial and detrimental aspects to this principle of "least psychological effort."

During the student strike at San Francisco State College in 1968, militant speakers kept repeating "If you're not part of the solution, you're part of the problem." The effectiveness of such a slogan as persuasive rhetoric—and as a polarizing tactic—is illustrative of the principle of psychological economy.

You can put this principle to work in persuasion by keeping your message as simple and straightforward as the subject matter will allow. Don't clutter up the message with tangential issues and digressions. Make it as easy as possible for the listener to follow your reasoning and to do what you want him to do.

BELIEF SYSTEMS

We tend to adjust our beliefs, and especially our simultaneously expressed beliefs (opinions), to make them consistent with one another. Logical consistency among beliefs means that the individual attempts to resolve apparent logical contradictions among related beliefs as he becomes aware of such contradictions and perhaps even in the absence of conscious awareness (McGuire, 1960).

This principle of belief consistency has been stated formally in many ways in the literature of attitude change and persuasion. Generally, the principle involves two types of consistency: purely logical consistency and what is sometimes called "psycho-logical" consistency. Psycho-logic refers to quasilogical reasoning that does not conform to the rules of formal logic. What appears reasonable in psycho-logic is therefore logically invalid in the formal sense. The term is attributable to Abelson and Rosenberg (1958) and is used in a broader and looser sense by Bem (1970).

Unlike Mr. Spock of "Star Trek," typical humans do not order their related beliefs into precisely logical belief systems. Their attempts to maintain apparent logical consistency often result in somewhat bizarre and idiosyncratic reasoning, more psycho-logical than logical. Consider the following exchange:

A: I'm against killing. I don't think it's ever justifiable to take another person's life.

B: OK, but suppose you had had an opportunity to take Hitler's life back in the thirties after you discovered some of the atrocities he had committed, thereby preventing him from murdering millions more.

A: Yeah. I see what you mean. But guys like Hitler are a special case in my book. I don't really consider them *human.*

This kind of Alice-in-Wonderland reasoning involves an apparent meaning change for the term *human* that takes place as if by magic in mid-discussion. It is a common ploy invoked when purely logical consistency is challenged. To maintain the appearance of logical consistency, person A invokes a psycho-logical prerogative, which might be stated: "It is OK to redefine a term in the middle of a line of reasoning in order to maintain apparent logical consistency."

There seem to be many common psycho-logical rules governing what individuals will accept as "reasonable" if not altogether logical. Frequently encountered logical fallacies suggest dozens of such rules of extrarational logic. One of the implications of psycho-logical consistency is that we tend to let our judgments generalize in nonlogical, if not altogether illogical, ways. Advertising appeals take advantage of this tendency. For example, popular sports stars are retained to endorse products ranging from panty hose to coffee makers on television. The strategy here is to induce us to transfer our favorable evaluations of the sports figures to the products they endorse. The assumption is that if

we like Joe Namath, and Joe Namath likes a particular brand of panty hose, we experience a psychological pressure toward consistency that requires us to find the same brand of panty hose preferable. A further assumption is that we will pay more attention to a well-known celebrity than to an unknown commercial narrator and that we'll experience more pressure to accept and comply with messages we listen to closely than to messages we give only cursory attention. These pressures are not necessarily predicated on logic and reasoning; they may be, but they may also rest on absurd violations of sound reasoning.

Osgood and Tannenbaum (1955) advance a mathematically stated theory concerning what typically happens when a source (speaker) makes an assertion about some object of judgment (concept or attitude object), as when Joe Namath endorses his favorite brand of panty hose. According to Osgood's theory, Namath's commercial message produces a gain in the popularity of the product at the expense of a small loss in Namath's own popularity. This holds true if Namath is generally evaluated as a more positive object of judgment than the product by the majority of listeners. It doesn't matter that the criteria against which we evaluate Joe Namath (as a quarterback) have nothing whatsoever to do with the criteria against which we evaluate the quality of panty hose. The gain in product popularity is purely attributable to psychological consistency and defies logical explanation.

Rokeach and Rothman (1965) propose a theory similar to Osgood's. They argue that a source-object assertion results in a wholly new attitude object—one that is characterized by the source—and that a listener's evaluation (attitude) toward this new object is not predictable on the basis of the listener's separate evaluations of source and object.

Advertisers know that they can influence buying behavior, not on the strength of rational arguments about product merits, but by literally selling a portion of the popularity of a known personality. A successful salesman will tell you that not only does he have to sell his product, he must sell himself. The persuasive speaker must do likewise. There may not be much logic in it, but a listener's attitude toward the source of a message influences his evaluation of the message itself. This holds true even when the context of the communication and the subject matter would seem to make the two judgments irrelevant. The credibility of the communicator always interacts with the content of the message to stimulate meaning in the listener. If you wish to persuade, you must generate confidence that you are competent, trustworthy, and of good character. All of your behavior, not just your message, will be judged in terms of credibility.

The legendary defense attorney Clarence Darrow is alleged to have offered the following advice: "Don't give the jury reasons to acquit your client. Make them *like* your client, and they'll find their own reasons." Darrow understood the principle of belief consistency and its application to credibility judgments, and he was an extremely persuasive speaker.

BELIEFS AND BEHAVIOR

On reflection, you will realize that most of us occasionally act in ways that are *inconsistent* with our professed opinions. We call it *hypocrisy* when it's the other guy whose actions don't fit with his words. For example, most people would probably agree that overeating, smoking, and drinking, and failing to get adequate exercise are unhealthy practices, yet many of these same people continue to overeat, tip a few too many, and lead sedentary lives. When confronted with the discrepancies between their opinions and their actions, people typically experience some degree of uneasiness or psychological discomfort. When pressed, they will frequently "rationalize" their actions, offering somewhat bizarre justifications to show that, after all, they are not being inconsistent. *Rationalization* is simply finding reasons that justify a decision or an act after the fact. The tendency to rationalize is most pronounced when individuals are called to account for apparent discrepancies between their actions and their beliefs.

Festinger (1957) has coined the term *cognitive dissonance* for the feeling of psychological discomfort that results when an individual recognizes a discrepancy between opinions and behavior or between opinions that seem to contradict each other, either logically or psychologically. For example, those who voted for Richard Nixon probably experienced cognitive dissonance over the Watergate disclosures, knowing that their *voting behavior* was inconsistent with their *beliefs* about appropriate conduct for politicians. Cigaret smokers who value their health yet believe that smoking is harmful would also experience cognitive dissonance. According to Festinger, the arousal of cognitive dissonance is at the root of all efforts to bring beliefs, attitudes, opinions, values, and behaviors into harmony with one another. Cognitive dissonance is uncomfortable and causes us to do psychological work; it is like a motivational itch that requires scratching. When we experience dissonance, we take steps to reduce or eliminate it. The principle of "least psychological effort" determines the way in which we go about reducing the dissonance. Whatever is easiest for us to change, we change. Sometimes it is easier to change a troublesome belief or attitude, sometimes a behavior. For example, if it is more difficult for an individual to quit smoking than to change his nagging belief that it is harmful to smoke, he is likely to find ways of eliminating the belief that to smoke is ultimately more harmful than to quit. Changing the troublesome belief often involves some circuitous reasoning such as "I know that smoking is harmful to my health, but it takes time for the harmful effects to happen. I'll quit later, before the damage is irreversible. Besides, nervous tension is also harmful, and right now I'm under a lot of pressure and smoking helps me relax. It's going to take a lot of effort to quit, and right now I just haven't got the energy to devote to stopping." Here the problem belief is not really eliminated, but the introduction of a time perspective helps reduce the dissonance temporarily, as does the introduction of some rationalizations.

Most of us at one time or another have announced New Year's resolutions to change some behavior that has been causing us to experience dissonance. Making the dissonance public is tantamount to confessing an inconsistency, thereby subjecting oneself to public ostracism unless the offending behavior is changed. For some individuals, such resolutions are an effective way of helping motivate the change. For others, ritual declarations of intent such as New Year's resolutions seem to melt away with the winter snow. Our next principle may help explain why.

TOLERANCE OF INCONSISTENCY

People differ in the extent to which they can tolerate and react to apparent inconsistencies among their beliefs and behaviors. Some individuals are openly embarrassed and humiliated when caught in self-contradiction. Others seem to enjoy publicly acclaiming their incongruities. Disclosure of seeming inconsistencies is an effective device for attracting attention to oneself. After a confrontation between members of the American Nazi Party and students in a speech class at San Francisco State University, one young woman secured an invitation to speak to the class by identifying herself—in all seriousness—as a Black, Jewish, pacifist Nazi, and a member of the clergy to boot.

Some individuals finding themselves exposed as inconsistent will resort to elaborate rhetorical rationalizations to justify their conflicting views and actions. Others will merely acknowledge the inconsistency with a broad grin and a wink and perhaps a reference to Emerson's oft-quoted remark: "A foolish consistency is the hobgoblin of little minds, adored by little statesmen and philosophers and divines."

These individual differences pose a problem for the persuader. Persuasive communication works by showing the listener the path to consistency. The message stimulates a feeling of psychological discomfort and prescribes a cure, the advocated change in behavior. The cure will be adopted only if the discomfort is sufficiently intense to motivate the listener, but a message that stimulates discomfort for one listener may not do so for another. This can happen either because the message does not stimulate the perception of inconsistency in the first place or because it does not produce enough inconsistency and discomfort to incite the listener to action. This is another reason it is vitally important for you to know your listener well enough to be able to gauge the kind and amount of inconsistency required to motivate the listener to act. Our next two principles illustrate some of the difficulties a persuader must overcome in stimulating discomfort based on the need for consistency.

WISHFUL THINKING

We tend to let our values, wishes, hopes, and aspirations interfere with our judgments of fact. Often called wishful thinking, this principle simply means that we sometimes tend to believe what we wish were true in spite of hard evidence to the contrary. Wishful thinking is illustrated in many kinds of peculiar reasoning, ranging from the commission of common logical fallacies to outright denials of facts so obvious as to cast doubts on the sanity of the wishful individual. McGuire (1960) has found experimental evidence of wishful thinking through experiments with formal deductive reasoning.

Wishful thinking is not just the reasoning of fools. Many of the noblest human achievements are attributable to an individual's persistent faith against overwhelming evidence. Goals that reasonable people have deemed unreachable have been accomplished. Anne Sullivan's work in helping Helen Keller acquire the gift of speech is an example. Recent advances in the treatment of cancer offer another vindication of raw hope in the face of doomsday logic. Many physicians now believe that all too frequently cancer patients die largely because they, their loved ones, and their physicians give up hope of the possibility of cure because of gloomy statistics from previous cases. There is a major persuasive campaign underway in the medical community to convince people, and their doctors, that cancer is in many instances completely curable and that the cure is frequently contingent on the patient's *belief* about the disease and the course of treatment prescribed.

In your efforts as a persuader, wishful thinking can work against you, so you must learn to recognize its symptoms. But it can work for you, too. You may never get involved in treating people for cancer, but you will find occasion in many persuasive situations to inspire your listener's confidence in faith and hope. Once again, knowledge of the listener is imperative. Find out what the listener *wants* to believe, and use it.

SELECTIVE EXPOSURE

We tend to protect and defend against contradiction and disconfirmation beliefs with which we've grown comfortable. This principle is manifested in the information-seeking and -avoiding behavior of individuals. We do not seek after new information indiscriminately; rather, we are selective in our attention to sources of new information. We read some newspapers and magazines while ignoring others. We listen to certain radio stations, watch particular TV programs, and avoid others. We affiliate with some people and not others. And even though we may affiliate with a fairly large number of people for different purposes, we do not communicate with all of them about the same subjects.

Not all of this selectivity is motivated by a desire, conscious or unconscious, to protect and defend our cherished beliefs against attack. But common sense and a substantial number of research findings indicate that some of our selectivity is so motivated. Several studies of communicator choice (our preferential choices of other persons with whom to interact) indicate that we tend to seek out others whose beliefs and attitudes are similar to our own. One explanation of this is that similar others do not threaten us with exposure to contrary views, which would generate discomfort and require us to do psychological work.

This principle is consistent with the principle of "least psychological effort." Imagine what it would be like to place yourself in a perpetual state of intellectual and emotional turmoil by actively seeking out information contrary to any and all of your convictions. An old Greek paradox is applicable here. There was once a wise old philosopher who taught the importance of skepticism — the persistent tendency to doubt the truth of one's beliefs. One day, as he walked in the garden with his protégé, the old scholar slipped and fell, becoming stuck head-first in a mudhole. The student suddenly found himself in a state of motivational paralysis, unable to act to save his teacher. He had immersed himself so deeply in skepticism that he couldn't decide whether it was worthwhile to extricate the old man to learn more about skepticism.

A certain amount of skepticism is a necessary condition for intellectual development, and natural consequences of skepticism in a healthy mind are inquisitiveness, curiosity, and the active pursuit of new information. Without skepticism, an individual can be exceptionally gullible, ripe prey for any new idea that comes along, or exceptionally dogmatic, closed to any outside influence that might threaten his petrified views. In the other extreme, skepticism robs an individual of a sense of purpose and meaning by stripping him of basic convictions of fact and value on which to predicate behavior.

By its very nature, skepticism breeds cognitive dissonance. It is likely, then, that the extent to which a given individual assumes a skeptical stance toward personal beliefs is related to a tolerance of inconsistency or dissonance. Some degree of willingness to reexamine one's beliefs is necessary if one is to be open to persuasive influence. On the other hand, if skepticism goes hand-in-hand with tolerance of inconsistency, then persuasive attempts based on the stimulation of inconsistency may be futile. When you pick your target listeners for persuasion, you should pick those people who are just skeptical enough to be open-minded, but not so skeptical that they are unable to make decisions.

Once again, always remember that since the assignment of meanings is accomplished by listeners, the effects of persuasive communication depend as much on the openness and receptivity of the receiver as on the argumentative skill of the sender. Approach persuasion as an effort to help someone else make intelligent choices, but remember that, frankly, some people will not permit themselves to be helped!

THE PRIORITY OF NEEDS

While we all share similar needs at the level of basic survival, we differ in the higher-order needs that become operative once lower-order needs are satisfied. Maslow (1954) argues that human needs form a hierarchy and that higher-order needs become dominant motivating forces when lower-order needs are fulfilled. In affluent cultures such as ours, many individuals seek gratification at higher levels. They are well fed, clothed, and sheltered. They enjoy the love of intimates and the companionship of friends. They enjoy considerable choice in creating their own advanced needs and finding ways of fulfilling them, unlike persons whose total daily output is required to eke out a meager subsistence.

In an advanced and pluralistic culture such as ours, there is considerable opportunity for persons to set different kinds of goals for themselves and undertake different means to achieve those goals. These differences are reflected in a wide variety of beliefs and preferred patterns of behavior. Several social scientists have attempted to identify such differences in needs and values. Morris (1956) and Rokeach (1968) have developed scales designed to measure preferred "ways of living" and values, both in terms of goals and means of achieving them. McClelland (1975) has investigated individual needs for achievement, affiliation, and power. If you're interested in studying motivation in depth, these sources are a good place to start.

It is beyond the scope of this chapter to elaborate fully on the implications of these theories and related research findings for persuasive communication. But you must recognize that effective persuasion must take advantage of the needs that motivate individual listeners, and these needs differ. *A fulfilled need no longer motivates.* Your persuasive strategies and tactics must be adapted to the needs of your listeners.

PERSUASIVE SPEAKING

When it's your turn to persuade an audience, be it an audience of one or many, base your strategies and tactics on the following considerations:

ESTABLISH YOUR CREDIBILITY

Let your message be evidence of your competence, trustworthiness, and character. Show your audience that you have a common ground — some common values and motives, and some common beliefs about the topic of persuasion. You must inspire your listeners' confidence that you understand and respect their needs.

Admit that you have a bias, a vested interest in achieving your persuasive purpose. To deny this fact is pointless and damaging to your case. No one attempts to persuade another person of anything without some personal motivation for doing so, some prospect of personal gain. Be candid about your motives, and show that they are compatible with those of your listener.

Demonstrate your awareness of real and potential issues on which you and your listeners may disagree. You must offer evidence that you are aware of alternative points of view and have examined your own position thoroughly in light of those alternatives.

Honor your listeners. You must convince your audience that you respect them for their intelligence and affirm both their ability and their right to make intelligent choices.

Present yourself and your message as attractively as possible. Compose your verbal message in language that is understandable, memorable, lively, and concise. Compose your nonverbal message to enhance your credibility, paying careful attention to such matters as dress, grooming, and general demeanor.

Judgments about your credibility are influenced by all these factors. Failing to consider any one may ruin your persuasive effort.

SPEAK TO THE NEEDS THAT ARE POWERFUL MOTIVATORS IN YOUR AUDIENCE

Analyze your audience to discover their unfulfilled needs at the time of your persuasive communication. Your analysis should enable you to cause each listener to believe that you are speaking directly to him or her.

Specify precisely why and how compliance with your message will produce benefits for the listener that are worth the costs of compliance, whatever the coinage of those costs may be.

Clearly state what you want the listener to do, and do everything in your power to make it possible for him or her to do it as soon as possible. The earlier you can obtain a behavioral commitment, the more successful your persuasion will be.

SHOW THAT YOUR PRESCRIPTION IS A REASONABLE PATH TO CONSISTENCY

Remember that the need to be consistent, both logically and psychologically, is a powerful motivating influence. Demonstrate that the behavior you advocate is a reasonable prescription in light of the facts you present and the motives to which you appeal. Your arguments should clearly indicate that *your* path to consistency is the most reasonable among available alternatives.

Finally, remember that persuasive communication is for interpretation by a whole human being. Whole human beings are motivated by many factors: psychological economy, consistency, wishfulness, selectivity, and a variety of need-states. Spend some time analyzing why you behave as you do, and persuade others as you would have others persuade you.

"I guess it's time to drag out the old speech about how we're just one happy family, and unionization would only cause divisiveness."

SUMMARY

Most human beings are rational individuals and, therefore, amenable to persuasion through logical arguments. At the same time, most individuals are motivated by factors that transcend logic and reasoning. An individual's beliefs, attitudes, and values influence his or her behavior, but the relationships among these elements cannot always be explained or predicted on a logical basis. Extrarational motivators help explain why an individual thinks, feels, and acts in particular ways.

The principle of psychological economy says we are motivated to minimize psychological effort in integrating beliefs, attitudes, values, and behavior. Our systems of belief and behavior are governed both by logical and psycho-logical rules of consistency. While all of us are motivated by a need for consistency, not all of us are so motivated to the same degree, and we do not all share the same psycho-logical rules governing what it means to be consistent.

Humans tend to think wishfully, believing what they want to believe even when rationality dictates otherwise. Too, individuals are selective in exposing themselves to information contrary to cherished beliefs, because such exposure causes discomfort from the perception of inconsistencies.

Finally, human beings are motivated by a variety of needs, some of which take precedence over others. These needs vary with time and circumstance, and an individual's susceptibility to persuasion varies accordingly.

These extrarational motivators must be considered in designing persuasive messages. Effective persuasion requires attention to all the factors that motivate human behavior, not just to our ability to calculate logically.

QUESTIONS

1. Why does persuasion involve more than just reasoning?
2. In what ways does the human need for consistency relate to reasoning and logic?
3. What is a belief? An attitude? A value?
4. How do beliefs, attitudes, and values influence behavior, and how does behavior influence beliefs, attitudes, and values?

5. What are some of the characteristics of human thinking and acting that influence persuasion in nonrational ways?
6. What are the essential elements of speaker credibility?
7. What are some of the factors that make a person open or closed to persuasive influence?

SUGGESTED READINGS

Bem, D. J. *Beliefs, attitudes, and human affairs.* Belmont, Calif.: Brooks/ Cole, 1970.

Boorstin, D. J. *The image.* New York: Atheneum, 1962.

Karlins, Marvin, and Herbert I. Abelson. *Persuasion: how opinions and attitudes are changed,* 2d ed. New York: Springer, 1970.

Maslow, A. *Motivation and personality.* New York: Harper & Row, 1954.

Polanyi, M. *Personal knowledge.* Chicago: The University of Chicago Press, 1958.

Rokeach, M. *Beliefs, attitudes, and values.* San Francisco: Jossey-Bass, 1968.

Zimbardo, P. G., E. Ebbesen and C. Masluch. *Influencing attitudes and changing behavior*, 2nd ed. Reading, Mass.: Addison-Wesley, 1977.

DONT

12

THE SPEAKER AND THE AUDIENCE

PREVIEW

In the first five chapters of Part Two we discussed basic approaches to the development and delivery of informative and persuasive speeches. In this chapter we consider typical issues on problems that arise in the *relationship* between *speaker* and the *audience*. Specifically, we focus on some of the legitimate questions that should surface in negotiating a speech. We also discuss the problems of managing the speaker's environment and the management of speaker-audience interactions.

OBJECTIVES

To identify basic issues that should be considered in negotiating a speech

To provide suggestions for managing the speaker's physical environment

To provide suggestions for managing special communication settings

To provide suggestions for managing speaker-audience interactions

TWELVE There are many basic similarities in the process of developing speeches for different audiences. At the same time each public speech poses its own unique set of circumstances. In negotiating a speech a speaker will need to consider the reasons for giving a particular speech as well as its suitability for a particular audience. A speaker will also need to consider the unique setting in which the speech is to be delivered, and the ways in which effective and productive speaker-audience interactions can be generated and managed.

NEGOTIATING THE PUBLIC SPEECH

A decision to give a public speech usually results from negotiations between a speaker and some social agent. The speaker can be any individual who is available and willing to prepare and deliver a speech. The social agent can be a club president, a business executive, a church leader, or any other individual representing a group that constitutes a potential audience. Prespeech negotiations may be initiated by either the speaker or the organizational representative. Occasionally speeches are negotiated by a third party such as the League of Women Voters.

SPEAKER-INITIATED SPEECHES

An individual may be able to achieve progress toward personal, professional, or social goals through public speaking, and therefore may wish to negotiate opportunities for speaking engagements. A business executive may wish to inform his employees of new developments within the business organization. The president of a professional organization may wish to appear before the community to explain why its members are on strike, or a member of a government agency may wish to meet with community representatives to explore the feasibility of constructing an atomic generator near that community. In any case, an individual who wishes to negotiate a public speech should consider some of the following issues:

1. What are the speaker's specific goals?
2. Which speech communication format is most conducive to achieving those goals?
3. What speech materials are needed to achieve the goals?
4. Which individuals should receive the speaker's messages or participate in the communication exchange?

Public speaking is expensive. It demands a considerable amount of the speaker's time and energy. It also can require the purchase or rental of audiovisual equipment, the rental of appropriate facilities, and the speaker's travel and living expenses. The effective speaker will want the greatest return on this investment. Accordingly, a speaker should be clear about goals, and should be selective in the choice of messages and the audiences who should hear those messages.

REQUESTED SPEECHES

An organization frequently can contribute to its purposes by contacting speakers. Typically, an organization will initiate negotiations with an individual who possesses needed information or skills. The members of an organization may desire special information from an expert in a given field; they may wish to learn more about a candidate for political office; or they may want an interesting speaker who can provide an entertaining after-dinner speech.

Although it is flattering to receive speaking invitations, the speaker should evaluate the implications of accepting a speaking engagement. He is entitled to accept only engagements that are likely to compliment his own personal, professional, and social values. Clearly, the speaker should understand the motives, interests, and expectations of the requesting group. Since speech preparation and delivery are demanding in terms of speaker time and energy, it also is reasonable for him to take some time to consider the potential payoffs in accepting a given invitation.

A speaker might accept an invitation to deliver a speech for a number of reasons. He may be in sympathy with the goals of the requesting organization; he may view the invitation as an opportunity to help fulfill his community responsibilities; or he may perceive the opportunity to gain exposure for his ideas. In some cases he may be attracted by a speaker's honorarium. On the other hand, the speaker may conclude that the payoff is minimal or, worse yet, that an appearance could compromise his own standards or contribute to unnecessary conflict and hostility.

CHECKLIST FOR NEGOTIATING A SPEECH

The following list identifies some of the important issues that should be considered in negotiating for and arranging a speech:

1. What is the purpose of the speech?
2. What is the nature of the audience?
3. Where and when is the speech to be given?
4. How much time will be allowed for the speech?
5. Will the speech be followed by two-way speaker-audience communication?
6. Is the speaker donating his services or is an honorarium provided?
7. Does the speaker introduce himself or is he introduced by someone else?
8. If the speaker is introduced by another person, does that person have adequate information about the speaker and his speech?

MANAGING THE SPEECH ENVIRONMENT

In addition to the problem of negotiating the right speech for the right audience, the public communicator often encounters unique problems in each speech setting or environment. The more information we can get on the speech setting before we have to use it, the more carefully we can adapt. Most environmental problems can be solved before the speech ever begins. A noted historian was asked to present a one-hour speech as part of an evening lecture series. The man was a fluent speaker with a superb grasp of historical materials. He had color slides of the site of a famous battle and had numerous examples and anecdotes to hold attention. His audience included people who enjoyed historical subjects. They also knew of the speaker's several books; his reputation and credibility were well established. Many ingredients were present for a successful communication event. Yet the speech failed, with the audience leaving two hours later shaking their heads. Why? The reasons lie in the speaker's neglect of the environment. He *assumed* that everything would be appropriately arranged for him and appeared only about five minutes ahead of time. This is what happened.

The room scheduled for the speech was already occupied by another group, an administrative foul-up. The program chairman hurriedly arranged for another room in an adjacent building. The audience and the speaker filed out of the building together and found the alternate room locked. Luckily, a brief search turned up a janitor who opened the door. As people settled into their chairs, the speaker began to look for an extension cord for the slide projector. The janitor again came to the rescue, but members of the audience had to help pass the cord under

their chairs to reach a wall socket. Volunteers from the audience also had to bring in more chairs from down the hall because this new room was not as large as the one originally scheduled. The speaker finally began about thirty minutes late, but his problems had just begun.

The new room had a podium but no reading light, and when the house lights were turned off for the slide presentation, the speaker could not read his notes. He moved near a red exit light to see the notes, and was then too far away to point at various features on the screen. The microphone was attached to the podium, and the volume kept changing as he continually moved from the podium to the exit light to the screen and back to the podium. Sometimes he was uncomfortably loud, and sometimes he was barely audible.

Finally, the speaker had not arranged in advance for someone to operate the slide projector (his projector had no remote or automatic slide-changing mechanism), so the program chairman, who had never operated such equipment before, agreed to run the projector. To change slides, the speaker called out "Next, please," and the audience waited awkwardly as the chairman-turned-projectionist struggled with the next slide, sometimes getting it in upside down or backwards. The planned hour lecture took about an hour and a half, and the chairman called off the previously announced question-and-answer session.

Here was a good speaker with an interesting topic, clear visual aids, and an enthusiastic audience — yet he failed in his communication effort because of poor management of the environment. This true story is typical of many speeches that fail due to unexpected problems. What can a speaker do to minimize the risk of such potentially disastrous disruptions? Following are some important guidelines.

GET ADVANCED INFORMATION

Ask people who may be familiar with the environment of your forthcoming speech: Will some prior arrangements be made? By whom? What are the room and seating characteristics? Will there be a loudspeaker system? A blackboard? Demonstration area? How many people are expected? Are distractions or interruptions likely? Will specified people be available to help with last-minute problems? These and other questions help eliminate the element of surprise; the speaker knows what to expect.

ARRIVE EARLY AND TRY OUT ALL ELECTRONIC EQUIPMENT IN ADVANCE

The speaker should arrive at least twenty to thirty minutes ahead of time and survey the scene before people begin arriving. A movie or slide projector, a videotape machine, or an overhead projector should be plugged in and tested so it will be ready to use with a simple flick of a switch. Similarly, the microphone should be tested, with another person standing at various places in the room to assure proper volume. The speaker should move to various positions around the podium to determine the microphone's sensitivity and how much freedom of movement will be possible without distorting sound reproduction. He can thus avoid awkward introductory comments like, "Is this thing on?" or the shout from the back of the room, "We can't hear you!"

GET USED TO THE LECTERN

Is a lectern needed? Is one available? Notice its height. Will it restrict audience vision of bodily movement or visual aids? Would a small portable lectern be more appropriate? If the speech involves physical demonstration of visual materials, where can notes be placed?

ANALYZE THE AUDIENCE SEATING ARRANGEMENT

In most cases, seating will be fixed, and the speaker must adapt to it. If so, survey the room, and notice places where some people may have trouble hearing or seeing. In a few cases, it may be possible to rope off certain sections or let people know where the best seats are. In some environments, the speaker can actually rearrange the seating—in classrooms, conference rooms, luncheon or banquet areas, churches, and public halls. Audiences tend to be more responsive if they are sitting closer together and nearer the speaker than if they are spread out over a large room. Avoid setting up chairs too far to either side of the podium; this arrangement will make eye contact with some people more difficult.

SURVEY THE TOTAL ENVIRONMENT FOR POTENTIAL DISTRACTIONS

Will some of the lights be uncomfortable for the speaker or audience? Is room temperature comfortable and can it be raised or lowered? Will open windows or doors admit distracting sights and sounds? Are the chairs the type that will become especially uncomfortable if the speech is lengthy? (Most folding chairs usually are.)

MANAGING SPECIAL COMMUNICATION SETTINGS

Some speaking situations require special adaptation. Students in a basic speech communication class conform to a fairly predictable laboratory environment—a short speech to a captive audience of peers and a teacher-evaluator, with a specific set of instructions and a known setting. While useful educationally, this format does not provide all the elements of real-world public communication. In-class activities help develop tools that we must then learn to apply to unique settings and events.

THE CONFERENCE OR BUSINESS MEETING

Though some conferences closely resemble the small work group, they may take the form of a one-to-many communication event. While ten to twenty people listen, one speaker with special information or expertise develops a comparatively complicated topic. Members of the audience are usually insiders in that they share the same language and background with the speaker and some of the same interests. Thus the message in this setting does not make so many compromises toward simpler language, nor does it explain in great depth the concepts that the audience should already know. The speaker may cover more material more quickly because of audience expertise. Interest in the topic also is likely to be higher because of special audience backgrounds, so devices to maintain attention may not be so numerous.

The conference speaker may be constrained by strict time limits. A fairly common instruction is, "At the next meeting, we'd like you to discuss your new proposal; you will have eight minutes." And the chairperson really does mean *eight* minutes, not nine or ten. The speaker must also be more concerned with precision of content; oversimplifications or minor errors are usually noticed. Message organization is equally important, for busy professionals have little patience with the rambling speaker.

THE BRIEFING

A *briefing* is a relatively short (thirty minutes or less) message that condenses a large amount of current information into capsule form. The usual objectives are to provide background materials, to describe situations and events, or to give instructions for future events. The briefing may provide feedback on how a particular project was carried out (sometimes called a *debriefing*). Briefings may occur in one-to-one or small-group situations and be relatively informal, but they are also useful in audience situations. The stereotyped briefing is the old war movie scene of a RAF wing commander telling the bomber crews of the day's mission over Germany. Actually, such speeches are not usually so dramatic and occur on an everyday basis in many professions and organizations.

The key to good briefing is accuracy and brevity; anything less, and the whole purpose of the activity has been negated. A good strategy is to include outlined or excerpted printed materials and perhaps some pictorial visual aids to accompany the oral message. The speaker should expect to be interrupted regularly with audience questions unless he indicates that he will leave time for audience feedback at the end. In some situations, the speaker has freedom to delete topics or data in the interest of manageability. However, a good briefing often demands that the speaker present all relevant topics because they are crucial to understanding an event or activity. If the speaker has only fifteen minutes to present about thirty minutes of material (a frequent problem), he must economize in language and elaboration rather than arbitrarily eliminating relevant points. This task of condensing large amounts of information is the fundamental challenge of briefing.

THE CLASSROOM

Entire courses are devoted to classroom methods. A person who plans to enter teaching should take such courses and do significant reading, study, and practice in instructional techniques. Here we simply provide some overviews.

The classroom instructor has several advantages—a captive audience, predictable facilities and environment, a series of meetings, reasonably large blocks of time, and usually some legitimacy in that the listeners tend to presume special speaker expertise. Whether in the public and private schools, business and government, or special training programs, however, the instructional speaker still must adapt to several problems.

An obvious advantage of having more time is that the informative speaker can cover topics in more depth and obtain more reliable feedback on communication outcomes. But the paradox of having plenty of time is that the speaker may waste too much of it. He does not prepare information carefully and economically. Too often the result is a rambling, disjointed message with irrelevant information, careless presentation or delivery, and limited audience appeal. Planning is just as important regardless of the available time. For example, if a speaker spends two of the eight hours allotted for a twenty-five member training session in casual meanderings and without planned teaching techniques, she has wasted fifty "people hours" with her poor preparation. She may also have bored her listeners. Or when a classroom teacher sheepishly admits, "I didn't have time to prepare any lesson for today, so let's just discuss the textbook," he may be indirectly suggesting that class time is not very important and that haphazard conversation serves as an acceptable substitute for prepared activities and objectives.

Unlike many informative situations, the classroom does not usually confront the speaker with continuous pressure to communicate well. Instructors get so used to the informal environment that they may not be psychologically "up" for the communicative effort. But we believe that the setting is no less important because of its familiarity and informality. Rather, we argue that an informative speaker can no more justify wasting the time of thirty students or trainees than he can rambling through a shoddy report to a corporate board of directors.

Another problem is that the classroom may be less suitable for maintaining continuous attention. As any teacher knows all too well, the captive audience may lose interest quickly, and the speaker must make special efforts to bring them back. Because the speech content is not usually as compelling as that discussed in, say, a business or professional setting, the teacher must be creative in developing interesting presentational techniques. Visual materials, variety in instructional activities, and the encouragement of group participation are some of the common devices to surmount this problem.

THE EXCEPTIONALLY LARGE AUDIENCE

Sometimes speakers address listeners numbering in the hundreds or thousands in large auditoriums. Such communication events include large college lecture classes, banquets, and special programs.

The large audience presents several problems. The speaker can rarely interact with the listeners, and audience participation is awkward. The effective use of visual aids and demonstration is more difficult. Subgroups within the audience may respond differently throughout the speech; people close to the speaker may see and hear easily and respond enthusiastically, while those farther away may become impatient and surly. Audience members are much less likely to share common backgrounds and interests to the extent that members of smaller groups do. The greater the number of people, the greater the chance that the level of information will be too complicated or too simple depending on the listener. A speaker's platform, podium, and public address system may keep the speaker locked to a tiny presentational area. (Pretesting of loudspeaker equipment, incidentally, is crucial!)

The speaker must develop materials with the average listener in mind, whose identity is, admittedly, based on a subjective guess. Casual prespeech interaction with people who will be in the audience can assist the speaker in determining an appropriate intellectual level for the presentation. Electronic projections will be among the more effective visual materials because size and sound can be varied. Expository goals may be achieved better by a speech lasting thirty minutes or less than by one running forty-five minutes or longer.

While the classroom speaker can encourage questions when anything is unclear, in an auditorium with two thousand people such techniques can become disruptive. Because informal feedback is difficult, the speech may need more careful structuring and elaboration. Clear presentation the first time through is the only reasonable solution. If the speaker will accept audience inquiries, he might ask an assistant to collect written questions from the audience and select some of them to answer. Finally, if the communicator regularly speaks to a particular audience, he may want to get systematic oral and written feedback *after* each speech to determine how to modify the next one.

MANAGING SPEAKER-AUDIENCE INTERACTIONS

A popular myth is that in a public communication event, the speaker is the active participant and the audience is passive. The fact is that the audience is rarely — if ever — totally passive. Listeners constantly engage in a variety of behaviors, some more noticeable than others, that may affect speech effectiveness. For example, interpersonal dyads may be operating within the audience during the speech, a small child may be crying, someone may be staring out the window or falling asleep, another may raise his hand for a question, and others may interrupt with applause, laughter, or comments. Someone may enter the room unexpectedly; someone else may get up and leave. The audience thus is a dynamic group engaging in continual activity, and the speaker is not simply "acting" but is *interacting* with audience behaviors.

The obvious implication is that the speaker must make regular spontaneous adaptations to the varied responses of the listeners. Unlike the stereotyped professor who enters the classroom, buries his head in notes, reads for an hour, and then walks out, most speakers will be continuously reminded of audience presence. The following are common occurrences and suggestions for adapting.

AUDIENCE NOISE OR COMMOTION

Noise or commotion frequently occurs when youngsters are present or when the speech situation involves a volatile emotional issue. Sometimes members of the audience who want to hear will try to silence others, but more often the speaker will have to intervene. Dogmatic statements like "Be quiet while I'm talking!" are usually too antagonistic to be productive, and a more friendly reaction might be, "Perhaps some people cannot hear because of side conversations; we will have time for comments and questions in a few minutes." In addition to being courteous, such comments should preserve the anonymity of the noisemakers. To single them out might encourage even more damaging behaviors. Only when the disturbance persists should the speaker single anyone out for comment. The key is to be as tactful and accommodating as possible for as long as possible. Do not alienate an audience with an unnecessary command or accusation.

SPONTANEOUS AUDIENCE QUESTIONS

Questions that arise spontaneously may interrupt the speaker's trend of thought. In any speech, we should decide in advance whether we want to permit questions during the planned presentation. If precise timing is not a factor, questions might be handled as they arise (a common classroom technique). However, the speaker should be wary of irrelevant questions that divert the listeners from the speech topic. He should also avoid belaboring a point by accepting too many questions on the same basic idea. A comment like, "Perhaps we've discussed this notion long enough and should get back to some of the things I wanted to mention," will usually have the approval of most of the audience.

If the speaker feels that questions during the speech will be disruptive to the flow of ideas, he may want to agree to answer all audience questions later on. For example, the speaker might say, "I'm going to talk to you for about thirty minutes. Then I shall be happy to spend a few minutes answering whatever questions you might have." If this tactic is used, however, the speaker *must* reserve the question-and-answer time. An audience is not amused when the speaker sheepishly concludes, "Well, I see I talked longer than I expected, and we won't have time for questions." For speakers attempting to persuade (like salespersons or politicians) this comment can be deadly to the achievement of objectives. Also, a speaker may defer the question to a later point in the speech. "If you don't mind, I'd like to come back to that important question when I discuss the issue later in the speech." That response is fine as long as the speaker does indeed refer to the question later. Evasive speakers sometimes use the reply as a strategy for ignoring a tough question, but the person who asked the question (and usually others in the audience as well) will remember what it was and may persist later on, leaving the speaker in a very awkward position.

A useful technique for fielding questions is for the speaker to pause at the end of each main point and ask for questions before moving on to the next. Whatever the strategy, however, we must realize that the public communication environment is increasingly becoming *two-way*, and presentational speaking with speaker-audience dialog is a growing trend that more and more audiences are coming to expect.

THE HECKLER

Though feared by many speakers, the heckler is actually quite rare in public communication. Politicians being covered by the news media may encounter antagonists who recognize an opportunity to make a point and to have it picked up on television, but most of our speeches are attended by reasonably well-mannered, considerate people who do not attempt to embarrass or destroy the speaker.

There is the occasional person, however, who obviously wants to interrupt, challenge, or heckle the speaker, and we cannot ignore him or his antics may increase. Remember, first, that the speaker usually has legitimacy, and the heckler does not. The person at the lectern, often with a microphone, has an enormous psychological advantage. Second, many audience members are frequently as embarrassed by the heckler's comments as is the speaker, and the speaker therefore can often count on the audience as an ally rather than an enemy.

Some people may not be aware of the inappropriateness of their behavior. A brief remark from the speaker may be all that is necessary to quiet them.

The following are potentially useful responses to the heckler:

> Though you are entitled to your opinions, you've been monopolizing the discussion, and I think we should give others a chance to participate.
>
> It's obvious that you don't want me to talk. Shall we let the audience decide whether they want to listen to you or listen to me? I'll tell you what. If you will let me finish my speech without interruption, I'll let you have the floor to answer my arguments.
>
> Sir, you are rude and obnoxious and are wasting the audience's time. I think you should be quiet or leave.

The speaker must be firm and attempt to maintain reasonable control! A grateful audience often will actually applaud and may even assist the speaker in managing the heckler.

INTERRUPTIONS FROM OUTSIDERS

Outside interruptions can come at any time. Waiters may begin clearing tables. A secretary may interrupt to announce an emergency phone call. Someone may enter the room by mistake. A janitor may choose the wrong time to vacuum the floors in an adjoining room. A latecomer may make a conspicuous entrance. A jet passing overhead or an ambulance siren may drown out the speaker.

We should not try to ignore such interruptions, pretending that they don't exist. The audience knows they are there and usually will be distracted momentarily. The speaker should suggest a strategy for dealing with them. The following are possible responses:

> I hope the table clearing won't be too distracting. Let me know if you can't hear me.
>
> Would someone shut the door? The hall noise is rather loud.
>
> Can someone help this man find the correct room?
>
> Would someone volunteer to go next door to tell the janitor that we are having a meeting?
>
> Hi! Come on in. There's a seat right over there.

The specific message depends on the situation, of course, but some response should be made. The more relaxed and informal the speaker's style, the easier and more appropriate such comments will be.

MAINTAINING AUDIENCE INTEREST

One of the most positive ways of managing desirable speaker-audience interaction is to develop a presentation that maintains audience interest. Most speakers will need to consider the unique concerns of a particular audience and will have to modify their presentation in order to tap those interests. The following discussion offers a variety of specific approaches to generating and maintaining audience interest. Their use, of course, does not guarantee success. The artistry and creativity with which they are employed, combined with their adaptation to a particular audience, will ultimately determine their effectiveness.

Vital Information We generate attention when messages appear crucial to our well-being. How does this topic directly affect the lives of others? What are the likely consequences if we fail to hear or heed the message? In addition to enhancing interest, vital information enhances a speaker's overall persuasiveness (Chapter Ten).

Familiarity Have you ever seen a movie that included a site with which you were familiar? There was a movie star walking where you had walked, and you told your companions, "Hey, I've been there!" The speaker can exploit the tendency to identify with the familiar. When an audience begins to tune out an abstract message, a familiar reference may bring them back.

Newness Just as we like to recall the past, so we are intrigued with the new and unique. New acquaintances fascinate us, new products lure us, and new ideas can capture us. One of the authors sat for hours at the television through the tedious countdowns of the U.S. space missions; the newness of space flight was of overwhelming interest. An advertising executive noted that she would rather sell a new, unfamiliar product than continue to sell an old, successful one because it was easier to get public attention on the latest merchandise. Though the ability to introduce novelty into the speech is limited by the topic, even the inventive phrasing of old ideas into new and exciting language is a possibility for any speech situation.

The Bizarre or Unusual Audiences cannot resist the odd or the extraordinary, as evidenced by the popularity of travelogs and magazines like *National Geographic* that cover strange lands and people, the continuing success of Ripley's "Believe It or Not," and the fascination with science fiction and the occult. These materials are usually topic-dependent, however, and their overuse may detract from a focus on common, here-and-now problems.

Suspense As with a good mystery novel that we can't put down, the feeling of uncertainty, of suspense, has enormous potency in holding audience interest. Some of the most successful public speakers have relied heavily on the extended narrative, a story with plot and characters. Sometimes suspense can be developed without a story, as with the speaker who promises early in the speech to present vital information at the end of his speech. The speaker must follow through however; we dare not leave the audience hanging with an unresolved mystery. Most important, we must use suspense as an attention-getting device only if its resolution is relevant to the main topic.

Conflict and Antagonism We can recall from grammar school days an occasional playground argument that ended in a fistfight. When it began, someone would yell "Fight! Fight!" and from every direction students would come running to watch the combatants. We simply cannot resist paying attention to competitive or hostile encounters. Thus, political debate is more interesting than a single speech, and a speech on a controversial subject is more compelling than one that describes an everyday activity. The speaker who dispassionately analyzes an issue is less appealing than one who contrasts competing arguments on that issue or refutes opposing ones. The teacher who simply explains ideas may not be as interesting as the one who plays "devil's advocate."

Humor Audiences enjoy humor in a speech if it is truly funny, is not offensive to the audience, and applies to the topic. We have all felt embarrassed for the speaker whose joke fell flat, and impatient with the would-be comedian who has forgotten the topic he was supposed to be discussing. Nevertheless, we cannot deny the power of good humor to gain almost total attention while it is being used. For example, though some students cannot remember a professor's main lecture points, they can recall and retell almost verbatim his jokes and anecdotes. If humor is to be a tool for *sustaining* attention, it should be periodic, appearing

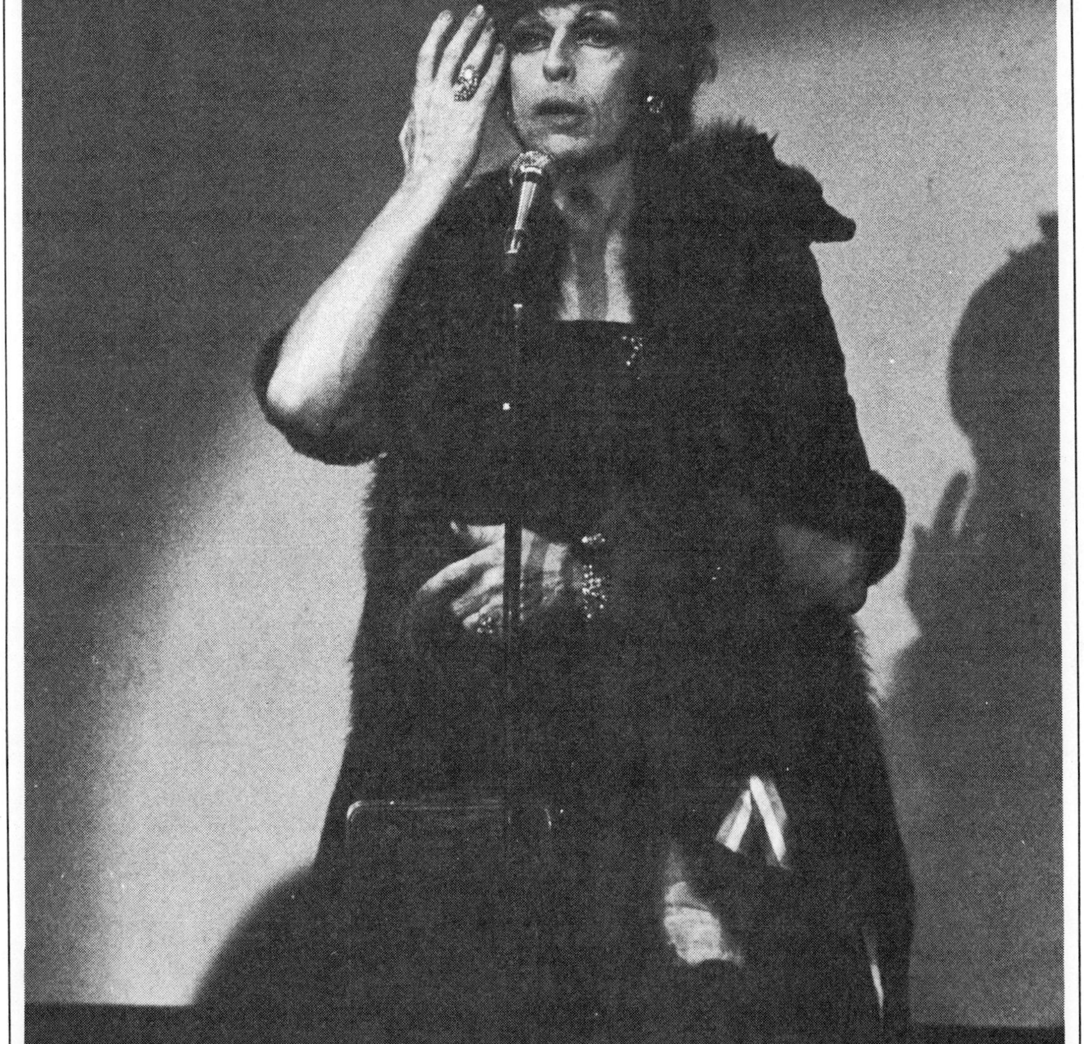

regularly throughout the speech. The speaker who begins with two or three jokes and then lapses into dry prose for the remainder of the speech will quickly lose whatever attention he gained with the humorous introduction. Finally, just as some people "can't tell a joke," so some speakers cannot use humor effectively, and we should frankly evaluate our innate ability to use this device.

The Emotional Appeal In Chapter Eleven, we explored the persuasive potential of appeals to emotion. Listeners become especially attentive when they hear ideas and materials that are shocking, frightening, romantic, poignant, sad, or sentimental. Certainly the emotional audience is not indifferent or bored. The question is whether they really grasp the speaker's main ideas or whether their emotional response distorts their impression of the message. Building pathos can be fruitful, however, if done sparingly and with close reference to specific points in the speech.

Specifics Our everyday lives are filled with concreteness, with tangible people and things. Much of our conversation deals with specific behavior, actual events, and well-defined environments. Speeches often deal with intangibles — ideas and arguments and issues — and the collective mind of the audience will wander unless the speaker can make these abstract concepts meaningful. Using real names of real people engaging in specific activities in precise environments can significantly improve audience tolerance for abstraction. Thus, instead of arguing that "college education must adapt to changing societal priorities," the speaker might instead note, "In 1975, Walter Jones graduated from State University with a bachelor's degree in political science. He began applying for jobs and could not find work. Today he is driving a taxicab." We cannot identify with "changing societal priorities," but we can certainly empathize with a college graduate who cannot find a job. Besides enhancing interest, specifics and clarity are functional to most any speech topic.

References to Audience Members We all like recognition. We like to hear our names mentioned. Some speakers are especially adept at using specific audience members as examples. The person mentioned shows interest as do others in the audience. Making personal references may backfire, of course, especially if the speaker's information about the listener is inaccurate or if that person prefers to remain anonymous. Used carefully, however, this technique can increase audience interest.

Audience Participation An obvious reason that some audiences lose interest is that they are cast in a relatively passive role. They listen quietly while another person speaks. If, on the other hand, the speaker encourages audience responses—if members of the audience actively participate with comments or movements—they also become more attentive. For example, the speaker might ask for a show of hands, ask particular people to stand up, ask specific questions for volunteers to answer, or select people to help in a demonstration. Participation may be embarrassing to some and can lead to unanticipated results (as when a volunteer from the audience botches up the speaker's demonstration), but with careful planning the technique can significantly improve audience interest.

Audience Feedback It is frustrating to be part of an audience in which everyone except the speaker realizes that the speech is dragging. People are showing all the nonverbal signs of boredom, and the speaker doesn't see them. As public communicators, we must be receptive to feedback. On the other hand, we should not magnify it out of proportion. In any sizable audience a few people are likely to yawn, whisper to a neighbor, show displeased facial expressions, or even show drowsiness. Hence, the speaker should judge at regular intervals whether *most* of the listeners appear to be attentive and responsive. If they are not, the speaker should consider spontaneous strategies for restoring attention—for example, taking a break, asking for questions, cutting out some of the prepared remarks, and increasing vocal variety and bodily movement.

Variety By far the most important factor for sustaining attention, variety, or change assures that no single attention-getting device will lose its effectiveness. Careful planning includes the use of several different interest appeals for any particular speech.

The suggestions in this section are mainly commonsense adaptations to the motives of the speaker, and to the needs of his or her audience. But such practical solutions are frequently overlooked; we urge speakers to develop systematic procedures for dealing with unique audiences.

SUMMARY

This chapter discussed some of the special problems of adapting to a particular audience.

In negotiating a speech, the speaker was encouraged to clarify personal and professional goals and their relation to specific speech opportunities. The speaker should consider his or her potential contribution to the needs of a particular audience.

Every public communication event is unique. Environmental factors often lead to unexpected problems for the speaker, problems that may negate the intended purpose of the speech. The speaker should obtain as much information about the setting as possible and arrange the physical environment so that it is appropriate to the needs of the speech.

We viewed the speaker as not simply "acting" but *interacting* with an audience, and a variety of techniques for managing desirable types of speaker-audience interaction were suggested. Speakers were encouraged to become familiar with reoccurring problems of speaker-audience interaction and to plan general as well as specific strategies for dealing with them.

QUESTIONS

1. What are some of the techniques that could be used to make a speech on the following topics more interesting?
   Improvements in Processing the U.S. Mail
   Toward a New Tax Reform Program
   State vs. National Presidential Primaries: An Analysis
   Conserving Energy
   Effective Sales Messages
2. Could there be conflicts between a speaker's interest in *adapting* closely to audience interests and *saying what needs to be said*, what his or her conscience dictates? How many compromises can a speaker make and still preserve integrity, candor, and honesty?
3. Discuss some of the unexpected problems that can arise in any speaker-audience setting. What specific problems have you observed?
4. Under what conditions should a speaker decline the opportunity to give a speech?
5. How can a speaker maximize speaker-audience interaction without losing too much control over the presentation and the purposes of the speech occasion?

SUGGESTED READINGS

Bormann, Ernest, and William Howell. *Presentational speaking in business and the professions.* New York: Harper & Row, 1971.

Clevenger, Jr., Theodore. *Audience analysis.* Indianapolis: Bobbs-Merrill, 1966.

Dickens, Milton. *Speech: dynamic communication*, 2d ed. New York: Harcourt, Brace & World, 1963.

Monroe, Alan H., and Douglas Ehninger. *Principles and types of speech communication,* 7th ed. Glenview, Ill.: Scott, Foresman, 1974.

Wilson, John F., and Carroll Arnold. *Public speaking as a liberal art*, 3rd ed. Boston: Allyn and Bacon, 1974.

CONCLUSION: RESPONSIBLE SPEECH COMMUNICATION

Human communication is behavior. It is behavior that we employ to achieve our goals, to get things done, to receive rewards, to learn new things, to seek emotional release, to demonstrate feelings for others. Literally, most of our activities as human beings involve speech communication. Throughout this text, you have found suggestions for making communication behavior more meaningful and productive. You have, we hope, enhanced your speech communication abilities in one-to-one, small-group, and one-to-many settings. Your skills and understanding should continue to improve throughout college and your career. The ways in which you communicate make a difference. The more competent you become, the more you are likely to have impact on other people's lives and, in turn, on your own life.

Consider the following hypothetical yet plausible example. Margaret and Bill are college classmates and close friends. They especially enjoy parties and dancing together. Margaret, an "A" student, just finished a big exam and wants to go dancing tonight at a local discotheque. She calls Bill and asks him to go with her. He replies, "I'd really like to, but I have a big chemistry exam tomorrow. I flunked the last exam, and if I don't do better on this one, I may fail the course. My grade point average can't take any more low grades." "Look," says Margaret, "we'll just go for an hour or so. It will do you good to take a break from studies. You'll probably study better if you are relaxed. Besides, you are the best dancer I know, and I really don't want to go with anyone but you." After some more arguments and flattery, Bill finally agrees to go. He returns home after two in the morning, totally exhausted, and not too steady after too many dances and too many beers. He grabs a quick four hours sleep, rushes off to his eight o'clock exam, and flunks it.

Angrily, he phones Margaret. "Look what you made me do! I was all ready to get in some good studying, you talked me into a party, and now I may flunk out of school! How could you have done this to me?"

"Wait just a minute!" Margaret responds. "You're a big boy now. You didn't have to go with me. I didn't drag you kicking and screaming from your room. Don't try to blame me for your low grades or your lack of willpower!" Bill and Margaret hang up on each other, no longer such close friends.

Is Margaret partly responsible for Bill's flunking the exam? Or are Bill's problems totally his own fault? Couldn't he have declined the offer? Couldn't he have left early after a few dances and had soft drinks instead of beer? And why was he waiting until the last minute to cram for the test anyway? Should Margaret have to accept the blame for Bill's shortcomings as a scholar? We cannot judge whether Margaret was right or wrong, but we, the authors, do argue this: *She should accept at least a portion of the responsibility for the results of her communication behavior.* That is, had she not called Bill or had she encouraged him to study after hearing of his grade problem, the outcome may have been different — not necessarily *better*, but *different.* Margaret used her communicative skill to change Bill's behavior. Whenever that happens, whenever the behavior of one person prompts behavioral responses from another, the initiator must recognize the role that that first action played in subsequent actions.

We shall not explore in depth the problem of *ethics*, the study of good or bad behavior, of right or wrong. We shall not delve into personal morality to any great extent. For one thing, such topics are better left to studies in philosophy and religion. For another, we should be presumptuous to suggest that we know, in specific situations, what is good or bad behavior for speech communicators. But we do think that everyone should give some thought to the implications of communicative responsibility.

We base our views on the premise that *speech is behavior; it is action.* Our society often tries to deny this premise. We hear phrases like: "Actions speak louder than words." "Talk is cheap — what can you deliver?" "I believe in deeds, not in words." "It's not what you *say* that counts but what you *do.*" "Sticks and stones may break my bones, but words will never hurt me." People will often refuse to accept an oral agreement and instead force others to behave more actively, to "sign on the dotted line," for example. We regret this cultural tendency to minimize the significance of oral behavior. Some cultures, such as those of native American or Asian peoples, place a much higher premium on spoken words. But general American culture — business, politics, and even interpersonal relationships — tends to separate physical acts and speech acts. We think this separation is meaningless. Behavior is behavior is behavior. Action is action, whether it is verbal or nonverbal. For example, hitting someone with your fists and criticizing him with your speech may be different in form, but they are the same in content. Both are behaviors that *you initiate*. Both are perceived and given meaning by another person. And both are actions that have some sort of result.

Remember that even so-called nonbehavior, or inaction, has effects. Try *not* answering an exam question or *not* paying your taxes to find out whether others notice, interpret, and respond to your passive behavior. As we've indicated before, you cannot not communicate and you cannot not behave. Both religion and the law recognize this principle by including sins and crimes of *omission* as well as *commission*. We once heard an interesting discussion on whether there was any real difference between (1) stealing food from a hungry person (active) and (2) refusing to give food to a hungry person (passive). Similarly, is there any difference between (1) saying something that hurts someone's feelings and (2) failing to say something that could have soothed hurt feelings?

Throughout this text we have argued that speech communication behavior, if noticed by another, will have some effect or response. The response may be important or insignificant, overt or unnoticeable, positive or negative, clear or ambiguous, permanent or short-range, conscious or unconscious. But a response will occur. And that response may then prompt further behavior by the initiator. Thus, we see the *interdependence* of communicative interaction and, by extension, the mutual, ongoing impact we have on each other. In essence, then, ethical or moral judgments are inevitable. We cannot escape them. Consciously or unconsciously, we make them every day. (Even the person who says "I shall not concern myself with ethical problems" has already rendered an ethical judgment.) We suggest that *responsible speech communication* occurs when one develops awareness of one's interdependence with others, of the kinds of message choices that are available, and of the possible results those choices might have. The responsible communicator welcomes the personal accountability that goes with interpersonal conduct, especially speech behavior.

ISSUES AND PROBLEMS IN RESPONSIBLE COMMUNICATION

Once we realize that our speech behavior has practical and moral consequences, we still must answer for ourselves several difficult questions. Our answers should then help determine how we communicate, which choices we select. Below we bring up a few of these questions. We suggest that you not try to answer them with a simple yes or no, but, rather, think of possible justifications for either point of view.

Do the Ends Justify the Means? Are we justified in saying things that may temporarily hurt or deceive if the long-run impact of those messages is beneficial? Or should we always justify our communication on a short-range basis as well as a long-range one?

Should We Use the Self-Reference Criterion When We Advise Others? Should we determine what is best for them according to what we think is best for us? For example, should we try to convince others that our beliefs and behaviors will help them because they helped us? Or should we encourage others according to what we guess their personal interests to be? Or should we perhaps just try to avoid advising or influencing others altogether.

Should Our Messages Be Based Primarily on Rational, Objective Grounds? Are we irresponsible if we urge others to behave according to their feelings, passions, sentiments, sensations? For example, are advertisers justified in pushing a product because it may "make us feel young, alive, and exciting?" Should politicians use appeals to fear to get our vote?

Is Responsible Communication Situational? Are our message choices always to be based on the context—the situation—or should some hard and fast rules never be broken? For instance, if we decide that we should always be totally open and honest with someone we love, are there times when we are justified in holding back information or even lying?

May We Send Messages that Were Created by Another Person? If we use an idea originally phrased by another and perhaps lead others to believe that it is our own, are we irresponsible? Is a politician justified in delivering a speech that has been ghostwritten by a staff of experts? If politicians or any other communicators truly *believe* what they say, does it matter who originally thought it up?

Does "Intentionality" Make a Difference? If I communicate in a way that harms other people, is my responsibility lessened if I did not realize what I was doing? What if it was not my *intention* to hurt others? What if I was simply naive, unaware of the consequences? Must I accept full responsibility for my behavior regardless of my intent?

Does Listener Receptivity Make a Difference? If a potential receiver does not seek my comments or does not prefer to listen to them, am I justified in initiating those comments anyway? For example, are door-to-door sales promotions or political campaigns examples of irresponsible communication when the receiver prefers to be left alone? Does a responsible speaker have any special obligations with an involuntary or captive audience? Or are there some things that others *need* to hear regardless of whether they *want* to hear (as in parent-child or teacher-student transactions)?

Is Secrecy Justifiable? Is it irresponsible to "talk behind someone's back?" To communicate secretly about other people? To make policy decisions in private—decisions that will eventually affect others? Are there times when more open communication could actually be irresponsible and dangerous?

Your answers to these questions are a product of your unique beliefs, attitudes, values, and experiences. We cannot always achieve consensus on what constitutes good or ethical communication. However, we can become more responsible communicators if we consider more carefully our own communication behaviors and their consequences for others and for ourselves.

GUIDELINES FOR RESPONSIBLE COMMUNICATION

We noted earlier that we cannot prescribe for you specific ethical behaviors for specific situations. On the other hand, we can outline guidelines that the responsible communicator may wish to use. We do not intend them as absolutes; we do not even expect you to agree with us, but we hope you will read them carefully and critically.

First, responsible communicators attempt to be *truthful*. They are honest. They avoid intentional deception. They frankly recognize the self-interest that motivates much of their message behavior, and they willingly disclose such motives to others. When attempting to persuade, they try to be empirically accurate and logically valid; they recognize that half-truths or partial distortions are really a kind of lie.

Second, responsible communicators are accommodative; they are *receiver-centered.* They compose messages according to the comprehension abilities of receivers, and they encourage open feedback — authentic two-way communication — to enhance shared meaning. They prepare messages with thought and care so as to justify the receivers' time and attention. They try to display empathy, to understand and appreciate the interests and feelings of others.

Our third point is that responsible communicators are also effects-oriented. They are concerned about the *results* of their communication behavior. They acknowledge their interdependence with others and willingly accept responsibility for the outcomes of their transactions.

Fourth, responsible communicators try to develop *listening skills.* They try to listen actively and empathically, assuring that they understand the speaker's personal perspective as well as the specific message. They provide accurate verbal and nonverbal feedback. They first seek shared meaning through good listening before responding with their own points of view.

Responsible communicators, last, recognize the *limitations of judgmental messages*, comments that evaluate other people. Such evaluation, though inevitable in interpersonal transactions, should be used cautiously, after the initiator obtains complete information. Good communicators do not judge another's feelings; a person's emotional responses can be described but not evaluated. And, of course, these communicators are concerned with the impact of their judgments on others.

We began this book with the belief that by developing awareness and improving skills in speech communication, you would not only be more *productive* (get tasks done) but would also find interaction more *satisfying* (develop meaningful human relationships). We conclude with the hope that you will discover the benefits of responsible and effective speech. But remember that these rewards cannot be assured by a single college course; rather, they result from a sincere and ongoing concern for quality communication between people.

REFERENCES

Applbaum, R., Edward Bodaken, Kenneth Sereno, and Karl Anatol. *The process of group communication*. Chicago: Science Research, 1974.

The art of not listening. *Time*, Jan. 24, 1969.

Baker, Eldon. An experimental study of speech disturbance for the measurement of stage fright in the basic speech course. *Southern Speech* 29 (Spring 1964), 232–43.

Bales, Robert. *Interaction process analysis: a method for the study of small groups*. Cambridge, Mass.: Addison-Wesley, 1950.

Barnlund, Dean C. Toward a meaning centered philosophy of communication. *Journal of Communication* 12 (December 1962), 197–211.

———.*Interpersonal communication: survey and studies*. Boston: Houghton Mifflin, 1968.

Bem, D. J. *Beliefs, attitudes, and human affairs*. Belmont, Calif.: Brooks/Cole, 1970.

Bernstein, B. *Class, codes and control*, vol. 1. London: Routledge, 1971.

Bohr, N. *Atomic physics and human knowledge*. New York: Science Editions, Wiley, 1961.

Bormann, Ernest G. *Discussion and group methods*. New York: Harper & Row, 1969.

———, and George Shapiro. Perceived confidence as a function of self-image. *Central States Speech Journal* 13 (Spring 1962), 253–6.

Brandes, Paul. A semantic reaction to the measurement of stage fright. *Journal of Communication* 17 (June 1967), 142–6.

Brilhart, John. *Effective group discussion*. Dubuque, Iowa: Wm. C. Brown, 1974.

Brooks, William. *Speech communication*, 2d ed. Dubuque, Iowa: Wm. C. Brown, 1974.

———, and Judith Strong. An investigation of improvement in bodily action as a result of the basic course in speech. *Southern Speech* 35 (Fall 1969), 9–15.

Buehler, E. C., and Wil A. Linkugel. *Speech: a first course*. New York: Harper & Row, 1962.

Carlson, R. E., et al. Improvements in the selection interview. *Personnel Journal* 50 (April 1971), 268–75, 317.

Clevenger, Theodore. A synthesis of experimental research in stage fright. *Quarterly Journal of Speech* 45 (1959), 134–45.

———, and Thomas King. Visible symptoms of stage fright. *Speech Monographs* 28 (November 1961), 296–8.

Dance, Frank E. X., and Carl Larson. *The functions of human communication*. New York: Holt, 1976.

——— and ———. *Fundamentals of interpersonal communication*. New York: Harper & Row, 1976.

Davitz, J. P. *The communication of emotional meaning*. New York: McGraw-Hill, 1964.

Dewey, John. *How we think*. Chicago: Heath, 1910.

Faircloth, Samuel. A descriptive study of 133 speech deficient college students. *Southern Speech* 32 (Winter 1966), 117–23.

Festinger, Leon. *A theory of cognitive dissonance*. Evanston, Ill.: Row-Peterson, 1957.

Fiedler, Fred. The contingency model: a theory of leadership effectiveness. In L. Berkowitz (ed.), *Advances in experimental social psychology,* I. New York: Holt, 1965, 538–51.

Fisher, B. Aubrey. Decision emergence: phases in group decision-making. *Speech Monographs* 37 (1970), 53–66.

———. *Small group decision making*. New York: McGraw-Hill, 1974.

Foulke, Emerson. Listening comprehension as a function of word rate. *Journal of Communication* 18 (September 1968), 198–206.

Freeley, Austin. *Argumentation and debate*, 3d ed. Belmont, Calif.: Wadsworth, 1971.

Friedrich, Gustav. An empirical explication of a concept of self-reported speech anxiety. *Speech Monographs* 37 (March 1970), 67–72.

Gaske, Paul. Elaborated and restricted codes: implications for communication research and theory. Paper presented to the Western Speech Communication Association, November 1975.

Hall, Edward. *The silent language*. Garden City, N.Y.: Doubleday, 1959.

———. *The hidden dimension*. Garden City, N.Y.: Doubleday, 1966.

Houston, Susan. Black english. *Psychology Today* 6 (March 1973), 45–8.

Huseman, Richard, James Lahiff, and John Hatfield. *Interpersonal communication in organizations*. Boston: Holbrook, 1976.

Jacobson, Wally D. *Power and interpersonal relations*. Belmont, Calif.: Wadsworth, 1972.

Jensen, J. Vernon. Communicative functions of silence. *ETC: A Review of General Semantics* 30 (September 1973), 259–63.

Klee, Bruce. The myth about stage fright. *Today's Speech* 12 (February 1964), 20.

Knapp, Mark. *Nonverbal communication in human interaction*. New York: Holt, 1972.

Laing, R. D., H. Phillipson, and A. R. Lee. *Interpersonal perception: a theory and a method of research*. New York: Springer, 1966.

Lomas, Charles. The psychology of stage fright. *Quarterly Journal of Speech* 23 (February 1937), 35–44.

Maslow, Abraham. *Motivation and personality*. New York: Harper & Row, 1954.

Mayfield, Eugene. The selection interview—A re-evaluation of published research. *Personnel Psychology* 17 (Autumn 1964), 239–60.

McClelland, David. *Power: the inner experience*. New York: Irvington, 1975.

McGuire, W. J. A syllogistic analysis of cognitive relationships. In C. I. Hovland, M. J. Rosenberg (eds), *Attitude, organization and change*. New Haven, Conn.: Yale University Press, 1960, 65–111.

Mehrabian, Albert. Communication without words. *Psychology Today* 2 (September 1968), 52–5.

Mental maps. *Newsweek*, Mar. 15, 1976, 71.

Morris, C. W. *Signs, language, and behavior*. Englewood Cliffs, N.J.: Prentice-Hall, 1946.

———. *Varieties of human value.* Chicago: The University of Chicago Press, 1956.

Mowrer, O. Hobart. Stage fright and self-regard. *Western Speech* 29 (Fall 1965), 197–200.

Osgood, C., and P. Tannenbaum. The principle of congruity in the prediction of attitude change. *Psychological Review* 62 (1955), 42–55.

Phillips, Gerald. *Communication and the small group.* Indianapolis: Bobbs-Merrill, 1966.

Powell, John. *Why am I afraid to tell you who I am?* Chicago: Argus Communications, 1969.

Rice, A. K. *Learning for leadership.* London: Associated Book Publishers, 1965.

Robinson, Edward. What can the speech teacher do about students' stage fright? *Speech Teacher* 8 (January 1959), 10–1.

Rogers, Carl. *On becoming a person.* Boston: Houghton Mifflin, 1961.

Rogers, Everett, and F. Floyd Shoemaker. *Communication of innovations.* New York: Free Press, 1971.

Rokeach, Milton. *Beliefs, attitudes and values.* San Francisco: Jossey-Bass, 1968.

———, and G. Rothman. The principle of belief congruence and the congruity principle as models of cognitive interaction. *Psychological Review* 72 (1965), 128–72.

Ross, Raymond. *Speech communication: fundamentals and practice.* Englewood Cliffs, N.J.: Prentice-Hall, 1974.

Shostrom, Everett. *Man, the manipulator.* New York: Abingdon, 1967.

Sieburg, Evelyn. Confirming and disconfirming communication in an organizational context. *The Personnel Woman* 18 (February 1974), 4–11.

Sommer, Robert. *Personal space.* Englewood Cliffs, N.J.: Prentice-Hall, 1969.

Stewart, John, ed. *Bridges, not walls.* Reading, Mass.: Addison-Wesley, 1973.

Sticht, Thomas, and Douglas Glasnapp. Effects of speech rate, selection difficulty, association strength and mental aptitude on learning by listening. *Journal of Communication* 22 (June 1974), 174–88.

Toulmin, Stephen. *The uses of argument.* Cambridge: Cambridge University Press, 1958.

Trenholm, S. Language code and interpersonal tactic choice: a descriptive study. Paper presented at the Western Speech Communication Association, 1973.

Watzlawick, Paul, Janet Beavin, and Don Jackson. *Pragmatics of human communication.* New York: W. W. Norton, 1967.

Weaver, Andrew, and Ordean Ness. *The fundamentals and forms of speech.* New York: Odyssey, 1963.

Williams, F., and R. C. Naremore. On the functional analysis of social class differences in modes of speech. *Speech Monographs* 36 (1969), 77–102.

Winterowd, W. Ross. *Rhetoric: a synthesis.* New York: Holt, 1968.

INDEX

†